'Beatty is an original and irreverent talent.'   *The Times*

'Paul Beatty's blistering *The Sellout* shares DNA with the work of Swift, as well as possessing some of the savagery of Wyndham Lewis, and the single-minded absurdity of Myles na gCopaleen.'   Jon Day, Man Booker Judge 2016

'There's satire and then there's satire, and without question Paul Beatty's caustic third novel, *The Sellout*, definitely falls into the latter category...Brutally honest and very funny.'
Independent

'An outrageous scattergun satire taking aim at racism and what racism has done to black Americans...*The Sellout* aims to do for race relations what Joseph Heller's *Catch-22* – a favourite novel of Beatty's – did for the Second World War... Beatty's sharp humour challenges pieties from all sides, while never losing sight of the fundamental issue: America's racism and the legacy of slavery. Intelligent and entertaining.'
Telegraph

'An eccentric mix of Swiftian satire and observational comedy...I was banned from reading in bed because I was laughing so much.'
Olivia Williams, Man Booker Judge 2016

'Not for the faint-hearted.'   *Daily Mail*

'Both riotously experimental and touching…erudite…and viscerally engaging…Exceptional comic writing makes the skeletal plotting work…Beatty's inspiring new novel about the impossibility of "post-racial" anything in America is much more than "scathing" – it is constructive.'

Times Literary Supplement

'Paul Beatty has always been one of the smartest, funniest, gutsiest writers in America, but *The Sellout* sets a new standard. It's a spectacular explosion of comic daring, cultural provocation, brilliant, hilarious prose, and genuine heart.'

Sam Lipsyte, author of *The Ask*

'[*The Sellout*] is among the most important and difficult American novels written in the 21st century…It is a bruising novel that readers will likely never forget.'

Los Angeles Times

'As Mark Twain so ably showed us, America…is rich with material worthy of ridicule. But where is today's Twain? The answer is Paul Beatty…Beatty has written a wild new book, an uproariously funny, deliciously profane and ferociously intelligent send-up of so much of our culture.'

San Francisco Chronicle

'I am glad that I read this insane book alone, with no one watching, because I fell apart with envy, hysterics, and flatout awe. Is there a more fiercely brilliant and scathingly hilarious American novelist than Paul Beatty?'

Ben Marcus, author of *The Flame Alphabet*

'Beatty's towering talent proves there's no subject, no matter how infuriatingly unjust, how outrageously sorrowful, which can't be made to glitter like gold in the hands of a brilliant writer.'

Big Issue

'[*The Sellout*] may end up being the smartest, funniest, and most important novel of 2015.'   *Flavorwire*

'Had we been granted a chunk of pages in this magazine to extol the virtues of Paul Beatty's uproarious new novel, *The Sellout*, we could've easily and gladly filled them – much as Beatty floods his 288-page racial satire with blistering comic flourishes.'   *Penthouse*

'The first 100 pages of [Paul Beatty's] new novel, *The Sellout*, are the most caustic and the most badass first 100 pages of an American novel I've read in at least a decade. I gave up underlining the killer bits because my arm began to hurt...The riffs don't stop coming in this land-mark and deeply aware comic novel...[It] puts you down in a place that's miles from where it picked you up.'   *New York Times*

'*The Sellout* isn't just one of the most hilarious American novels in years, it also might be the first truly great satirical novel of the century...[It] is a comic mas-terpiece, but it's much more than just that-it's one of the smartest and most honest reflections on race and identity in America in a very long time.'   NPR.org

'Beatty, author of the deservedly highly praised *The White Boy Shuffle*, here outdoes himself and possibly ev-erybody else in a send-up of race, popular culture, and politics in today's America...Beatty hits on all cylin-ders in a darkly funny, dead-on-target, elegantly written satire...[*The Sellout*] is frequently laugh-out-loud funny and, in the way of the great ones, profoundly thought provoking. A major contribution.'   *Booklist*

ABOUT THE AUTHOR

PAUL BEATTY is the author of the novels *Slumberland*, *Tuff*, *The White Boy Shuffle* and *The Sellout*, which won the Man Booker Prize in 2016. He is also the author of two poetry collections, *Big Bank Take Little Bank* and *Joker, Joker, Deuce*, and is the editor of *Hokum: An Anthology of African-American Humor*. He lives in New York City.

ALSO BY PAUL BEATTY

FICTION
Slumberland
Tuff
The White Boy Shuffle

NONFICTION
Hokum: An Anthology of African-American Humor (editor)

POETRY
Joker, Joker, Deuce
Big Bank Take Little Bank

THE SELLOUT

PAUL BEATTY

ONEWORLD

A Oneworld Book

First published in the United Kingdom and Australia by
Oneworld Publications, 2016
Reprinted eight times 2016

Copyright © Paul Beatty 2015

ISBN: 978-1-78607-015-9
ISBN: 978-1-78607-017-3 (Export)
ISBN: 978-1-78607-147-7 (Hardback)
ISBN: 978-1-78607-016-6 (eBook)

Printed and bound in Great Britain by Clays Ltd, St Ives plc
Designed by Jonathan D. Lippincott

Oneworld Publications
10 Bloomsbury Street
London WC1B 3SR
England

Stay up to date with the latest books,
special offers, and exclusive content from
Oneworld with our monthly newsletter

Sign up on our website
oneworld-publications.com

For Althea Amrik Wasow

THE SELLOUT

Prologue

This may be hard to believe, coming from a black man, but I've never stolen anything. Never cheated on my taxes or at cards. Never snuck into the movies or failed to give back the extra change to a drugstore cashier indifferent to the ways of mercantilism and minimum-wage expectations. I've never burgled a house. Held up a liquor store. Never boarded a crowded bus or subway car, sat in a seat reserved for the elderly, pulled out my gigantic penis and masturbated to satisfaction with a perverted, yet somehow crestfallen, look on my face. But here I am, in the cavernous chambers of the Supreme Court of the United States of America, my car illegally and somewhat ironically parked on Constitution Avenue, my hands cuffed and crossed behind my back, my right to remain silent long since waived and said goodbye to as I sit in a thickly padded chair that, much like this country, isn't quite as comfortable as it looks.

Summoned here by an officious-looking envelope stamped IMPORTANT! in large, sweepstakes-red letters, I haven't stopped squirming since I arrived in this city.

"Dear Sir," the letter read.

"Congratulations, you may already be a winner! Your case has been selected from hundreds of other appellate cases to be heard by the Supreme Court of the United States of America. What a glorious honor! It's highly recommended that you arrive at least two hours early for your hearing scheduled for 10:00 a.m. on the morning of March 19, the year of our Lord . . ." The letter closed with directions to the Supreme Court building from the airport, the train station, I-95, and a set of clip-out coupons to various attractions, restaurants, bed-and-breakfasts, and the like. There was no signature. It simply ended . . .

Sincerely yours,
   The People of the United States of America

Washington, D.C., with its wide streets, confounding round-abouts, marble statues, Doric columns, and domes, is supposed to feel like ancient Rome (that is, if the streets of ancient Rome were lined with homeless black people, bomb-sniffing dogs, tour buses, and cherry blossoms). Yesterday afternoon, like some sandal-shod Ethiop from the sticks of the darkest of the Los Angeles jungles, I ventured from the hotel and joined the hajj of blue-jeaned yokels that paraded slowly and patriotically past the empire's historic landmarks. I stared in awe at the Lincoln Memorial. If Honest Abe had come to life and somehow managed to lift his bony twenty-three-foot, four-inch frame from his throne, what would he say? What would he do? Would he break-dance? Would he pitch pennies against the curbside? Would he read the paper and see that the Union he saved was now a dysfunctional plutocracy, that the people he freed were now slaves to rhythm, rap, and predatory lending, and that today his skill set would be better suited to the basketball court than the White House? There he could catch the rock on the break, pull up for a bearded three-pointer, hold the pose, and talk shit as the ball popped the net. The Great Emancipator, you can't stop him, you can only hope to contain him.

Not surprisingly, there's nothing to do at the Pentagon except start a war. Tourists aren't even allowed to take photos with the building in the background, so when the sailor-suited family of Navy veterans four generations deep handed me a disposable camera and asked me to follow at a distance and secretly take photos of them while they snapped to attention, saluted, and flashed peace signs for no apparent reason, I was only too happy to serve my country. At the National Mall there was a one-man march on Washington. A lone white boy lay on the grass, fucking with the depth perception in such a way that the distant Washington Monument looked like a massive, pointy-tipped, Caucasian hard-on streaming from his unzipped trousers. He joked with passersby, smiling into their camera phones and stroking his trick photography priapism.

At the zoo, I stood in front of the primate cage listening to a woman marvel at how "presidential" the four-hundred-pound gorilla looked sitting astride a shorn oaken limb, keeping a watchful eye over his caged brood. When her boyfriend, his finger tapping the informational placard, pointed out the "presidential" silverback's name coincidentally was Baraka, the woman laughed aloud, until she saw me, the other four-hundred-pound gorilla in the room, stuffing something that might have been the last of a Big Stick Popsicle or a Chiquita banana in my mouth. Then she became disconsolate, crying and apologizing for having spoken her mind and my having been born. "Some of my best friends are monkeys," she said accidentally. It was my turn to laugh. I understood where she was coming from. This whole city's a Freudian slip of the tongue, a concrete hard-on for America's deeds and misdeeds. Slavery? Manifest Destiny? *Laverne & Shirley*? Standing by idly while Germany tried to kill every Jew in Europe? Why some of my best friends are the Museum of African Art, the Holocaust Museum, the Museum of the American Indian, the National Museum of Women in the Arts. And furthermore, I'll have you know, my sister's daughter is married to an orangutan.

All it takes is a day trip through Georgetown and Chinatown. A slow saunter past the White House, Phoenix House, Blair House, and the local crackhouse for the message to become abundantly clear. Be it ancient Rome or modern-day America, you're either citizen or slave. Lion or Jew. Guilty or innocent. Comfortable or uncomfortable. And here, in the Supreme Court of the United States of America, fuck if between the handcuffs and the slipperiness of this chair's leather upholstery, the only way I can keep from spilling my ass ignominiously onto the goddamn floor is to lean back until I'm reclined at an angle just short of detention-room nonchalance, but definitely well past courtroom contempt.

Work keys jangling like sleigh bells, the Court officers march into the chambers like a two-by-two wagonless team of crew-cut Clydesdales harnessed together by a love of God and country. The lead dray, a proud Budweiser of a woman with a brightly colored sash of citations rainbowed across her chest, taps the back of my seat. She wants me to sit up straight, but the legendary civil disobedient that I am, I defiantly tilt myself even farther back in the chair, only to crash to the floor in a painful pratfall of inept nonviolent resistance. She dangles a handcuff key in my face and, with one thick hairless arm, hoists me upright, scooting my chair in so close to the table that I can see my suit and tie's reflection in its shiny, lemony-fresh mahogany finish. I've never worn a suit before, and the man who sold me this one said, "You're going to like the way you look. I guarantee it." But the face in the table staring back at me looks like what any business-suit-wearing, cornrowed, dreadlocked, bald-headed, corporate Afro'd black man whose name you don't know and whose face you don't recognize looks like—he looks like a criminal.

"When you look good, you feel good," the salesman also promised me. Guaranteed it. So when I get home I'm going to ask for my $129 back, because I don't like the way I look. The way I feel. I feel like my suit—cheap, itchy, and coming apart at the seams.

Most times cops expect to be thanked. Whether they've just given you directions to the post office, beaten your ass in the backseat of the patrol car, or, in my case, uncuffed you, returned your weed, drug paraphernalia, and provided you with the traditional Supreme Court quill. But this one has had a look of pity on her face, ever since this morning, when she and her posse met me atop the Supreme Court's vaunted forty-fourth stair. Under a pediment inscribed with the words EQUAL JUSTICE UNDER LAW they stood shoulder-to-shoulder, squinting into the morning sun, windbreakers dotted with the dandruff of fallen cherry blossoms, blocking my entrance into the building. We all knew that this was a charade, a last-minute meaningless show of power by the state. The only one not in on the joke was the cocker spaniel. His retractable leash whirring behind him, he bounded up to me, excitedly sniffed my shoes and my pant legs, nuzzled my crotch with his wet snot-encrusted nose, then obediently sat down beside me, his tail proudly pounding the ground. I've been charged with a crime so heinous that busting me for possession of marijuana on federal property would be like charging Hitler with loitering and a multinational oil company like British Petrolum with littering after fifty years of exploding refineries, toxic spills and emissions, and a shamelessly disingenuous advertising campaign. So I clear my pipe with two loud raps on the mahogany table. Brush and blow the gummy resin onto the floor, stuff the bowl with homegrown, and like a firing squad commander lighting a deserter's last cigarette, the lady cop obligingly flicks her BIC and sparks me up. I refuse the blindfold and take the most glorious toke ever taken in the history of pot smoking. Call every racially profiled, abortion-denied, flag-burning, Fifth Amendment taker and tell them to demand a re-trial, because I'm getting high in the highest court in the land. The officers stare at me in amazement. I'm the Scopes monkey, the missing link in the evolution of African-American jurisprudence come to life. I can hear the cocker spaniel whimpering in the corridor, pawing at the door, as I blow an A-bomb mushroom-cloud-sized plume of smoke into the faces that line the giant friezes on the ceiling. Hammurabi, Moses, Solomon—these veined Spanish marble incantations of democracy and fair play—Muhammad, Napoleon, Charlemagne, and some buffed ancient Greek frat boy in a toga stand above me, casting their stony judgmental gazes down upon me. I wonder if they looked at the Scottsboro Boys and Al Gore, Jr., with the same disdain.

Only Confucius looks chill. The sporty Chinese satin robe with the big sleeves, kung fu shoes, Shaolin sifu beard and mustache. I hold the pipe high overhead and offer him a hit; the longest journey starts with a single puff . . .

"That 'longest journey' shit is Lao-tzu," he says.

"All you motherfucking philosopher-poets sound alike to me," I say.

It's a trip being the latest in the long line of landmark race-related cases. I suppose the constitutional scholars and cultural paleontologists will argue over my place on the historical timeline. Carbon-date my pipe and determine whether I'm a direct descendant of Dred Scott, that colored conundrum who, as a slave living in a free state, was man enough for his wife and kids, man enough to sue his master for his freedom, but not man enough for the Constitution, because in the eyes of the Court he was simply property: a black biped "with no rights the white man was bound to respect." They'll pore over the legal briefs and thumb through the antebellum vellum and try to determine whether or not the outcome of this case confirms or overturns *Plessy v. Ferguson*. They'll scour the plantations, the projects, and the Tudor suburban subdivision affirmative-action palaces, digging up backyards looking for remnants of the ghosts of discrimination past in the fossilized dice and domino bones, brush the dust off the petrified rights and writs buried in bound legal volumes, and pronounce me as "unforeseen hip-hop generation precedent" in the vein of Luther "Luke Skyy-

walker" Campbell, the gap-toothed rapper who fought for his right
to party and parody the white man the way he'd done us for years.
Though if I'd been on the other side of the bench, I would've
snatched the fountain pen from Chief Justice Rehnquist's hand
and written the lone dissenting opinion, stating categorically that
"any wack rapper whose signature tune is 'Me So Horny' has no
rights the white man, or any other B-boy worth his suede Pumas,
was bound to respect."

The smoke burns the inside of my throat. "Equal Justice Under
Law!" I shout to no one in particular, a testament to both the po-
tency of the weed and my lightweight constitution. In neighborhoods like the one I grew up in, places that are poor in praxis but
rich in rhetoric, the homies have a saying—I'd rather be judged by
twelve than carried by six. It's a maxim, an oft-repeated rap lyric,
a last-ditch rock and hard place algorithm that on the surface is
about faith in the system but in reality means shoot first, put your
trust in the public defender, and be thankful you still have your
health. I'm not all that streetwise, but to my knowledge there's no
appellate court corollary. I've never heard a corner store rough-
neck take a sip of malt liquor and say, "I'd rather be reviewed by
nine than arbitrated by one." People have fought and died trying
to get some of that "Equal Justice Under Law" advertised so blithely
on the outside of this building, but innocent or guilty, most of-
fenders never make it this far. Their courtroom appeals rarely go
beyond a mother's tearful call for the Good Lord's mercy or a second mortgage on grandma's house. And if I believed in such slo-
gans, I'd have to say I've had more than my share of justice, but
I don't. When people feel the need to adorn a building or a com-
pound with an *"Arbeit Macht Frei,"* a "Biggest Little City in the
World," or "The Happiest Place on Earth," it's a sign of insecurity, a
contrived excuse for taking up our finite space and time. Ever been
to Reno, Nevada? It's the Shittiest Little City in the World, and if
Disneyland was indeed the Happiest Place on Earth, you'd either

keep it a secret or the price of admission would be free and not equivalent to the yearly per capita income of a small sub-Saharan African nation like Detroit.

I didn't always feel this way. Growing up, I used to think all of black America's problems could be solved if we only had a motto. A pithy *Liberté, egalité, fraternité* we could post over squeaky wrought-iron gateways, embroider onto kitchen wall hangings and ceremonial bunting. It, like the best of African-American folklore and hairstyles, would have to be simple, yet profound. Noble, and yet somehow egalitarian. A calling card for an entire race that was raceless on the surface, but quietly understood by those in the know to be very, very black. I don't know where young boys come up with such notions, but when your friends all refer to their parents by their first names, there's the sense that something isn't quite right. And wouldn't it be nice, in these times of constant connniption and crisis, for broken Negro families to gather around the hearth, gaze upon the mantelpiece, and take comfort in the uplifting words inscribed on a set of lovingly handcrafted commemorative plates or limited-edition gold coins purchased from a late-night infomercial on an already maxed-out credit card?

Other ethnicities have mottos. "Unconquered and unconquerable" is the calling card of the Chickasaw nation, though it doesn't apply to the casino gaming tables or having fought with Confederates in the Civil War. *Allahu Akbar. Shikata ga nai. Never again. Harvard class of '96. To Protect and to Serve.* These are more than just greetings and trite sayings. They are reenergizing codes. Linguistic chi that strengthens our life force and bonds us to other like-minded, like-skinned, like-shoe-wearing human beings. What is that they say in the Mediterranean? *Stessa faccia, stessa razza.* Same face, same race. Every race has a motto. Don't believe me? You know that dark-haired guy in human resources? The one who acts white, talks white, but doesn't quite look right? Go up to him. Ask him why Mexican goalkeepers play so recklessly or if the food at the taco truck parked outside is really safe to eat. Go ahead. Ask him. Prod him. Rub the back of his flat *indio* skull and see if he doesn't turn around with the *pronunciamiento ¡Por La Raza—todo! ¡Fuera de La Raza—nada!* (For the race, everything! Outside the race, nothing!)

When I was ten, I spent a long night burrowed under my comforter, cuddled up with Funshine Bear, who, filled with a foamy enigmatic sense of language and a Bloomian dogmatism, was the most literary of the Care Bears and my harshest critic. In the musty darkness of that rayon bat cave, his stubby, all-but-immobile yellow arms struggled to hold the flashlight steady as together we tried to save the black race in eight words or less. Putting my homeschool Latin to good use, I'd crank out a motto, then shove it under his heart-shaped plastic nose for approval. My first effort, *Black America: Veni, vidi, vici—Fried Chicken!* peeled back Funshine's ears and closed his hard plastic eyes in disappointment. *Semper Fi, Semper Funky* raised his polyester hackles, and when he began to paw the mattress in anger and reared up on his stubby yellow legs, baring his ursine fangs and claws, I tried to remember what the Cub Scout manual said to do when confronted by an angry stuffed cartoon bear drunk on stolen credenza wine and editorial power. "If you meet an angry bear—remain calm. Speak in gentle tones, stand your ground, get large, and write in clear, simple, uplifting Latin sentences."

> *Unum corpus, una mens, una cor, unum amor.*
> One body, one mind, one heart, one love.

Not bad. It had a nice license plate ring to it. I could see it in cursive, circumnavigating the rim of a race war medal of honor. Funshine didn't hate it, but from the way he wrinkled his nose right before falling asleep that night, I could tell he felt my slogan implied a certain groupthink, and weren't black people always complaining about being labeled as monolithic? I didn't ruin his dreams by telling him that black people do all think alike. They won't admit it, but every black person thinks they're better than every other black person. I never heard back from the NAACP or the Urban League, so the black credo exists only in my head, impatiently waiting on a movement, a nation, and, I suppose, since nowadays branding is everything, a logo.

Maybe we don't need a motto. How many times have I heard someone say, "Nigger, you know me, my motto is . . ."? If I were smart, I'd put my Latin to use. Charge ten dollars a word. Fifteen if they aren't from the neighborhood or want me to translate "Don't hate the player, hate the game." If it's true that one's body is one's temple, I could make good money. Open up a little shop on the boulevard and have a long line of tattooed customers who've transformed themselves into nondenominational places of worship: ankhs, sankofas, and crucifixes fighting for abdominal space with Aztec sun gods and one-star Star of David galaxies. Chinese characters running down shaved calves and spinal columns. Sinological shout-outs to dead loved ones that they think means "Rest in peace, Grandma Beverly," but in reality reads "No tickee! No Bilateral Trade Agreement!" Man, it'd be a goldmine. High as the price of cigarettes, they'd come at all hours of the night. I could sit behind a thick Plexiglas window and have one of those sliding metal drop boxes that the gas station attendants use. I'd slide out the drawer, and like prisoners passing jailhouse kites, my clientele would surreptitiously hand me their affirmations. The harder the man, the neater the handwriting. The more softhearted the woman, the more pugnacious the phrase. "You know me," they'd say, "my motto is . . ." and drop the cash and quotations from Shakespeare and *Scarface*, biblical passages, schoolyard aphorisms, and hoodlum truisms written in every medium from blood to eyeliner into the drawer. And whether it was scribbled on a crumpled-up bar napkin, a paper plate stained with BBQ sauce and potato salad, or was a page carefully torn from a secret diary kept since a stir in juvenile hall that if I tell anyone about it'll be my ass, *Ya estuvo* (whatever that means), I'd take the job seriously. For these are a people for whom the phrase "Well, if you put a gun to my head . . ." isn't theoretical, and when someone has pressed a cold metal muzzle to the yin and yang symbol tattooed on your temple and you've lived to tell about it, you don't need to have read the *I Ching* to appreciate the cosmic balance of the universe and the power of the tramp stamp. Because what else could your motto possibly be but "What goes around, comes around . . . *Quod circumvehitur, revehitur.*"

When business is slow, they'll come by to show me my handiwork. The olde English lettering glistening in the streetlight, its orthography parsed on their sweaty tank- and tube-topped musculatures. Money talks, bullshit walks . . . *Pecunia sermo, somnium ambulo.* Dative and accusative clauses burnished onto their jugulars, there's something special about having the language of science and romance surf the tidal waves of a homegirl's body fat. Strictly dickly . . . *Austerus verpa.* The shaky noun declension that would ticker-tape across their foreheads would be the closest most of them ever get to being white, to reading white. *Crip up or grip up . . . Criptum vexo vel carpo vex.* It's nonessential essentialism. Blood in, blood out . . . *Minuo in, minuo sicco.* It's the satisfaction of looking at your motto in the mirror and thinking, Any nigger who isn't paranoid is crazy . . . *Ullus niger vir quisnam est non insanus ist rabidus* is something Julius Caesar would've said if he were black. Act your age, not your shoe size . . . *Factio vestri aevum, non vestri calceus amplitudo.* And if an increasingly pluralistic America ever decides to commission a new motto, I'm open for business, because I've got a better one than *E pluribus unum.*

Tu dormis, tu perdis . . . You snooze, you lose.

Someone takes the pipe from my hand. "C'mon, man. That shit is cashed. It's time to make the donuts, homie." Hampton Fiske, my lawyer and old friend, calmly wafts away the last of the pot smoke, then engulfs me in an antifungal cloud of spray-can air freshener. I'm too high to speak, so we greet each other with chin-up, what's-up nods, and share a knowing smile, because we both recognize the scent. Tropic Breeze—same shit we used to hide the evidence from our parents because it smelled like angel dust. If moms came home, kicked off the espadrilles, and found the crib redolent of Apple Cinnamon or Strawberries and Cream, she'd know we'd been smoking, but if the crib smelled like PCP, then the stench could be blamed on "Uncle Rick and them," or alternatively, she could say nothing, too tired to deal with the possibility that her only child was addicted to sherm, and hope the problem would simply go away.

Arguing cases in front of the Supreme Court isn't Hamp's bailiwick. He's an old-school criminal defense attorney. When you call his office, you invariably get put on hold. Not because he's busy or there's no receptionist, or you've called at the same time as some other sap who saw his ad on a bus stop bench or the 800 number (1-800-FREEDOM) scratched by paid transients onto metal holding-cell mirrors and backseat police car Plexiglas. It's because he likes to listen to his answering machine, a ten-minute recitation of his legal triumphs and mistrials.

"You have reached the Fiske Group—Any Firm Can List the Charges, We Can Beat the Charges. Not Guilty—Murder. Not Guilty—DUI. Not Guilty—Assault of a Police Officer. Not Guilty—Sexual Abuse. Not Guilty—Child Abuse. Not Guilty—Elderly Abuse. Dismissed—Theft. Dismissed—Forgery. Dismissed—Domestic Violence (more than one thousand cases). Dismissed—Sexual Conduct with a Minor. Dismissed—Involving a Child in Drug Activity. Dismissed—Kidnapping . . ."

Hamp knows that only the most desperate of the accused will have the patience to sit through that litany of damn near every criminal statute in the Los Angeles County penal code, first in English, then in Spanish, then in Tagalog. And those are the people he likes to represent. The wretched of the Earth, he calls us. People too poor to afford cable and too stupid to know that they aren't missing anything. "If Jean Valjean had me representing him," he likes to say, "then *Les Misérables* would've only been six pages long. Dismissed—Loaf of Bread Pilfery."

My crimes aren't listed on the answering machine. At the arraignment in district court right before the judge asked me to enter a plea, he read the list of felonious charges against me. Allegations that in summation accused me of everything from desecration of the Homeland to conspiracy to upset the apple cart just when things were going so well. Dumbfounded, I stood before the court, trying to figure out if there was a state of being between "guilty" and "innocent." Why were those my only alternatives? I thought. Why couldn't I be "neither" or "both"?

After a long pause, I finally faced the bench and said, "Your Honor, I plead human." For this I received an understanding snicker from the judge and a citation for contempt of court, which Hamp instantly got reduced to time served, right before making an innocent plea on my behalf and half-jokingly requesting a change of venue, suggesting Nuremburg or Salem, Massachusetts, as possible locales given the serious nature of the charges. And while he never said anything to me, my guess is that the ramifications of what he'd previously thought would be a simple case of standard black inner-city absurdity suddenly struck him, and he applied for admission to the Supreme Court bar the very next day.

But that's old news. For now, I'm here in Washington, D.C., dangling at the end of my legal rope, stoned on memory and marijuana. My mouth bone-dry and feeling like I've just woken up on the #7 bus, drunk as fuck after a long futile night of carousing and chasing Mexican babes at the Santa Monica pier, looking out the window and coming to the slow, marijuana-impaired realization that I've missed my stop and have no idea where I am or why everybody is looking at me. Like this woman in the Court's front row, leaning over the wooden banister, her face a knotted and twisted burl of anger as she flips her long, slender, manicured, press-on-nailed middle fingers in my direction. Black women have beautiful hands, and with every "fuck you" cocoa-butter stab of the air, her hands become more and more elegant. They're the hands of a poet, one of those natural-haired, brass-bangled teacher-poets whose elegiac verse compares everything to jazz. Childbirth is like jazz. Muhammad Ali is like jazz. Philadelphia is like jazz. Jazz is like jazz. Everything is like jazz except for me. To her I'm like a remixed Anglo-Saxon appropriation of black music. I'm Pat Boone in blackface singing a watered-down version of Fats Domino's "Ain't That a Shame." I'm every note of nonpunk British rock 'n' roll plucked and strummed since the Beatles hit that mind-reverberating chord that opens "A Hard Day's Night." But what about Bobby "What You Won't Do for Love" Caldwell, Gerry Mulligan, Third Bass, and Janis Joplin? I want to shout back at her. What about Eric Clapton? Wait, I take that back. Fuck Eric Clapton. Ample bosoms first, she hops the rail, bogarts her way past the cops, and bolts toward me, her thumb-sucking charges clinging desperately to her "Don't You See How Insanely Long, Soft, Shiny, and Expensive This Is? Motherfucker, YOU WILL Treat Me Like a Queen!" Toni Morrison signature model pashmina shawl trailing behind her like a cashmere kite tail.

Now she's in my face, mumbling calmly but incoherently about black pride, the slave ships, the three-fifths clause, Ronald Reagan, the poll tax, the March on Washington, the myth of the drop-back quarterback, how even the white-robed horses of the Ku Klux Klan were racist, and, most emphatically, how the malleable minds of the ever-increasingly redundant *young* black *youth* must be protected. And lo, the mind of the little waterheaded boy with both arms wrapped about his teacher's hips, his face buried in her crotch, definitely needs a bodyguard, or at least a mental prophy-

lactic. He comes up for air looking expectantly to me for an explanation as to why his teacher hates me so. Not getting one, the pupil
returns to the warm moistness of his happy place, oblivious to the
stereotype that black males don't go down there. What could I
have said to him? "You know how when you play Chutes and Lad-
ders and you're almost at the finish line, but you spin a six and
land on that long, really curvy red slide that takes you from square
sixty-seven all the way back to number twenty-four?"

"Yes, sir," he'd say politely.

"Well," I'd say, rubbing his ball-peen-hammer head, "I'm that
long red slide."

The teacher-poet slaps me hard across the face. And I know
why. She, like most everyone here, wants me to feel guilty. Wants
me to show some contrition, to break down in tears, to save the
state some money and her the embarrassment of sharing my blackness. I, too, keep waiting for that familiar, overwhelming sense of
black guilt to drop me to my knees. Knock me down peg by meaningless idiomatic peg, until I'm bent over in total supplication to
America, tearfully confessing my sins against color and country,
begging my proud black history for forgiveness. But there's nothing. Only the buzz of the air conditioner and my high, and as
security escorts her back to her seat, the little boy trailing behind
her, holding on to her scarf for dear life, the sting in my cheek that
she hopes will smart in perpetuity has already faded and I find
myself unable to conjure up a single guilty pang.

That's the bitch of it, to be on trial for my life, and for the first
time ever not feel guilty. That omnipresent guilt that's as black as
fast-food apple pie and prison basketball is finally gone, and it
feels almost white to be unburdened from the racial shame that
makes a bespectacled college freshman dread Fried Chicken Fridays
at the dining hall. I was the "diversity" the school trumpeted so
loudly in its glossy literature, but there wasn't enough financial aid
in the world to get me to suck the gristle from a leg bone in front of

the entire freshman class. I'm no longer party to that collective guilt that keeps the third-chair cellist, the administrative secretary, the stock clerk, the not-really-all-that-attractive-but-she's-black beauty pageant winner from showing up for work Monday morning and shooting every white motherfucker in the place. It's a guilt that has obligated me to mutter "My bad" for every misplaced bounce pass, politician under federal investigation, every bug-eyed and Rastus-voiced comedian, and every black film made since 1968. But I don't feel responsible anymore. I understand now that the only time black people don't feel guilty is when we've actually done something wrong, because that relieves us of the cognitive disso-nance of being black and innocent, and in a way the prospect of going to jail becomes a relief. In the way that cooning is a relief, voting Republican is a relief, marrying white is a relief—albeit a temporary one.

Uncomfortable with being so comfortable, I make one last at-tempt to be at one with my people. I close my eyes, place my head on the table, and bury my broad nose in the crook of my arm. I focus on my breathing, shutting out the flags and the fanfare, and cull through my vast repository of daydream blackness until I dredge up the scratchy archival footage of the civil rights struggle. Handling it carefully by its sensitive edges, I remove it from its sacred canister, thread it through mental sprockets and psycho-logical gates, and past the bulb in my head that flickers with the occasional decent idea. I flip on the projector. There's no need to focus. Human carnage is always filmed and remembered in the highest definition. The images are crystal-clear, permanently burned into our memories and plasma television screens. That in-cessant Black History Month loop of barking dogs, gushing fire hoses, and carbuncles oozing blood through two-dollar haircuts, colorless blood spilling down faces shiny with sweat and the light of the evening news, these are the pictures that form our collective 16 mm superego. But today I'm all medulla oblongata and I can't concentrate. The film inside my head begins to skip and sputter. The sound cuts out, and protesters falling like dominoes in Selma, Alabama, begin to look like Keystone Negroes slipping en masse on an affirmative-action banana peel and tumbling to the street, a tangled mess of legs and dreams akimbo. The marchers on Washington become civil rights zombies, one hundred thousand strong, somnambulating lockstep onto the mall, stretching out their stiff, needy fingers for their pound of flesh. The head zombie looks exhausted from being raised from the dead every time someone wants to make a point about what black people should and shouldn't do, can and cannot have. He doesn't know the mic is on, and under his breath he confesses that if he'd only tasted that unsweetened swill that passed for iced tea at the segregated lunch counters in the South he would've called the whole civil rights thing off. Before the boycotts, the beatings, and the killings. He places a can of diet soda on the podium. "Things go better with Coke," he says. "It's the real thing!"

Still, I don't feel guilty. If I'm indeed moving backward and dragging all of black America down with me, I couldn't care less. Is it my fault that the only tangible benefit to come out of the civil rights movement is that black people aren't as afraid of dogs as they used to be? No, it isn't.

The Marshal of the Court rises, pounds her gavel, and begins to incant the Court's invocation: *"The honorable, the Chief Justice and the Associate Justices of the Supreme Court of the United States."*

Hampton lifts me shakily to my feet, and we, along with all those in attendance, rise in ministerial solemnity as the Justices enter the courtroom, trying their level best to look impartial, with their Eisenhower-era hairstyles and "another day, another dollar" blank workaday expressions. Too bad it's impossible not to come off as pompous when you're wearing a silk black robe and the Negro Justice has absentmindedly forgotten to take off his $50,000 platinum Rolex. I suppose if I had better job security than Father Time, I'd be smug as a motherfucker, too.

Oyez! Oyez! Oyez!

At this point, after five years of endless decisions, reversals, appeals, postponements, and pretrial hearings, I don't even know if I'm the plaintiff or the defendant. All I know is that the sour-faced Justice with the post-racial chronometer won't stop looking at me. His beady eyes fixed in this unblinking and unforgiving stare, he's angry that I've fucked up his political expediency. Blown up his spot like a little kid visiting the city zoo for the first time and, frustrated at having walked past cage after seemingly empty reptile cage, finally stops at an enclosure and shouts, "There he is!"

There he is, *Chamaeleo africanus tokenus* hidden way in the back among all the shrubbery, his slimy feet gripped tightly around the judicial branch in a cool torpor, silently gnawing on the leaves of injustice. "Out of sight, out of mind" is the black working-man's motto, but now the entire country can see this one, our collective noses pressed to the glass in amazement that he's been able to camouflage his Alabama jet-black ass against the red, white, and blue of the American flag for so long.

"All persons having business before the honorable, the Supreme Court of the United States, are admonished to draw near and give their attention, for the Court is now sitting. God save the United States and this honorable Court!"

Hamp kneads my shoulder, a reminder not to sweat the nappy-headed magistrate or the republic for which he stands. This is the Supreme Court, not the People's Court. I don't have to do anything. I don't need copies of dry cleaner receipts, police reports, or a photograph of a dented bumper. Here the lawyers argue, the judges question, and I get to simply kick back and enjoy my high.

The Chief Justice enters the case. His dispassionate midwestern demeanor goes a long way toward easing the tension in the room. "We'll hear argument first this morning in case 09-2606 . . ."

He pauses, rubs his eyes, then composes himself. "In case 09-2606, *Me v. the United States of America*." There's no outburst. Only giggling and eye rolling accompanied by some loud "Who this motherfucker think he is?" teeth sucking. I admit it, *Me v. the United States* sounds a little self-aggrandizing, but what can I say? I'm Me. Literally. A not-so-proud descendant of the Kentucky Mees, one of the first black families to settle in southwest Los Angeles, I can trace my roots all the way back to that first vessel to escape state-sanctioned southern repression—the Greyhound bus. But when I was born, my father, in the twisted tradition of Jewish entertainers who change their names and the uptight, underachieving black men who envy them, decided to truncate the family name, dropping that last unwieldy *e* like Jack Benny dropped Benjamin Kubelsky, Kirk Douglas—Danielovitch, like Jerry Lewis dropped Dean Martin, Max Baer dropped Schmeling, Third Bass dropped science, and Sammy Davis, Jr., dropped Judaism all together. He wasn't going to let that extra vowel hold me back like it did him. Pops liked to say that he didn't Anglicize or Africanize my surname, but actualized it, that I was born having reached my full potential and could skip Maslow, third grade, and Jesus.

Knowing that the ugliest movie stars, the whitest rappers, and the dumbest intellectuals are often the most respected members of their chosen profession, Hamp, the defense lawyer who looks like a criminal, confidently sets his toothpick on the lectern, runs his tongue over a gold-capped incisor, and straightens his suit, a baby-tooth-white, caftan-baggy, double-breasted ensemble that hangs on his bony frame like an empty hot-air balloon and, depending on your taste in music, either matches or clashes with his asp-black, Cleopatra chemical perm and the first-round Mike Tyson knockout darkness of his skin. I half expect him to address the court with "Fellow pimps and pimpettes, you may have heard that my client is dishonest, but that's easy for them to say, because my client is a crook!" In an age where social activists have television shows and millions of dollars, there aren't many left like Hampton Fiske, those pro-bono assholes who believe in the system and in the Constitution, but who can see the gap between reality and rhetoric. And while I don't really know if he truly believes in me or not, I know that when he starts to defend the indefensible, it won't make a difference, because he's a man whose business card motto is "For the poor every day is casual Friday."

Fiske has barely uttered "May it please the Court," when the black Justice moves almost imperceptibly forward in his seat. No one would've noticed, but a squeaky wheel on his swivel chair gave him away. And with each referral to some obscure section of the Civil Rights Act or precedent-setting case, the Justice shifts impatiently, causing his chair to squeak louder and louder with each transfer of his restless body weight from one flabby diabetic butt cheek to the other. You can assimilate the man, but not the blood pressure, and the vein pulsating angrily down the middle of his forehead gives him away. He's giving me that crazy, red-eyed penetrating look that back home we call the Willowbrook Avenue Stare, Willowbrook Avenue being the four-lane river Styx that in 1960s Dickens separated white neighborhoods from black, but now, post-white, post-anybody-with-two-nickels-to-rub-together-flight, hell lies on both sides of the street. The riverbanks are dangerous, and while standing at the crosswalk waiting for the light to change, your life can change. Some drive-by homie, representing some color, clique, or any one of the five stages of grief, can stick his gauge out the passenger-side window of a two-tone coupe, give you the Negro Supreme Court Justice glare, and ask, "Where you from, fool?"

The correct answer, of course, is "Nowhere," but sometimes they don't hear you over the loud, sputtering, unmuffiered engine, the contentious confirmation hearing, the liberal media's questioning of your credentials, the conniving black bitch accusing you of sexual harassment. Sometimes "Nowhere" just isn't a good enough answer. Not because they don't believe you, because "everybody's from somewhere," but because they don't want to believe you. And now, having lost his veneer of patrician civility, this screw-faced magistrate, sitting in his high-backed swivel chair, is no different from the gangbanger cruising up and down Willowbrook Avenue calling and sitting "shotgun" because he has one.

And for the first time in his long tenure on the Supreme Court, the black Justice has a question. He's never interjected before, so he doesn't quite know how. Looking to the Italian Justice for permission, he slowly raises his puffy, cigar-fingered hand in the air, but too infuriated to wait for approval, he blurts out, "Nigger, are you crazy?" in a voice surprisingly high-pitched for a black man his size. Now void of objectivity and equanimity, his ham-sized fists pound the bench so hard the fancy, giant, gold-plated clock suspended from the ceiling above the Chief Justice's head begins to pendulum back and forth. The black Justice moves in too close to his microphone, yelling into it, because although I'm seated only a few feet away from the bench, our differences are light-years apart. He's demanding to know how it is that in this day and age a black man can violate the hallowed principles of the Thirteenth Amendment by owning a slave. How could I willfully ignore the Fourteenth Amendment and argue that sometimes segregation brings people together. Like all people who believe in the system, he wants answers. He wants to believe that Shakespeare wrote all those books, that Lincoln fought the Civil War to free the slaves and the United States fought World War II to rescue the Jews and keep the world safe for democracy, that Jesus and the double feature are coming back. But I'm no Panglossian American. And when I did what I did, I wasn't thinking about inalienable rights, the proud history of our people. I did what worked, and since when did a little slavery and segregation ever hurt anybody, and if so, so fucking be it.

Sometimes, when you're high as I am, the line between thought

and speech blurs, and judging by the way the black Justice is froth-
ing at the mouth, I've said that last bit out loud, ". . . so fucking be
it." He stands up like he wants to fight. A wad of spit hocked from
the deepest regions of his Yale Law School education chambered
on the tip of his tongue. The Chief Justice calls out his name, and
the black Justice catches himself and plops back into his chair.
Swallowing his saliva, if not his pride. "Racial segregation? Slavery?
Why you bitch-made motherfucker, I know goddamn well your
parents raised you better than that! So let's get this hanging party
started!"

THE SHIT YOU SHOVEL

One

I suppose that's exactly the problem—I wasn't raised to know any better. My father was (Carl Jung, rest his soul) a social scientist of some renown. As the founder and, to my knowledge, sole practitioner of the field of Liberation Psychology, he liked to walk around the house, aka "the Skinner box," in a laboratory coat. Where I, his gangly, absentminded black lab rat was homeschooled in strict accordance with Piaget's theory of cognitive development. I wasn't fed; I was presented with lukewarm appetitive stimuli. I wasn't punished, but broken of my unconditioned reflexes. I wasn't loved, but brought up in an atmosphere of calculated intimacy and intense levels of commitment.

We lived in Dickens, a ghetto community on the southern outskirts of Los Angeles, and as odd as it might sound, I grew up on a farm in the inner city. Founded in 1868, Dickens, like most California towns except for Irvine, which was established as a breeding ground for stupid, fat, ugly, white Republicans and the chihuahuas and East Asian refugees who love them, started out as an agrarian community. The city's original charter stipulated that "Dickens shall remain free of Chinamen, Spanish of all shades, dialects, and hats, Frenchmen, redheads, city slickers, and unskilled Jews." However, the founders, in their somewhat limited wisdom, also provided that the five hundred acres bordering the canal be forever zoned for something referred to as "residential agriculture," and thus my neighborhood, a ten-square-block section of Dickens unofficially known as the Farms was born. You know when you've entered the Farms, because the city sidewalks, along with your rims, car stereo, nerve, and progressive voting record, will have vanished into air thick with the smell of cow manure and, if the wind is blowing the right direction—good weed. Grown men slowly pedal dirt bikes and fixies through streets clogged with gaggles and coveys of every type of farm bird from chickens to peacocks. They ride by with no hands, counting small stacks of bills, looking up just long enough to raise an inquisitive eyebrow and mouth: "Wassup? Q'vo?" Wagon wheels nailed to front-yard trees and fences lend the ranch-style houses a touch of pioneer authenticity that belies the fact that every window, entryway, and doggie door has more bars on it and padlocks than a prison commissary. Front porch senior citizens and eight-year-olds who've already seen it all sit on rickety lawn chairs whittling with switchblades, waiting for something to happen, as it always did.

For the twenty years I knew him, Dad had been the interim dean of the department of psychology at West Riverside Community College. For him, having grown up as a stable manager's son on a small horse ranch in Lexington, Kentucky, farming was nostalgic. And when he came out west with a teaching position, the opportunity to live in a black community and breed horses was too good to pass up, even if he'd never really been able to afford the mortgage and the upkeep.

Maybe if he'd been a comparative psychologist, some of the horses and cows would've lived past the age of three and the tomatoes would've had fewer worms, but in his heart he was more interested in black liberty than in pest management and the well-being of the animal kingdom. And in his quest to unlock the keys to mental freedom, I was his Anna Freud, his little case study, and

when he wasn't teaching me how to ride, he was replicating famous social science experiments with me as both the control and
the experimental group. Like any "primitive" Negro child lucky
enough to reach the formal operational stage, I've come to realize
that I had a shitty upbringing that I'll never be able to live down.

I suppose if one takes into account the lack of an ethics committee to oversee my dad's childrearing methodologies, the experiments started innocently enough. In the early part of the twentieth
century, the behaviorists Watson and Rayner, in an attempt to
prove that fear was a learned behavior, exposed nine-month-old
"Little Albert" to neutral stimuli like white rats, monkeys, and
sheaves of burned newsprint. Initially, the baby test subject was
unperturbed by the series of simians, rodents, and flames, but after Watson repeatedly paired the rats with unconscionably loud
noises, over time "Little Albert" developed a fear not only of white
rats but of all things furry. When I was seven months, Pops placed
objects like toy police cars, cold cans of Pabst Blue Ribbon, Richard Nixon campaign buttons, and a copy of *The Economist* in my
bassinet, but instead of conditioning me with a deafening clang, I
learned to be afraid of the presented stimuli because they were
accompanied by him taking out the family .38 Special and firing
several window-rattling rounds into the ceiling, while shouting,
"Nigger, go back to Africa!" loud enough to make himself heard
over the quadraphonic console stereo blasting "Sweet Home Alabama" in the living room. To this day I've never been able to sit
through even the most mundane TV crime drama, I have a strange
affinity for Neil Young, and whenever I have trouble sleeping, I
don't listen to recorded rainstorms or crashing waves but to the
Watergate tapes.

Family lore has it that from ages one to four, he'd tied my right
hand behind my back so I'd grow up to be left-handed, right-
brained, and well-centered. I was eight when my father wanted to
test the "bystander effect" as it applies to the "black community."

He replicated the infamous Kitty Genovese case with a prepubescent me standing in for the ill-fated Ms. Genovese, who, in 1964,
was robbed, raped, and stabbed to death in the apathetic streets of
New York, her plaintive *Psychology 101* textbook cries for help ignored by dozens of onlookers and neighborhood residents. Hence,
the "bystander effect": the more people around to provide help, the
less likely one is to receive help. Dad hypothesized that this didn't
apply to black people, a loving race whose very survival has been
dependent on helping one another in times of need. So he made
me stand on the busiest intersection in the neighborhood, dollar
bills bursting from my pockets, the latest and shiniest electronic
gadgetry jammed into my ear canals, a hip-hop heavy gold chain
hanging from my neck, and, inexplicably, a set of custom-made
carpeted Honda Civic floor mats draped over my forearm like a
waiter's towel, and as tears streamed from my eyes, my own father
mugged me. He beat me down in front of a throng of bystanders,
who didn't stand by for long. The mugging wasn't two punches to
the face old when the people came, not to my aid, but to my father's. Assisting him in my ass kicking, they happily joined in with
flying elbows and television wrestling throws. One woman put me
in a well-executed and, in retrospect, merciful, rear-naked choke-
hold. When I regained consciousness to see my father surveying
her and the rest of my attackers, their faces still sweaty and chests
still heaving from the efforts of their altruism, I imagined that, like
mine, their ears were still ringing with my high-pitched screams
and their frenzied laughter.

"How satisfied were you with your act of selflessness?"
Not at all   Somewhat satisfied   Very satisfied
1   2   3   4   5

On the way home, Pops put a consoling arm around my aching shoulders and delivered an apologetic lecture about his failure
to take into account the "bandwagon effect."

Then there was the time he wanted to test "Servility and Obedience in the Hip-hop Generation." I must've been about ten when my father sat me down in front of a mirror, pulled a Ronald Reagan Halloween mask over his head, pinned a defunct pair of Trans World Airlines captain wings to his lab coat, and proclaimed himself a "white authority figure." "The nigger in the mirror is a stupid nigger," he explained to me in that screechy, cloying "white voice" comedians of color use, while attaching a set of electrodes to my temples. The wires led to a sinister-looking console filled with buttons, dials, and old-fashioned voltage gauges.

"You will ask the boy in the mirror a series of questions about his supposed nigger history from the sheet on the table. If he gets the question wrong or fails to answer in ten seconds, you will press the red button, delivering an electric shock that will increase in intensity with each wrong answer."

I knew better than to beg for mercy, for mercy would be a rant about getting what I deserved for reading the one comic book I ever owned. Batman #203, *Spectacular Secrets of the Batcave Revealed*, a moldy, dog-eared back issue someone had thrown into the farmyard and I brought inside and nursed back to readability like a wounded piece of literature. It was the first thing I had ever read from the outside world, and when I whipped it out during a break in my homeschooling, my father confiscated it. From then on, whenever I didn't know something or had a bad day in the neighborhood, he'd wave the comic's half-torn cover in my face. "See, if you weren't wasting your life reading this bullshit, you'd realize Batman ain't coming to save your ass or your people!"

I read the first question.

"Prior to declaring independence in 1957, the West African nation of Ghana was comprised of what two colonies?"

I didn't know the answer. I cocked my ears for the roar of the rocket-propelled Batmobile screeching around the corner, but could only hear my father's stopwatch ticking down the seconds.

I gritted my teeth, placed my finger over the red button, and waited for the time limit to expire.

"The answer is Togoland and the Gold Coast."

Obediently, as my father predicted, I pressed the button. The needles on the dial and my spine both straightened, while I watched myself in the mirror jitterbug violently for a second or two.

Jesus.

"How many volts was that?" I asked, my hands shaking uncontrollably.

"The subject will ask only the questions that are listed on the sheet," my dad said coldly, reaching past me to turn a black dial a few clicks to the right, so that the indicator now rested on XXX. "Now, please read the next question."

I began to suffer from a blurring of vision I suspected was psychosomatic, but nonetheless everything was as out of focus as a five-dollar bootleg video on a swap-meet flat screen, and to read the next question I had to hold the quivering paper to my nose.

"Of the 23,000 eighth-grade students who took the entrance exam for admission into Stuyvesant High, New York's most elite public high school, how many African-Americans scored high enough to qualify for admission?"

When I finished reading, my nose began to bleed, red droplets of blood trickling from my left nostril and plopping onto the table in perfect one-second intervals. Eschewing his stopwatch, my father started the countdown. I glanced suspiciously at him. The question was too topical. Obviously he'd been reading *The New York Times* at breakfast. Prepping for the day's experiment by looking for racial fodder over a bowl of Rice Krispies. Flipping from page to page with a speed and rage that caused the paper's sharp corners to snap, crackle, and pop in the morning air.

What would Batman do if he rushed into the kitchen right then and saw a father electrocuting his son for the good of science? Why, he'd open up his utility belt and bust out some of those tear-gas pellets, and while my dad was choking on the fumes, he'd finish asphyxiating him, assuming there was enough bat rope to tie around his fat-ass hot-dog neck; then he'd burn out his eyeballs with the laser torch, use the miniature camera to take some pictures for bat-posterity, then steal Pop's classic, only-driven-on-trips-to-white-neighborhoods sky-blue Karmann Ghia convertible with the skeleton keys, and we'd bone the fuck out. That's what Batman would've done. But me, cowardly batfag that I was and still am, I could only think to question the question's shoddy methodology. For instance, how many black students had taken the admissions test? What was the average class size at this Stuyvesant High?

But this time, before the tenth drop of blood had landed on the table, and before my father could blurt out the answer (seven), I pressed the red button, self-administering a nerve-shattering, growth-stunting electric shock of a voltage that would've frightened Thor and lobotomized an already sedated educated class, because now I, too, was curious. I wanted to see what happens when you bequeath a ten-year-old black boy to science.

What I discovered was that the phrase "evacuate one's bowels" is a misnomer, because the opposite was true, my bowels evacuated me. It was a feces retreat comparable to the great evacuations of history. Dunkirk. Saigon. New Orleans. But unlike the Brits, the Vietnamese capitalists, and flooded-out residents of the Ninth Ward, the occupants of my intestinal tract had nowhere to go. What runny parts of that fetid tidal wave of shit and urine that didn't encamp itself about my buttocks and balls ran down my legs and pooled in and around my sneakers. Not wanting to hinder the integrity of his experiment, my father simply pinched his nose shut and motioned for me to proceed. Thank goodness, I knew the answer to the third question, "How many Chambers are in the Wu-Tang?" because if I hadn't, my brain would be the ash-gray color and consistency of a barbecue briquette on the Fifth of July.

My crash course in childhood development ended two years

later, when Dad tried to replicate Drs. Kenneth and Mamie Clark's study of color consciousness in black children using white and black dolls. My father's version, of course, was a little more revolutionary. A tad more modern. While the Clarks sat two cherubic, life-sized, saddle-shoe-shod dolls, one white and one colored, in front of schoolchildren and asked them to choose the one they preferred, my father placed two elaborate dollscapes in front of me and asked me, "With whom, with what social-cultural subtext are you down with, son?"

Dollscape I featured Ken and Malibu Barbie dressed in matching bathing suits, appropriately snorkeled and goggled, cooling by the Dream House pool. In Dollscape II, Martin Luther King, Jr., Malcolm X, Harriet Tubman, and a brown-skinned, egg-shaped Weeble toy were running (and wobbling) through a swampy thicket from a pack of plastic German shepherds leading an armed lynch party comprised of my G.I. Joes hooded in Ku Klux Klan sheets. "What's that?" I asked, pointing to a small white Christmas ornament that spun slowly over the bog, glittering and sparkling like a disco ball in the afternoon sun.

"That's the North Star. They're running toward the North Star. Toward freedom."

I picked up Martin, Malcolm, and Harriet, teasing my dad by asking, "What are these, *inaction* figures?" Martin Luther King, Jr., looked okay. Stylishly dressed in a glossy black tight-fitting suit, a copy of Gandhi's autobiography glued to one hand and a microphone in the other. Malcolm was similarly outfitted, but was bespectacled and holding a burning Molotov cocktail that was slowly melting his hand. The smiling, racially ambiguous Weeble, which looked suspiciously like a boyhood version of my father, stayed true to its advertising slogan by wobbling and never falling down, whether balanced precariously in the palm of my hand or chased by the knights of white supremacy. There was something wrong with Ms. Tubman, though. She was outfitted in a form-fitting burlap sack, and I don't remember any of my history primers describing the woman known as Moses as being statuesque with a 36–24–36 hourglass figure, long silky hair, plucked eyebrows, blue eyes, dick-sucking lips, and pointy titties.

"Dad, you painted Barbie black."

"I wanted to maintain the beauty threshold. Establish a baseline of cuteness so that you couldn't say one doll was prettier than the other."

Plantation Barbie had a string coming out of her back. I pulled it. "Math is hard, let's go shopping," she said in a squeaky singsong voice. I set the black heroes back down in the kitchen table swamp, moving their limbs so that they resumed their runaway poses.

"I'm down with Ken and Barbie."

My father lost his scientific objectivity and grabbed me by the shirt. "What? Why?" he yelled.

"Because the white people got better accessories. I mean, look. Harriet Tubman has a gas lantern, a walking stick, and a compass. Ken and Barbie have a dune buggy and speedboat! It's really no contest."

The next day my father burned his "findings" in the fireplace. Even at the junior college level it's publish or perish. But more than the fact he'd never get a parking space with his name on it or a reduced course load, I was a failed social experiment. A statistically insignificant son who'd shattered his hopes for both me and the black race. He made me turn in my dream book. Stopped calling my allowance "positive reinforcement" and began referring to it as "restitution." While he never stopped pushing the "book learning," it wasn't long after this that he bought my first spade, pitchfork, and sheep-shearing razor. Sending me into the fields with a pat on the tush and Booker T. Washington's famous quote pinned to my denim overalls for encouragement, "Cast down your bucket where you are."

•

If there is a heaven worth the effort that people make to get there, then I hope for my father's sake there's a celestial psychology journal. One that publishes the results of failed experiments, because acknowledging unsubstantiated theories and negative results is just as important as publishing studies proving red wine is the cure-all we'd always pretended it was.

My memories of my father aren't all bad. Though technically I was an only child, Daddy, like many black men, had lots of kids. The citizens of Dickens were his progeny. While he wasn't very good with horses, he was known around town as the Nigger Whisperer. Whenever some nigger who'd "done lost they mother-fucking mind" needed to be talked down from a tree or freeway overpass precipice, the call would go out. My father would grab his social psychology bible, *The Planning of Change*, by Bennis, Benne, and Robert Chin, a woefully underappreciated Chinese-American psychologist my dad had never met but claimed as his mentor. Most kids got bedtime stories and fairy tales; I had to fall asleep to readings from chapters with titles like "The Utility of Models of the Environments of Systems for Practitioners." My father was nothing if not a practitioner. I can't remember a time when he didn't bring me along on a nigger whisper. On the drive over he'd brag that the black community was a lot like him—ABD.

"All but dissertation?"

"All but defeated."

When we arrived, he'd sit me on the roof of a nearby minivan or stand me atop an alleyway Dumpster, hand me a legal pad, and tell me to take notes. Among all the flashing sirens, the crying and broken glass crunching softly under his buckskin shoes, I'd be so scared for him. But Daddy had a way of approaching the unapproachable. His face sympathetic and sullen, palms turned up like a dashboard Jesus figurine, he'd walk toward some knife-wielding lunatic whose pupils were dilated to the size of atoms smashed by a quart of Hennessy XO and a twelve-pack light-beer chaser. Ignoring the bloodstained work uniform caked in brain and fecal matter, he'd hug the person like he was greeting an old friend. People thought it was his selflessness that allowed him to get so close, but to me it was his voice that got him over. Doo-wop bass deep, my father spoke in F-sharp. A resonant low-pitched tone that rooted you in place like a bobby-socked teenager listening to the Five Satins sing "In the Still of the Night." It's not music that soothes the savage beast but the systematic desensitization. And Father's voice had a way of relaxing the enraged and allowing them to confront their fears anxiety-free.

When I was in grade school, I knew from how the taste of the pomegranates would bring you to tears, from the way the summer sun turned our Afros blood-orange red, and from how giddy my father would get whenever he talked about Dodger Stadium, white Zinfandel, and the latest green flash sunset he'd seen from the summit of Mount Wilson that California was a special place. And if you think about it, pretty much everything that made the twentieth century bearable was invented in a California garage: the Apple computer, the Boogie Board, and gangster rap. Thanks to my dad's career in nigger-whispering, I was there for the birth of the latter, when at six o'clock on a cold, dark ghetto morning two blocks down from where I live, Carl "Kilo G" Garfield, hallucinating high on his own supply and Alfred Lord Tennyson's brooding lyricism, burst out of his garage squinting into his Moleskin, a smoldering crack pipe dangling from fingertips. It was the height of the crack rock era. I was about ten when he clambered into the bed of his tricked-out, hot-rod yellow Toyota pickup truck, the TO and the TA buffed out and painted over so that the brand name on the tailgate read just YO, and began reciting his verse at the top of his lungs, the slurred iambic pentameter punctuated with gun claps from his nickel-plated .38 and pleas from his mama to take his naked ass inside.

THE CHARGE OF THE LIGHT-SKINNED SPADE

> Half a liter, half a liter,
>   Half a liter onward
> All in the alley of Death
>   Rode the Olde English Eight Hundred.
> Forward, the Light-skinned Spade!
>   "Charge for the Bloods!" he said:
> Into the alley of Death
>   Rode the Olde English Eight Hundred . . .

When the SWAT team finally arrived on the scene, taking cover behind patrol car doors and the sycamore trees, clutching their assault rifles to their chests, none of them could stop giggling long enough to take the kill shot.

> Theirs not to reason what the fuck,
> Theirs but to shoot and duck:
>
> Niggers to the right of them
> Niggers to the left of them,
> Niggers in front of them
> Partied and blundered
> Bumrush'd at caps and hollow point shell
> While hooptie and hoodlum fell
> They that had banged so well
> Came thro' the jaws of Death
> Back from the ho's of Hell,
> All that was left of them
>   Left of the Olde English Eight Hundred.

And when my father, the Nigger Whisperer—that beatific smile splashed across his face—eased his way past the police barricade, put a tweed-jacketed arm around the broken-down drug dealer, and spoke some whispered profundity into his ear, Kilo G blinked blankly like a stage-show volunteer struck dumb by an Indian casino hypnotist, then calmly handed over his gun and the keys to his heart. The police closed in for the arrest, but my father asked them to stay back, beckoning Kilo to finish his poem, even joining in at the end of each line, pretending he knew the words.

> When can their shine and buzz fade?
> Oh the buckwild charge they made!
> All the motherfuckin' world wondered.
> Respect the charge they made
> Respect the charge of the Light-skinned Spade
>   The noble now empty Olde English Eight Hundred.

The police vans and cruisers disappeared into the morning haze, leaving my father, godlike, alone in the middle of the street, reveling in his humanitarianism. Cockily, he turned toward me. "You know what I said to get that psychotic motherfucker to lower his gun?"

"What did you say, Daddy?"

"I said, 'Brother, you have to ask yourself two questions, Who am I? And how may I become myself?' That's basic person-centered therapeutics. You want the client to feel important, to feel that he or she is in control of the healing process. Remember that shit."

I wanted to ask him why he never spoke to me in the same reassuring tone that he used with his "clients," but I knew, instead of an answer, I'd get the belt, and my healing process would involve Mercurochrome and, in place of being grounded, a sentence of five to no less than three weeks of Jungian active imagination. In the distance, hurtling away from me like some distant spiral galaxy, the red and blue sirens spun silently but brilliantly, lighting up the mist of the morning marine layer like some inner-city aurora borealis. I fingered a bullet hole in the tree bark, thinking that like the slug buried ten rings deep in the trunk, I'd never leave this neighborhood. That I'd go to the local high school. Graduate in the middle of my class, another Willie Lump Lump with a six-line résumé rife with spelling errors, trekking back and forth between the Job Center, the strip club parking lot, and the civil service exam tutorials. I'd marry, fuck, and kill Marpessa Delissa Dawson, the bitch next door and my one and only love. Have kids. Threaten them with military school and promises not to bail them out if they ever got arrested. I'd be the type of nigger who played pool at the titty bar and cheated on his wife with the blond cheese girl from the Trader Joe's on National and Westwood Boulevards. I'd stop pestering my father about my missing mother, finally admitting to myself that motherhood, like the artistic trilogy, is overrated. After a lifetime of beating myself up for never having been breast-fed or finishing *The Lord of the Rings*, *Paradise*, and *The Hitchhiker's Guide to the Galaxy*, eventually, like all lower-middle-class Californians, I'd die in the same bedroom I'd grown up in, looking up at the cracks in the stucco ceiling that've been there since the '68 quake. So introspective questions like "Who am I? And how can I be that person?" didn't pertain to me then, because I already knew the answer. Like the entire town of Dickens, I was my father's child, a product of my environment, and nothing more. Dickens was me. And I was my father. Problem is, they both disappeared from my life, first my dad, and then my hometown, and suddenly I had no idea who I was, and no clue how to become myself.

Two

Westside, nigger! What?

Three

The three basic laws of ghetto physics are: Niggers in your face tend to stay in your face; no matter where the sun is in the sky, the time is always "Half past a monkey's ass and a quarter to his balls"; and the third is that whenever someone you love has been shot, invariably you will be back home on winter break, halfway through your junior year of college, taking the horse on a little afternoon ride to rendezvous with your father for a meeting of the Dum Dum Donut Intellectuals, the local think tank, where he and the rest of the neighborhood savants will ply you with cider, cinnamon rolls, and conversion therapy. (Not that your dad thinks that you're gay, but he's worried that you never stay out past eleven and the word "booty" doesn't seem to be in your vocabulary.) It's a cold night. You're minding your own business, savoring the last of your vanilla shake, when you come upon a drove of detectives huddled around the body. You dismount. Step closer and recognize a shoe, or a shirtsleeve, or a piece of jewelry. My father was facedown in the intersection. I recognized him by his fist, cocked and knuckled up tight, the veins on the back of his hand still bulging and full. I compromised the crime scene by picking lint off his matted Afro, straightening the rumpled collar of his Oxford shirt, brushing the pebbles of gravel from his cheek, and, according to the police report, most egregiously by sticking my hand in the blood pooled around his body, which to my surprise was cold. Not hot, roiling with the black anger and lifelong frustration of a decent, albeit slightly crazy man who never became what he thought he was.

"You the son?"

The detective looked me up and down. His brow wrinkled, his eyes flicking back and forth from identifying feature to identifying feature. Behind the dismissive smirk I could almost see his brain cross-referencing my scars, height, and build with some database of wanted felons filed inside his head.

"Yes, I am."

"You something special?"

"Huh?"

"The officers involved said that when he charged them, he shouted, and I quote, 'I'm warning you, you anal-retentive, authoritarian archetypes, you don't know who my son is!' So, you someone special?"

Who am I? And how can I be that person?

"No, I'm no one special."

You're supposed to cry when your dad dies. Curse the system because your father has died at the hands of the police. Bemoan being lower-middle-class and colored in a police state that protects only rich white people and movie stars of all races, though I can't think of any Asian-American ones. But I didn't cry. I thought his death was a trick. Another one of his elaborate schemes to educate me on the plight of the black race and to inspire me to make something of myself, I half expected him to get up, brush himself off, and say, "See, nigger, if this could happen to the world's smartest black man, just imagine what could happen to your dumb ass. Just because racism is dead don't mean they still don't shoot niggers on sight."

Now, if I had my druthers, I couldn't care less about being black. To this day, when the census form arrives in the mail, under the "RACE" question I check the box marked "Some other race" and proudly write in "Californian." Of course, two months later, a census worker shows up at my door, takes one look at me, and says, "You foul nigger. As a black man, what do you have to say for yourself?" And as a black man, I never have anything to say for myself. Hence, the need for a motto, which, if we had, I'd raise my fist, shout it out, and slam the door in the government's face. But we don't. So I mumble Sorry and scribble my initials next to the box marked "Black, African-American, Negro, coward."

No, what little inspiration I have in life comes not from any sense of racial pride. It stems from the same age-old yearning that has produced great presidents and great pretenders, birthed captains of industry and captains of football; that Oedipal yen that makes men do all sorts of shit we'd rather not do, like try out for basketball and fistfight the kid next door because in this family we don't start shit but we damn sure finish it. I speak only of that most basic of needs, the child's need to please the father.

Many fathers foster that need in their children through a wanton manipulation that starts in infancy. They dote on the kids with airplane spins, ice cream cones on cold days, and weekend custody trips to the Salton Sea and the science museum. The incessant magic tricks that produced dollar pieces out of thin air and the open-house mind games that made you think that the view from the second-floor Tudor-style miracle in the hills, if not the world, would soon be yours are designed to fool us into believing that without daddies and the fatherly guidance they provide, the rest of our lives will be futile Mickey Mouseless I-told-ya-so existences. But later in adolescence, after one too many accidental driveway basketball elbows, drunken midnight slaps to the upside of our heads, puffs of crystal meth exhaled in our faces, jalapeño peppers snapped in half and ground into our lips for saying "fuck" when you were only trying to be like Daddy, you come to realize that the frozen niceties and trips to the drive-thru car wash were bait-and-switch parenting. Ploys and cover-ups for their reduced sex drives, stagnant take-home pay, and their own inabilities to live up to their father's expectations. The Oedipal yen to please Father is so powerful that it holds sway even in a neighborhood like mine, where fatherhood for the most part happens in absentia, yet nevertheless the kids sit dutifully by the window at night waiting for Daddy to come home. Of course, my problem was that Daddy was always home.

After all the evidence photos had been taken, the witnesses interviewed, and macabre homicide jokes cracked, without dropping my shake, I lifted my father's bullet-riddled body up by the underarms and dragged his heels through the chalk outline, through the yellow numbered shell-casing markers, through the intersection, the parking lot, and the glass double doors. I sat my father down at his favorite table, ordered his "usual," two chocolate frosteds and a large milk, and placed it in front of him. Since he had arrived thirty-five minutes late and dead, the meeting was already in progress, chaired by Foy Cheshire, fading TV personality, erstwhile friend of my father, and a man all too anxious to fill the void in leadership. There was a brief moment of awkwardness. The skeptical Dum Dums looking at the heavyset Foy like the nation must have looked to Andrew Johnson after Lincoln had been assassinated.

I loudly slurped up the dregs of my shake. The signal to carry on, because that's the way my father would've wanted it.

The Dum Dum Donut revolution must go on.

My father founded the Dum Dum Donut Intellectuals way back when, when he noticed that the local Dum Dum Donuts franchise was the only non-Latino or black-owned business that wasn't burned and pillaged in the riots. In fact, looters, police officers, and firemen alike used the twenty-four-hour drive-thru window to fuel up on crullers, cinnamon twists, and the surprisingly good lemonade as they fought off the conflagration, the fatigue, and the

pesky news crews who asked anyone within arm's length of a microphone, "Do you think the riots will change anything?"

"Well, I'm on TV, ain't I, bitch?"

In all its years of existence, Dum Dum Donuts has never been
robbed, burglarized, egged, or vandalized. And to this day, the franchise's art deco facade remains graffiti and piss-stain free. Customers don't park in the handicapped spot. Bicyclists leave their
vehicles unlocked and unattended, stuffed neatly into the rack like
Dutch cruisers parked at an Amsterdam train station. There's something tranquil, almost monastic, about the inner-city donut shop.
It's clean. Spotless. The employees are always sane and respectful.
Maybe it's the muted lighting or the bright decor, whose color
scheme is designed to be emblematic of a maple frosted with rainbow sprinkles. Whatever it is, my father recognized the donut shop
was the one place in Dickens where niggers knew how to act. People
passed the non-dairy creamer. Strangers politely pointed to the tip
of your nose and made the universal sign for "Brush the powdered
sugar off your face." In 7.81 square miles of vaunted black community, the 850 square feet of Dum Dum Donuts was the only place
in the "community" where one could experience the Latin root of
the word, where a citizen could revel in common togetherness. So
one rainy Sunday afternoon, not long after the tanks and media
attention had left, my father ordered his usual. He sat at the table
nearest the ATM and said aloud, to no one in particular, "Do you
know that the average household net worth for whites is $113,149
per year, Hispanics $6,325, and black folks $5,677?"

"For real?"

"What's your source material, nigger?"

"The Pew Research Center."

Motherfuckers from Harvard to Harlem respect the Pew Research Center, and hearing this, the concerned patrons turned
around in their squeaky plastic seats as best they could, given that
donut shop swivel chairs swivel only six degrees in either direc-

tion. Pops politely asked the manager to dim the lights. I switched on the overhead projector, slid a transparency over the glass, and together we craned our necks toward the ceiling, where a bar graph titled "Income Disparity as Determined by Race" hovered overhead like some dark, damning, statistical cumulonimbus cloud threatening to rain on our collective parades.

"I was wondering what that li'l nigger was doing in a donut shop with a damn overhead projector."

Next thing the people knew, my father, interspersed with a macroeconomics circulation flowchart there, a sketch of Milton Friedman here, was facilitating an impromptu seminar about the evils of deregulation and institutional racism. How it wasn't the Keynesian lapdogs so beloved by the banks and the media who predicted the most recent financial meltdown but the behavioral economists who knew that the market isn't swayed by interest rates and fluctuations in GDP, rather by greed, fear, and fiscal illusion. The discussion grew animated. Their mouths stuffed with pastries, their lips flaked with coconut shavings, the Dum Dum Donuts patrons decried low-interest checking and the nerve of the goddamn cable company to charge late fees for not promptly paying ahead of time in July for services not rendered until August. One woman, her jowls filled to near bursting with macaroons, asked my father, "How much the Chinos make?"

"Well, Asian men earn more than any other demographic."

"Even the faggots?" shouted the assistant manager. "You sure Asians make more than the faggots? 'Cause I hear faggots be making cash hand over fist."

"Yes, even the homosexuals, but remember, Asian men have no power."

"And what about the gay Asian males? Have you done a regression analysis controlling for race and sexual orientation?" That insightful comment came from Foy Cheshire, about ten years older than my dad, standing next to the water fountain, hands in his pockets, and wearing a wool sweater, even though it was 75 de-grees outside. This was way before the money and fame. Back then he was an assistant professor in urban studies, at UC Brentwood, living in Larchmont with the rest of the L.A. intellectual class, and hanging out in Dickens doing field research for his first book, *Blacktopolis: The Intransigence of African-American Urban Pov-erty and Baggy Clothes*. "I think an examination of the confluence of independent variables on income could result in some interest-ing r coefficients. Frankly, I wouldn't be surprised by p values in the .75 range."

Despite the smug attitude, Pops took a liking to Foy right away. Though Foy was born and raised in Michigan, it wasn't often Dad found somebody in Dickens who knew the difference between a t-test and an analysis of variance. After debriefing over a box of donut holes, everyone—locals and Foy included—agreed to meet on a regular basis, and the Dum Dum Donut Intellectuals were born. But where my father saw an opportunity for information exchange, public advocacy, and communal counsel, Foy saw a midlife springboard to fame. Things between the two of them started amicably enough. They strategized and chased women to-gether. But after a few years, Foy Cheshire got famous and my fa-ther never did. Foy was no deep thinker, but back then he was infinitely better organized than my dad, whose main strength was also his biggest weakness—he was way ahead of his time. While my dad was writing incomprehensible and unpublishable theories linking black oppression, game and social learning theory, Foy hosted a television talk show. Interviewing B-list celebrities and political figures, writing magazine articles, and taking meetings in Hollywood.

Once, while watching my father typing away at his desk, I asked him where his ideas came from. He turned around, his tongue thick with Scotch whiskey, and said, "The real question is not where do ideas come from but where do they go."

"So where do they go?"

"Punk motherfuckers like Foy Cheshire steal them and make not-so-small fortunes off your shit and invite you to the launch party like nothing happened."

The idea that Foy stole from my father was an award-winning Saturday-morning cartoon called *The Black Cats 'n' Jammin' Kids*, a show that had been syndicated around the world, dubbed into seven languages, and in the late mid-90s made Foy enough money to buy a dream house in the hills. My father never said anything in public. Never confronted Foy at the meetings, because, as he put it, "our people are in dire need of everything except acrimony." And in later years, when L.A. had turned Foy out like the small-town runaway he was at heart, after he'd lost his bankroll to a drug habit and a series of freckle-faced Creole L.A. women, been cheated out of his residuals by the production company, and had everything but his house and car seized by the IRS for tax evasion, my father kept quiet. When, gun to temple, Foy, flat broke and embarrassed, called to ask my dad to nigger-whisper him out of his suicidal funk, my father maintained patient-doctor confidentiality. Kept silent about the night sweats, the voices, the narcissistic personality disorder diagnosis, and the three-week psychiatric hospitalization. And the night my devoutly atheist father died, Foy prayed and spoke over him, hugged his lifeless body to his chest, and then acted as if the blood on his sparkling white Hugo Boss shirt was his own. You could see in his face that, despite his speech and poignant words about my father's death symbolizing black injustice, deep down he was happy my dad was gone. Because, with my dad's death, his secrets were safe, and maybe his grandiose Robespierre pipe dreams about the Dum Dum Donut Intellectuals being the black equivalent to the Jacobins might come true.

As the Dum Dums debated how to mete out a measure of revenge, I adjourned the meeting early by dragging my dad's body past the drink cooler and placing his corpse on the rear end of my

horse, facedown on the rump, like in the cowboy movies, his arms
and legs dangling in the air. At first the members tried to stop me.
Because how dare I remove the martyr before they had an opportunity for a photo op. Then the police took their turn, blocking the
streets with their cars so that I couldn't pass. I cried and cursed.
Circled my mount in the intersection and threatened anyone who
came near me with a horseshoe kick to the forehead. Eventually
the call went out for the Nigger Whisperer, but the Nigger Whisperer
was dead.

The crisis negotiator, Police Captain Murray Flores, was a man
my dad had worked with on many a nigger-whispering. He knew
his job well enough not to soft-soap the situation. And after raising
my father's head up to look him in face, he spat on the ground in
disgust and said, "What can I say?"

"You can tell me how it happened."

"It was 'accidental.'"

"And 'accidental' means?"

"Off the record, it means your dad pulled up behind plain-
clothes officers Orosco and Medina, who were stopped at a traffic
light, talking to a homeless woman. After the light changed from
green to red a couple of times, your dad zipped around them and,
while making a louie, yelled something, whereupon Officer Orosco
issued a traffic ticket and a stern warning. Your father said . . ."

" 'Either give me the ticket or the lecture, but you can't give me
both.' He stole that from Bill Russell."

"Exactly. You know your father. The officers took exception,
pulled their guns, your dad ran like any sensible person would,
they fired four shots into his back and left him for dead in the
intersection. So now you know. You just have to allow me to do my
job. You have to let the system hold the men responsible for this
accountable. So just give me the body."

I asked Captain Flores a question my father had asked me
many times: "In the history of the Los Angeles Police Department,

do you know how many officers have been convicted of murder while in the line of duty?"

"No."

"The answer is none, so there is no accountability. I'm taking him."

"Where?"

"I'm going to bury him in the backyard. You do what you have to do."

I don't think I'd ever seen a cop blow a whistle before. Not in real life. But Captain Flores blew his brass-plated whistle and waved the other officers, Foy, and the Dum Dum Donut protesters off. The blockade parted and I led a very slow-moving funeral procession to 205 Bernard Avenue.

It'd always been my father's dream to own 205 Bernard Avenue outright. "The Ponderosa," he called it. "Sharecropping, transracial adoption, and 'renting to own' is for suckers," he liked to say while he pored through real estate and no-money-down investment books, punching imaginary mortgage scenarios into the calculator. "My memoir . . . that'll be an easy twenty thousand upfront . . . We can pawn your mama's jewelry for five, six thou . . . and even though there's an early-withdrawal penalty on your college fund, if we cash that mug out now, home ownership will be right around the corner."

There never was any memoir, only titles shouted out while he was in the shower fucking some nineteen-year-old bubble-gum-blowing "colleague from the university." He'd stick his wet head out the door and, through the steam, ask what did I think about "The Interpretation of Niggers" or my favorite, "I'm Ai'ight. You're Ai'ight." And there was no jewelry. My mother, a former *Jet* magazine Beauty of the Week, had no baubles or trinkets on in the faded tearsheet pasted above my headboard. She was a modestly coiffed, curvy expanse of thighs and lip gloss lounging on a backyard diving board in a gold lamé bikini. All I knew about her was the extensive biographical information listed in the bottom right-hand corner of the photo. "Laurel Lescook is a student from Key Biscayne, Florida, who enjoys biking, photography, and poetry." Later in life I would track Ms. Lescook down. She was a paralegal in Atlanta who remembered my father as a man whom she'd never met, but who, after her one photo pictorial came out in September of '77, inundated her with marriage proposals, creepy poetry, and Kodak Instamatic photos of his erect penis. Given that my college savings amounted to $236.72, the total take from my sparsely attended black mitzvah, and that both my father's manuscript and my mother's jewelry collection were nonexistent, you'd think we'd never come to own that house, but as luck would have it, given my father's wrongful death at the hands of the police, and the $2 million settlement I'd later received, in a sense he and I bought the farm on the same day.

At first blush, his purchase of the proverbial farm seems the more metaphorical of the two transactions. But as even the most cursory of those early annual inspections by the California Department of Food and Agriculture bore out, to call 205 Bernard Avenue, that two-acre, just-this-side-of-lunar-surface fertile parcel of land in the most infamous ghetto in Los Angeles County with its hollowed-out 1973 Winnebago Chieftain motor home for a barn, a dilapidated-overcrowded-Section-8-henhouse-topped-by-a-weathervane-so-rusted-in-place-that-the-Santa-Ana-winds-El-Niño-and-the-'83-tornado-couldn't-move-it, medfly-infested-two-tree-lemon-grove, three horses, four pigs, a two-legged goat with shopping-cart wheels for back hooves, twelve stray cats, one cow herd of livestock, and the ever-present cumulonimbus cloud of flies that circled the inflatable "fishing" pond of liquefied swamp gas and fermented rat shit that I pulled out of foreclosure on the very same day my dad decided to tell the undercover police officer Edward Orosco to "move his piece o' shit Ford Crown Victoria and stop blocking the goddamn intersection!" with funds borrowed against what the courts would later determine to be a $2 million settlement for gross miscarriage of justice, to call that unsubsidized tract of inner-city Afro-agrarian ineptitude a "farm" would be to push the limits of literality. Had me and Pops founded Jamestown instead of the Pilgrims, the Indians would have looked at our wilted, meandering, labyrinthlike rows of maize and kumquats and said, "Today's corn planting seminar is canceled, because you niggers ain't going to make it."

When you grow up on a farm in the middle of the ghetto, you come to see that what your father always told you during morning chores was true: People eat the shit you shovel them. That like the pigs, we all have our heads in the trough. While the hogs don't believe in God, the American dream, or the pen being mightier than the sword, they do believe in the feed in the same desperate way we believe in the Sunday paper, the Bible, black urban radio, and hot sauce. On his off days, he'd often invite the neighborhood over just to watch me work. Though the Farms was zoned for agriculture, most of the families had long abandoned the salt-of-the-earth farming lifestyle for backyard acreage that featured full-sized basketball and tennis courts and maybe a guest cottage in the corner. And although a few families still maintained chicken coops and maybe raised a cow, or ran an equestrian school for at-risk youth, we were the only family giving full-scale farming a go. Trying to cash in on some forgotten post–Civil War promise. Forty acres and a fool. "This little nigger not going be like the rest of you niggers," my father would crow, one hand on his dick, the other pointing at me. "My son going to be a Renaissance nigger. A modern-day Galileo out this motherfucker!" Then he'd crack open a bottle of bumpy-face, hand out the paper cups, ice cubes, and splashes of lemon-lime soda, and from the back porch they'd watch me pick strawberries, snow peas, or whatever the fuck was in season. Cotton was the worst. Forget the stooping, the thorns, the droning Paul Robeson spirituals that he played loud enough to drown out the Lopezes' ranchero music coming from next door, or that planting, watering, and harvesting cotton was a complete waste of time, because the only gin we had was the Styrofoam cup of Seagram's in his hand, picking cotton sucked because it made Daddy nostalgic. A sentimental drunk and full of gin 'n' juice pride, he'd brag to our black neighbors how I'd never spent a day in day care or had a sandbox play date. Instead, he swore up and down I was nannied and mammied by a sow named Suzy Q and was the loser in a sibling "piglet versus niglet" rivalry to a porcine genius named Savoir Faire.

Daddy's friends would watch me expertly pluck cotton bolls from the dried stems, waiting for me to snort and overthrow the Orwellian social order, and thus confirm my hog-tied upbringing.

1. Whatever goes upon two legs is an enemy.
2. Whatever goes on four legs, or six wings and a biscuit, is a friend.
3. No Pigger shall wear shorts in the fall, much less the winter.
4. No Pigger shall be caught sleeping.
5. No Pigger shall drink presweetened Kool-Aid.
6. All Piggers are created equal, but some Piggers ain't shit.

I don't remember my father tying my right hand behind my back or being babysat in the pigpen, but I do remember pushing Savoir Faire, one hand on each prickly milk-fattened hindquarter, up the wooden ramp and into the trailer. The last driver on Earth to use hand signals, my father took the corners slowly, lecturing me on how fall was the best time to kill a pig because there were less flies and the meat would keep for a while outside, because once you freeze it, the quality starts to go down. Unbuckled, like any child raised before car seats and airbags, I knelt in the seat facing backward, looking out that tiny rear window at Savior Faire, the doomed, cloven-hoofed genius squealing like a four-hundred-pound bitch the whole way to the slaughterhouse. "You done won your last game of Connect Four, you fucking getting mucus on the pieces, 'I sunk your battleship,' 'King me!' son of a bitch." At stoplights Daddy would stick his arm out of the window, bent at the elbow, hand toward the ground, palm facing the rear. "People eat the shit you shovel them!" he'd shout over the radio music, somehow shifting, steering, turning on the blinker, making the hand signal, a left turn, singing along to Ella Fitzgerald, and reading the *L.A. Times* bestseller list all at the same time.

People eat the shit you shovel them.

I'd like to say, "I buried my father in the backyard and that day I became a man," or some other droll American bullshit, but all that happened was that day I became relieved. No more trying to look uninvolved as my own father fought for parking spaces at the Farmers Market. Shouting down Beverly Hills dowagers asserting their luxury sedan right of way by nosing their gigantic cars into spaces marked COMPACT ONLY. *You stupid overmedicated bitch. If you don't back that fucking jalopy out my space, I swear to God, I'm going to punch you in your anti-aging-cold-cream face and permanently reverse five hundred years of white privilege and five hundred thousand dollars of plastic surgery.*

People eat the shit you shovel them. And sometimes, when I pull up to the drive-thru window on horseback or return the disbelieving stares of a convertible carload of out-of-town *vatos* pointing at the black *vaquero* grazing his livestock in the trash-strewn fields underneath the power lines that stretch Eiffel Tower–like alongside West Greenleaf Boulevard, I think about all the lines of ad infinitum bullshit my father shoveled down my throat, until his dreams became my dreams. Sometimes, while I'm sharpening the plowshare and shearing the sheep, I feel like every moment of my life isn't mine but one of his "déjà vus." No, I don't miss my father. I just regret that I never had the nerve to ask him if it was really true that I'd spent the sensorimotor and preoperational stages of my life with one hand tied behind my back. Talk about starting life off with a handicap. Fuck being black. Try learning to crawl, ride a tricycle, cover both eyes while playing peek-a-boo, and constructing a meaningful theory of mind, all with one hand.

Four

You won't find Dickens, California, on the map, because about five years after my father died, and a year after I graduated college, it, too, perished. There was no loud send-off. Dickens didn't go out with a bang like Nagasaki, Sodom and Gomorrah, and my dad. It was quietly removed like those towns that vanished from maps of the Soviet Union during the Cold War, atomic accident by atomic accident. But the city of Dickens's disappearance was no accident. It was part of a blatant conspiracy by the surrounding, increasingly affluent, two-car-garage communities to keep their property values up and blood pressures down. When the housing boom hit in the early part of the century, many moderate-income neighborhoods in Los Angeles County underwent real estate makeovers. Once pleasant working-class enclaves became rife with fake tits and fake graduation and crime rates, hair and tree transplants, lipo- and cholosuctions. In the wee hours of the night, after the community boards, homeowner associations, and real estate moguls banded together and coined descriptive names for nondescript neighborhoods, someone would bolt a large glittery Mediterranean-blue sign high up on a telephone pole. And when the fog lifted, the residents of the soon-to-be-gentrified blocks awoke to find out they lived in Crest View, La Cienega Heights, or

Westdale. Even though there weren't any topographical features like crests, views, heights, or dales to be found within ten miles. Nowadays Angelenos who used to see themselves as denizens of the west, east, and south sides wage protracted legal battles over whether their two-bedroom, charming country cottages reside within the confines of Beverlywood or Beverlywood Adjacent.

Dickens underwent a different type of transition. One clear South Central morning, we awoke to find that the city hadn't been renamed but the signs that said WELCOME TO THE CITY OF DICKENS were gone. There was never an official announcement, an article in the paper, or a feature on the evening news. No one cared. In a way, most Dickensians were relieved to not be from anywhere. It saved them the embarrassment of having to answer the small-talk "Where are you from?" question with "Dickens," then watching the person apologetically back away from you. "Sorry about that. Don't kill me!" Rumor had it the county had revoked our charter because of the admittedly widespread local political corruption. The police and fire stations were closed down. You'd call what used to be city hall and a foul-mouthed teenager named Rebecca would answer, *Don't no niggers name Dickens live here, so don't be calling here no more!* The autonomous school board dismantled. Internet searches turned up only references to "Dickens, Charles John Huffam" and to a dust bowl county in Texas named after some unfortunate sap who may or may not have died at the Alamo.

In the years after my father died, the neighborhood looked to me to be the next Nigger Whisperer. I wish I could say that I answered the call to duty out of a sense of familial pride and communal concern, but the truth was, I did it because I had no social life. Nigger-whispering got me out of the house and away from the crops and the animals. I met interesting people and tried to convince them that no matter how much heroin and R. Kelly they had in their systems, they absolutely could not fly. When my father nigger-whispered, it didn't look so hard. Unfortunately, I wasn't blessed with my father's sonorous, luxury-car-commercial voiceover bass profundo. I'm squeamishly shrill and possess all the speaking gravitas of the "shiest" member of your favorite boy band. The skinny, soft-spoken one who in the music video sits in the backseat of the convertible and never gets the girl, much less a solo, so I was issued a bullhorn. Ever try to whisper through a bullhorn?

Up until the city's disappearance, the workload wasn't so bad. I was an every-other-month crisis negotiator, a farmer doing a little nigger-whispering on the side. But since Dickens's erasure I found myself in my pajamas, at least once a week, standing bare-foot in an apartment complex courtyard, bullhorn in hand, star-ing up at some distraught, partially hotcombed-headed mother dangling her baby over a second-floor balcony ledge. When my father did the whispering, Friday nights were the busiest. Every pay-day he'd be inundated by teeming hordes of the bipolar poor, who having spent it all in one place, and grown tired and unsated from the night's notoriously shitty prime-time television lineup, would unwedge themselves from between the couch-bound obese family members and the boxes of unsold Avon beauty products, turn off the kitchen radio pumping song after song extolling the virtues of Friday nights living it up at the club, popping bottles, niggers, and cherries in that order, then having canceled the next day's appoint-ment with their mental health care professional, the chatterbox cosmetologist, who after years doing heads, still knows only one hairstyle—fried, dyed, and laid to the side—they'd choose that Friday, "day of Venus," goddess of love, beauty, and unpaid bills, to commit suicide, murder, or both. But under my watch people tend to snap on Wednesday. Hump day. And so sans juju, gris-gris, and the foggiest notion of what to say, I'll press the trigger, and with a loud squeal of ear-piercing feedback, the bullhorn buzzes to stat-icky life. Half the unchosen tribe waiting for me to say the magic words and save the day; the other half waiting expectantly for a bathrobe to fly open and some milk-engorged titties to come popping out.

Sometimes I open with a little humor, remove a slip of paper from a large manila envelope, and in my best impersonation of a sensationalist afternoon-talk-show host announce, "When it comes to eight-month-old Kobe Jordan Kareem LeBron Mayweather III, I am *not* the father . . . but I wish I were," and providing I don't look too much like the baby's real father, the mother will laugh and drop the little crumb-snatcher, shit-filled diaper and all, into my waiting arms.

Usually it isn't so simple. Most times there's so much Nina Simone "Mississippi Goddam" despondency in the night air it becomes hard to focus. The deep purple contusions about the face and arms. The terry-cloth robe finally falling seductively off the shoulders, revealing the woman to be a man; a man with hormonally induced breasts, shaved pubes, surprisingly shapely hips, and a tire-iron-brandishing significant other, who, underneath that bulky sweatshirt and baseball cap cocked to the side, might be a man, or just mannish, but either way is manically pacing the carport, threatening to bash in my skull if I say the wrong thing. The baby, swaddled in blue because blue is for Crip-centric boys, will be either too fat or too skinny, crying its little lungs out so loudly you'd wish it'd shut up, or even worse, so bone-chillingly quiet that under the circumstances you think it must already be dead. And invariably, softly in the background, billowing the curtains through the parted sliding glass doors, there's always Nina Simone. These are the women my father warned me about. The drug-and-asshole-addled women who sit in the dark, hard up and lovesick, chain-smoking cigarettes, phones pressed to their ears, speed-dialing K-Earth 101 FM, the oldies station, so they can request Nina Simone or the Shirelles' "This Is Dedicated to the One I Love," aka "This Is Dedicated to Niggers That Beat Me Senseless and Leave." "Stay away from bitches who love Nina Simone and have faggots for best friends," he'd say. "They hate men."

Swinging by its tiny heels, the baby carves giant, parabolic, fast-pitch softball, windmill circles in the air. And I stand there useless, a vacant look on my face, a nigger whisperer without secrets and sweet nothings to whisper. The crowd murmurs that I don't know what I'm doing. And I don't.

"You don't stop fucking around, man, you gonna get that baby kilt."

"Killed."

"Whatever, nigger. Just say something."

They all think that after my dad died I went away to college, majored in psychology, and returned to continue his good work. But I have no interest in psychoanalytic theory, ink splotches, the human condition, and in giving something back to the community. I went to the University of California at Riverside because it had a decent agricultural studies department. Majored in animal sciences with dreams of turning Daddy's land into a hatchery where I could sell ostriches to all the early-nineties heavy rotation rappers, first-round draft choices, and big-budget movie sidekicks, eager to invest their "skrilla," and who, after flying first-class for the first time in their lives, laid down the dog-eared financial section of the in-flight magazine in their laps and thought to themselves, "Shit, ostrich meat is indeed the future!" It sounds like a financial no-brainer. A nutritious FDA-approved ostrich steak sells for twenty dollars a pound, the feathers go for five dollars apiece, and those bumpy brown leather hides are worth two hundred bucks each. But the real money would be on my end in selling breeders to the nouveau-nigger-riche, because the average bird yields only about forty pounds of edible meat, because Oscar Wilde is dead and no one wears plumage and feathered hats anymore except for drag queens over forty, Bavarian tuba players, Marcus Garvey impersonators, and mint-julep-sipping-Kentucky-Derby-trifecta-betting southern belles, who wouldn't buy black if you were selling the secret to ageless wrinkle-free skin and nine inches of dick. I knew full well the birds are impossible to raise, and I didn't have the start-up capital, but let's just say my sophomore year, the UC Riverside Small Farm Program was missing a few two-legged dissertations, because like the drug dealers say, "If I don't do it, somebody else will." And believe me when I tell you that, to this day, the cracked and abandoned nest eggs of many a bankrupt one-hit wonder run wild in the San Gabriel Mountains.

"I don't know what to say."

"Didn't you major in psychology like your daddy?"

"All I know is a little animal husbandry."

"Shit, being married to these animals is what gets these bitches into trouble in the first place, so you best say something to this heifer."

I minored in crop sciences and management, because Professor Farley, my intro to agronomy teacher, said that I was a natural horticulturist. That I could be the next George Washington Carver if I wanted to be. All I needed to do was apply myself and find my own equivalent to the peanut. A legume of my own, she joked, placing a single *phaseolus vulgaris* into my palm. But anyone who'd ever been to Tito's Tacos and tasted a warm cupful of the greasy, creamy, refried frijole slop covered in a solid half-inch of melted cheddar cheese knew the bean had already reached genetic perfection. I remember wondering why George Washington Carver. Why couldn't I have been the next Gregor Mendel, the next whoever it was that invented the Chia Pet, and even though nobody remembers Captain Kangaroo, the next Mr. Green Jeans? So I chose to specialize in the plant life that had the most cultural relevance to me—watermelon and weed. At best I'm a subsistence farmer, but three or four times a year, I'll hitch a horse to the wagon and clomp through Dickens, hawking my wares, Mongo Santamaría's "Watermelon Man" blasting from the boom box. That song pounding in the distance has been known to stop summer league basketball games mid–fast break, end many a ding-dong-ditch, double-Dutch marathon early, and force the women and children waiting at the intersection of Compton and Firestone for the last weekend visitation bus to the L.A. County Jail to make a difficult decision.

Although they're not hard to grow, and I've been selling them for years, folks still go crazy at the sight of a square watermelon. And like that black president, you'd think that after two terms of looking at a dude in a suit deliver the State of the Union address, you'd get used to square watermelons, but somehow you never do. The pyramidal shapes are big sellers also, and around Easter I sell bunny rabbit–shaped ones that I've genetically altered so that if you squint, the dark lines in the rind spell out *Jesus Saves.* Those I can't keep on the wagon. But it's the taste that keeps them coming back. Think of the best watermelon you've ever had. Now add a hint of anise and brown sugar. Seeds that you're reluctant to spit out because they cool your mouth like the last sweet remnants of a cola-covered ice cube melting on the tip of your tongue. I've never seen it, but they say people have bitten into my watermelon and fainted straightaway. That paramedics fresh from CPR rescues of customers nearly drowned in six inches of blue backyard plastic wading pool water don't ask about heatstroke or a family history of heart disease. Their faces covered in sticky red remnants of mouth-to-mouth resuscitation nectar, their cheeks freckled with black seeds, they stop licking their lips only long enough to ask, "Where did you get the watermelon?" Sometimes, when I'm in an unfamiliar neighborhood, looking for a stray goat on the Latino side of Harris Avenue, a click of peewees, fresh out of cholo school, their newly shorn scalps gleaming in the sun, will step to me, grab me by the shoulders, and with a forceful reverence say, *"Por la sandía . . . gracias."*

But even in sunny California you can't grow watermelon year-round. The winter nights are colder than people think. Twenty-pound melons take forever to mature, and they suck nitrate out of the soil like it's sodium crack. So it's the marijuana that's my

mainstay. I rarely sell it. Weed isn't a cash crop, but more like a gas
money one, plus I don't want motherfuckers running up on me
in the middle of the night. Occasionally, I'll pull out an eighth, and
the unsuspecting homie who's been weaned on the Chronic,
and who now lies on my front lawn covered in dirt and grass, laughing his ass off, his legs entwined in the frame of the bicycle he's
forgotten how to ride, will proudly hold up the joint he never
dropped and ask me, "What this shit called?"

"Ataxia," I'll say.

On the house party dance floor, when La Giggles, whom I've
known since second grade, finally stops staring incessantly into
her compact mirror at a face she likes but doesn't quite recognize,
she turns to me and asks three questions. Who am I? And who
this nigger sticking his tongue in my ear grinding on my ass? And
what the fuck am I smoking? The answers to her questions are:
Bridget "La Giggles" Sanchez, your husband, and Prostopagnosia.
Sometimes folks wonder why I *always* have the kine bud. But any
suspicious curiosity can be allayed with a shrug of the shoulders
and a deadpan "Oh, I know some white boys . . ."

Light up a joint. Exhale. Weed that smells bad is good. And a
dank, wispy cloud of smoke that smells like red tide at Huntington
Beach, dead fish, and seagulls roasting in the hot sun will make a
woman stop twirling her baby. Offer her a hit, sloppy-end first.
She'll nod. It's Anglophobia, a strain that I've just developed, but
she doesn't need to know that. Anything that will allow me to
come closer is a good thing. Approach in peace, and climb the ivy-
covered latticework or stand on some big nigger's shoulders and
put myself within arms' reach, so that I can touch her. Stroke her
with techniques that are basically the same ones I used on the
thoroughbreds at school after a work-study day of galloping and
breezing horses in the fields. Rub her ears. Blow gently into her
nostrils. Work her joints. Brush her hair. Shotgun weed smoke
into her pursed and needy lips. When she hands me the baby, and

I descend the stairs into the applause of the waiting crowd, I'd like to think that Gregor Mendel, George Washington Carver, and even my father would be proud, and sometime while they're being strapped to the gurney or consoled by a distraught grandmother, I'll ask them, "Why Wednesday?"

Five

Dickens's evanesce hit some folks harder than others, but the citizen who needed my services the most was old man Hominy Jenkins. Hominy had always been a little unstable, but my father never really dealt with him. I don't think he thought losing a gray-haired relic to Uncle Toms past would be any great loss to the neighborhood, so it'd be up to me to "go get that fool nigger." I guess, in a sense, Hominy was my first nigger whisperee. I can't count how many times I had to wrap a blanket around him because he was trying to commit suicide-by-gangbanger by wearing red in the blue neighborhoods, blue in the red, or shouting, *"¡Yo soy el gran pinche mayate! ¡Julio César Chávez es un puto!"* in the brown. He used to climb palm trees and recite Tarzan lines to the natives, "Me Tarzan, you Shaniqua!" And I'd have to beg every woman in the neighborhood to lower her gun and coax Hominy down with a phony contract from a long-dead movie studio, front-loaded with beer and smokehouse almond signing bonuses. One Halloween he yanked the doorbell wires from his living room wall and attached them to his testes, so when the trick-or-treaters rang the buzzer, instead of candy and an autographed photo, they got blood-curdling screams that continued until I fought my way through the sadistic throng of fairy godmothers and superheroes and pulled

She-Hulk's green eight-year-old finger away from the ringer long enough for me to talk Hominy into pulling his pants up and the shades down.

As the supposed Murder Capital of the World, Dickens never got much tourist trade. Occasionally, a pack of college kids vacationing in Los Angeles for the first time would stop at a busy intersection just long enough to shoot twenty seconds of shaky handheld video of them jumping up and down, whooping like crazed savages, shouting, "Check us out! We're in Dickens, California. What you know about that, fool?" then post the footage of their urban safari on the Internet. But when all the WELCOME TO DICKENS signs were removed, there was no Blarney Stone to kiss, the urban voyeurs stopped coming. Sometimes genuine sightseers did come through. Mostly old and pensioned, they'd troll the streets in their out-of-state license-plated RVs looking for the last link to their youths. Those halcyon days the campaign politicians always promise to take us back to when America was powerful and respected, a land of morals and virtue and cheap gas. And asking a local, "Excuse me, do you know where I can find Hominy?" was like asking some penny-ante lounge singer if they knew the way to San Jose.

Hominy Jenkins is the last surviving member of the Little Rascals, that madcap posse of street urchins who, from the Roaring Twenties until the Reaganomics eighties, flummoxed potbellied coppers, ditching school seven days a week and twice on Sundays on matinee movie screens and after-school televisions around the world. Signed by Hal Roach Studios in the mid-1930s at a reputed $350 a week to be Buckwheat Thomas's understudy, Hominy cashed his checks and bided his time by playing minor roles: the silent little brother who had to be babysat while Mother was away visiting Papa in jail, the colored kid on the ass-end of the runaway mule. He made do delivering the occasional throwaway one-liner from the back of the one-room schoolhouse. Acknowledging talking babies, wild men from Borneo, and Alfalfa's soap-bubble solos with an exaggerated roll of the eyeballs and his trademark "Yowza!" The underutilization of his sooty black cuteness made bearable with the knowledge that one day soon he'd step into the oversized, curly-toed genie shoes of the great pickaninnies that preceded him. Take his rightful place in the wisecracking pantheon of Farina, Stymie, and Buckwheat, and carry the legacy of bowler-hatted, ragamuffin racism well into the 1950s. But the era of the human golliwog and the one-reeler died before his turn came. Hollywood had all the blackness it needed in the demi-whiteness of Harry Belafonte and Sidney Poitier, the brooding Negritude of James Dean, and the broad, gravity-defying, Venus hot-to-trot roundness of Marilyn Monroe's ass.

When they found his house, Hominy would greet his devotees with a wide Polident smile and an arthritic finger-wiggling high sign. Inviting them in for Hi-C Fruit Punch and, if they were lucky, slices of my watermelon. I doubt that he told his aging fan base the same stories he shared with us. It's hard to say what started the love affair between me and Marpessa Delissa Dawson. She's three years older than me and I've known her all my life. A lifelong resident of the Farms, her mother ran the Sun to Sun Equestrian and Polo School from their backyard. They used to call me whenever they were short a show jumper or a Number 4 on the Junior Spear-chukkers. I wasn't much good at either, because Appaloosas are shitty jumpers and using your left hand is illegal in polo. When we were younger, me, Marpessa, and the rest of the kids on the block would jet over to Hominy's house after school, because what could be cooler than watching an hour of *Little Rascals* with a Little Rascal? In those days, when remote control television was your father screaming, "Shawn! Don! Mark! One of you motherfuckers come downstairs and change this goddamn channel," fine-tuning a fickle ultra-high-frequency station like Channel 52, KBSC-TV Corona, Los Angeles, on a beat-up black-and-white portable missing one rabbit ear antenna and all its dials required a vascular surgeon's touch.

It took forever to finagle a set of plumbing pliers around the stubby metal knobs, looking for any angularity that might result in the weest bit of channel-changing torque or vertical and horizontal hold. But when the opening title sequence, accompanied by the drunken warbling horns in the *Our Gang* theme song, popped up on the TV, we'd settle in around gray-haired Hominy and those red-hot space heater coils like slave children gathered 'round ol' Remus and his fire.

"Tell us another story, Uncle Remus, we means Hominy."

"I ever tell you all about the time I fucked the shit out of Darla on the He Man Woman Hater's Club set during our twentieth reunion?"

I didn't realize it then, but Hominy, like any other child star still standing in the klieg light afterglow of a long-ago canceled career, was bat-shit crazy. We thought that he was being funny; dry humping the TV with every low-angle shot of Darla's exposed lace panties. "In real life that bitch wasn't as stingy with the pussy as she was in the movies." Slamming his pelvis into the screen, shouting, "That's for Alfalfa, Mickey, Porky, Chubby, Froggy, Butch, that stuck-up punk Wally, and the rest of the gang!" punctuating his blue-balls roll call with increasingly violent thrusts. Needless to say, there's an anger to Hominy. One that comes from not being as famous as you think you should be.

When he wasn't reminiscing about his sexual conquests, Hominy liked to brag about how he was fluent in four languages, because they shot each short four times, once in English, French, Spanish, and German. The first time he told us this, we laughed in his face, because all his mentor, Buckwheat, did was flash his greasy gap-toothed grin and say "O'tay, 'Panky," in that marble-mouthed pickaninny pluperfect of his, and "Okay, Spanky" is "Okay, Spanky" in any fucking language.

Once, one of my favorites episodes, "Mush and Milk," was on, and to prove his boast, Hominy turned down the volume just as the gang sat around the Bleak Hill Boarding School breakfast table.

Kindly Old Cap was waiting on his back pension. The house mother, wrinkled and as temperamental as a dog pound shar-pei, spat and hissed at the kids, one of whom, having screwed up the morning chores, whispers into another urchin's ear a line we didn't need sound to hear, because we'd heard it a million times.

"Don't drink the milk," we said aloud.

"Why?" A towheaded white boy mouthed.

"It's spoiled," we whispered in unison.

Don't drink the milk. Pass it on. And Hominy did just that, dubbing each waif's warning to the next rascal down in a different language.

"*No bebas la leche. ¿Porqué? Está mala.*"

"*Ne bois pas le lait. Pourquoi? C'est gate.*"

"*Trink die Milch nicht! Warum? Die ist schlecht.*"

Don't drink the milk. Why? It's spoiled.

The milk was spoiled because in reality it was liquefied plaster of paris that hadn't yet hardened into a sight gag, and child stardom spoiled Hominy. Sometimes after a particularly abrupt edit for the sake of political correctness, he'd stomp his feet and pout. "I was in that scene! They edited me out! Spanky finds Aladdin's lamp, he rubs it and says, 'I wish Hominy was a monkey. I wish Hominy was a monkey!' And lo and motherfucking behold, I'm a motherfucking monkey."

"A monkey?"

"A capuchin, to be exact, and my method-acting monkey-ass hit the streets running, baby! And I comes across a nigger soda jerk making time with his old lady, he closes his eyes, leans in for a little loving; she sees me, splits, and that fool plants a wet one right on my big pink simian lips. That had them rolling in the aisles. 'A Lad in a Lamp,' most screen time I ever had. I fought the whole damn police force, and by the end of the picture, me and Spanky eating cake 'n' shit, and running the whole goddamn town. And let me tell you, Spanky was without question the coolest motherfuckering white boy ever. Yowza!"

It was hard to determine if he'd been turned into a real monkey or if Hal Roach Studios, never known for its extravagant special effects, just opened up the timeless cookbook of Classic American Stereotyping and turned to the one-step recipe for Negro Monkeyshines: 1. Just add tail. Whatever the case, as the celluloid snippets of censored slapstick racism piled up on the cutting room floor, it became apparent that Hominy was a sort of *Little Rascals* stunt coon. His film career was a compendium of unseen outtakes where he's doused with all things white: sunny-side-up eggs, paint, and pancake flour avalanches. Eyeballs bulging with fear and hyperthyroidism, sometimes the sight of a ghost in an abandoned house or a congregation of newly baptized holy ghost Negroes speaking in tongues and somnambulating through the thick of the local forest, or a white nightshirt blowing eerily on a clothesline like a hoodoo ghost come to billowing life would scare the shit out of Hominy. Turn him albino white. Blow out his Afro to freakishly long, scared-straight proportions and send him running headlong into a swamp tree, through a wooden fence or a plate-glass window. And he was constantly being electrocuted, both by his own ineptitude and by acts of a God whose supposedly random lightning strikes somehow never failed to miss the crack of his suspender-pants-covered ass. In "Frankly, Ben Franklin," after the prototype is chewed up by Petey the Pitbull, who else but Hominy would volunteer to be the bespectacled Spanky's kite? Sewn spread-eagle onto a giant Betsy Ross flag, wearing nothing but a set of tattered slave britches, a tricorne hat with a metal rod sticking out of its crown, and a placard hanging from his neck that in runny ink reads THESE ARE THE TIMES THAT FRY MEN'S SOULS— NATHAN HAIL, he soars high in the sky, a flying black squirrel sailing through the stinging rain, gale-force winds, and a fusillade of lightning bolts. There's a thunderclap, followed by a cloud of sparks, and Spanky examining a glowing, electrified skeleton key attached to the kite string. "Eureka," he's about to say, before he's rudely interrupted from up above, where Hominy, stuck in the tree branches, a smoldering ashen heap, smoke billowing from every orifice, eyes and teeth forever phosphorescent, delivers the longest line of his career, "Yowza! I done discobered electbicidy."

Over time, with the advent of cable television, home video games, and Melanie Price's bodacious eighth-grade bosoms, which she liked to show off in bedroom window striptease acts that started at the exact same time the *Little Rascals* did, one by one the gang stopped visiting Hominy after school, until it was only me and Marpessa left. I'm not sure why she stayed. She had her own fifteen-year-old tube-top breasts to show off. Sometimes the older guys would come up to the door and ask her to come outside to talk. But she'd always wait until the *Little Rascals* was over. Leaving the homeboys on Hominy's porch. I'd like to think that Marpessa liked me even then. But I know it was probably pity and a sense of safety that kept her around from three thirty to four. Munching on grapes and watching the gang put on extravagant backyard variety shows featuring raspy-voiced seven-year-olds and colored kids tap-dancing up a storm, what harm could a thirteen-year-old home-schooled farm boy and superannuated coon do?

"Marpessa?"

"Huh?"

"Wipe your chin, it's wet."

"Let me tell you, that's not all that's wet. That's how good these goddamn grapes is. You really grow these yourself?"

"Yup."

"Why?"

"Homework."

"Your father's fucking crazy."

I suppose that's what I first loved about Marpessa, her unabashed inappropriateness. I guess I loved her titties, too. Although, like she said whenever she caught me staring at them, I wouldn't know what to do with them if I ever had half the chance. Eventually the lure of older boys with drug money and sperm counts outweighed the sonorous charms of Alfalfa in a cowboy hat singing "Home on the Range," and for the longest time, it was just me, Hominy, and the grapes. I never regretted passing up the side-yard peepshows with my friends. I always figured that if Marpessa kept eating my grapes and drooling nectar down her ample chest, sooner or later those drill-bit hard nipples would bore through the wet spots on her shirt.

Sadly, I never saw a three-dimensional mammary until the eve of my sixteenth birthday, when I woke up one night to find Tasha, one of my dad's "teaching assistants," sitting on the edge of my bed, naked, reeking of postcoital must and muscatel, and reading Nancy Chodorow aloud: "Mothers are women, of course, because a mother is a female parent . . . We can talk about a man 'mothering' a child, if he is this child's primary nurturing figure, or is acting in a nurturant manner. But we would never talk about a woman 'fathering' a child." To this day, whenever I'm lonely, I touch myself, thinking about Tasha's titty and about how Freudian hermeneutics doesn't apply to Dickens. A place where, often as not, it's the child who raises the parents, where the Oedipus and Electra complexes are simple, sons, daughters, stepparents, or play-cousins, it doesn't matter, since everybody's fucking each other over and penis envy doesn't exist because sometimes niggers just got *too much* dick.

I don't know exactly why, but I felt like I owed Hominy something for all those afternoons Marpessa and I spent at his house. That there's something about the craziness that he had to go through that's kept me relatively sane. And one blustery Wednesday morning, about three years ago, during a well-earned afternoon nap, I heard Marpessa's voice in my sleep. "Hominy" was all she said. After scrambling outside, I found a hastily written sign Scotch-taped to Hominy's screen door fluttering in the breeze. *I'z in de back*, it read, his penmanship typical Little Rascal, squiggly, yet surprisingly legible. The back was Hominy's memorabilia room. A small fifteen-by-fifteen add-on that was once crammed with a treasure trove of *Our Gang* props, headshots, and costumes. There weren't many memories left. Most, like the suit of armor from which Spanky recited Mark Antony's soliloquy in "Shivering Shakespeare" under a barrage of peashooters, the lock of Alfalfa's personality, the top hat and tails Buckwheat wore when he conducted the Club Spanky Big Band and made "hundreds and thousands of dollars" in the "Our Gang Follies of 1938," the long-ass hook-'n'-ladder scrap-metal fire engine used to win Jane back from the rich kid with the real fire engine, and the kazoos, flutes, and spoons that made up the wind and rhythm sections of the International Silver String Band had been long pawned and auctioned off.

As advertised, Hominy was indeed "in de back," buck naked and hanging by his neck from a wooden beam. Two feet away from him sat a folding chair marked RESERVED, and on its seat a photocopy playbill for "Curtain Call," a one-act of desperation. The noose was a bungee cord stretched to its bike rack limit, so much so that if he'd worn anything bigger than a size-eight shoe, his toes would've touched the ground. His face turning a deep shade of blue, I watched him twist in the draft. I had half a mind to let him die.

"Cut my penis off and stuff it into my mouth," he rasped with what air was left in his lungs.

Apparently, asphyxiation makes your penis hard, and his brown member sprouted like a twig from a frizzy snowball of shock-white pubic hair. Like an antique whirligig, he kicked about frantically as much from his simultaneous attempt to burn himself in effigy as from the paucity of oxygen reaching his already-Alzheimered brain. Fuck the White Man's Burden, Hominy Jenkins was my burden, and I knocked the can of kerosene and the lighter from his hand. Walked, not ran, back home to look for the gardening shears and some skin lotion. Taking my sweet time, because I knew that racist Negro Archetypes, like Bebe's Kids, don't die. They multiply. Because the kerosene splashed on my shirt smelled like Zima, but mostly because my father said he never panicked when someone from the neighborhood tried to hang themselves, because, "for the life of them, black people can't tie knots for shit."

I cut the self-lynching drama queen down. Lowered him gently to the rayon-carpeted floor and coddled his scraggly head. He filled my armpit with snot and tears as I rubbed cortisone into his rope-chafed neck and flipped through the playbill. On page two was a publicity shot of our boy chilling with the Marx Brothers on the set of the unreleased sequel to *A Day at the Races*, called *A Day Among the Races*. The Marx Brothers sit in backward-facing director's chairs labeled GROUCHO, CHICO, HARPO, and ZEPPO. At the lineup's far end is a high chair whose back reads DEPRESSO. In it, sitting cross-legged, is six-year-old Hominy, a thick white Groucho mustache painted on his upper lip. The photo is signed *To Hominy Jenkins, the Shvartze Sheep of the Family. Best Wishes from the Marxes—Groucho, Karl, Skid, et al.* Below this was Hominy's bio. A sad listing of his meager screen credits that read like a suicide note:

Hominy Jenkins (Hominy Jenkins)—Hominy's happy to make both his theatrical debut and his swan song at the Back Room Repertory Theater. In 1933 Hominy first put his wild, unkempt Afro to good use when he debuted as the wailing, abandoned Native Baby Boy in the original *King Kong*. He went on to survive that near Skull Island stomping and has since specialized in portraying black boys from the ages of eight to eighty, including most notably in *Black Beauty*—Stable Boy (uncredited), *War of the Worlds*—Paper Boy (uncredited), *Captain Blood*—Cabin Boy (uncredited), *Charlie Chan Joins the Klan*—Bus Boy (uncredited). Every film shot in Los Angeles between 1937 and 1964—Shoeshine Boy (uncredited). Other credits include various roles as Messenger Boy, Bell Boy, Bus Boy, Pin Boy, Pool Boy, House Boy, Box Boy, Copy Boy, Delivery Boy, Boy Toy (stag film), Errand Boy, and token Aerospace Engineer Boy in the Academy Award–winning film *Apollo 13*. He wishes to thank his many fans who have supported him throughout the years. What a long, strange trip it's been.

If that naked old man crying in my lap had been born elsewhere, say Edinburgh, maybe he'd be knighted by now. "Arise, Sir Hominy of Dickens. Sir Jig of Boo. Sir Bo of Zo." If he were Japanese and had managed to survive the war, the economic bubble and Shonen Knife, then it's quite possible he'd be one of those octogenarian Kabuki actors who, when he enters during the second act of *Kyô Ningyô*, the play comes to a reverential halt as the announcer introduces him to great fanfare and a government stipend. "Playing the role of Courtesan Oguruma, the Kyoto Doll, is Japanese Living National Treasure Hominy 'Kokojin' Jenkins VIII." But he had the misfortune of being born in Dickens, California, and in America Hominy is no source of pride: he's a Living National Embarrassment. A mark of shame on the African-American legacy, something to be eradicated, stricken from the racial record, like the hambone, Amos 'n' Andy, Dave Chappelle's meltdown, and people who say "Valentime's Day."

I placed my mouth to the waxy folds of Hominy's ear.

"Why, Hominy?"

I couldn't tell if he'd understood me. There was only that minstrel smile, pearly white, wide and servile, beaming blankly back at me. It's crazy how, in a way, child actors never seem to age. There's always one feature that refuses to grow old and marks them forever young, if not forgotten. Think Gary Coleman's cheeks, Shirley Temple's pug nose, Eddie Munster's widow's peak, Brooke

Shields's flat-chestedness, and Hominy Jenkins's effervescent smile.

"Why, massa? Because when Dickens disappeared, I disappeared. I don't get fan mail anymore. I haven't had a visitor in ten years, 'cause don't nobody know where to find me. I just want to feel relevant. Is that too much for an old coon to ask, massa? To feel relevant?"

I shook my head no, but I had one more question.

"And why Wednesdays?"

"You don't know? You don't remember? It was the last talk your father gave at the Dum Dum Donuts meetin'. He said that the vast majority of slave revolts took place on Wednesdays because traditionally Thursday was whippin' day. The New York Slave Revolt, the L.A. riots, the *Amistad*, all them shits," Hominy said, grinning woodenly from ear to ear like a ventriloquist's dummy. "Been this way ever since we first set foot in this country. Someone's getting whipped or stopped and frisked, whether or not anyone done anything wrong. So why not make it worthwhile and act a fool Wednesday if you gonna get beat on Thursday, right, massa?"

"Hominy, you're not a slave and I'm definitely not your master."

"Massa," he said, the smile evaporating from his face, and shaking his head in that pitiable way people who you think you're better than do when they catch you thinking that you're better than them, "sometimes we just have to accept who we are and act accordingly. I'm a slave. That's who I am. It's the role I was born to play. A slave who just also happens to be an actor. But being black ain't method acting. Lee Strasberg could teach you how to be a tree, but he couldn't teach you how to be a nigger. This is the ultimate nexus between craft and purpose, and we won't be discussing this again. I'm your nigger for life, and that's it."

Unable to distinguish between himself and the corny "I owe you my life, I'll be your slave" trope, Hominy had finally lost his

mind, and I should've hospitalized him right then and there. Called
the police and had him 5150'd. But once during an afternoon visit
to the Cinematheque Hollywood Home for the Aged, Forgetful
and Forgotten, he made me promise that I'd never institutionalize
him, because he didn't want to be exploited like his old friends
Slicker Smith, Chattanooga Brown, and Beulah "Mammy" Mc-
Queenie. Who, chasing one last film credit before heading up to
that green room in the sky, auditioned from their deathbeds for
novice film students from the UCLA Extension Program, looking to attach a star, even a faded-out senile one, to their certificate-
earning final projects.

The next morning, Thursday, I awoke to Hominy, standing in
my front yard, shirtless and barefoot and lashed to the curbside
mailbox, demanding that I whip him. I don't know who tied his
hands, but I do know that Hominy had tied mine.

"Massa."

"Hominy, stop."

"I want to thank you for saving my life."

"You know I'd do anything for you. Your work with the Little
Rascals made my childhood bearable."

"You want to make me happy?"

"Yes, you know that."

"Then beat me. Beat me to within an inch of my worthless black
life. Beat me, but don't kill me, massa. Beat me just enough so that
I can feel what I'm missing."

"Isn't there another way? Isn't there something else that would
make you happy?"

"Bring back Dickens."

"You know that's impossible. When cities disappear, they don't
come back."

"Then you know what to do."

They say it took three sheriff's deputies to pull me off his black
ass, because I whipped the shit out of that nigger. Daddy would've

said that I was suffering from "dissociative reaction." That's what he always attributed my beatings to. Opening up the *DSM I*, a holy book of mental disorders so old it defined homosexuality as "libidinal dylexsia," he'd point to "Dissociative Reaction," then clean his glasses and begin explaining himself slowly, "Dissociative reaction is like a psychic circuit breaker. When the mind experiences a power surge of stress and bullshit, it switches off, just shuts your cognition down and you blank out. You act but are unaware of your actions. So you see, even though I don't remember dislocating your jaw . . ."

I'd love to say that I awoke from my own fugue state and remembered only the stinging fizz of my wounds as Hominy gently dabbed at my police-inflicted abrasions with cotton balls soaked in hydrogen peroxide. But as long as I live, I'll never forget the sound of my leather belt against the Levi Strauss denim as I unsheathed it from my pants. The whistle of that brown-and-black reversible whip cutting through the air and raining down hard in loud skin-popping thunderclaps on Hominy's back. The teary-eyed joy and the thankfulness he showed me as he crawled, not away from the beating, but into it; seeking closure for centuries of repressed anger and decades of unrequited subservience by hugging me at the knees and begging me to hit him harder, his black body welcoming the weight and sizzle of my whip with groveling groans of ecstasy. I'll never forget Hominy bleeding in the street and, like every slave throughout history, refusing to press charges. I'll never forget him walking me gently inside and asking those who'd gathered around not to judge me because, after all, who whispers in the Nigger Whisperer's ear?

"Hominy."

"Yes, massa."

"What would you whisper in my ear?"

"I'd whisper that you're thinking too small. That saving Dickens nigger by nigger with a bullhorn ain't never going to work.

That you have to think bigger than your father did. You know the phrase 'You can't see the forest for the trees'?"

"Of course."

"Well, you have to stop seeing us as individuals, 'cause right now, massa, you ain't seeing the plantation for the niggers."

Six

They say "pimpin' ain't easy." Well, neither is slaveholdin'. Like children, dogs, dice, and overpromising politicians, and apparently prostitutes, slaves don't do what you tell them to do. And when your eighty-some-odd-year-old black thrall has maybe fifteen good minutes of work in him a day and enjoys the shit out of being punished, you don't get many of the plantation perks you see in the movies either. No woe is me, "Go Down Moses" field singing. No pillowy soft black breasts to nuzzle up to. No feather dusters. No one says "by 'n' by." No fancy dinners replete with candelabra and endless helpings of glazed ham, heaping spoonfuls of mashed potatoes, and the healthiest-looking greens known to mankind. I never got to experience any of that unquestioned trust between master and bondman. I just owned a wizened old black man who knew only one thing—his place. Hominy couldn't fix a wagon wheel. Hoe a fucking row. Tote barge or lift bale. But he could genuflect his ass off, and from 1:00 p.m. to 1:15 p.m., or thereabouts, hat in hand, he'd show up for work. Doing whatever he felt like doing. Sometimes work consisted of donning a shiny pair of emerald green and pink silks, holding a gas lamp at arm's length, and posing in my front yard as a life-size lawn jockey. Other times, he liked to serve as a human footstool, and when the spirit of servitude moved him, he'd drop to all fours at the foot of my horse or the base of the pickup truck and stay there until I stepped on his back and took an unwanted trip to the liquor store or the Ontario livestock auction. But mostly Hominy's work consisted of watching me work. Biting into Burbank plums whose tartness to sweetness to skin thickness ratios took me six years to get just right, and exclaiming, "Damn, massa, these plums sho' am good. They Japanese you say? Well, you musta stuck yo' hand up Godzilla's asshole, cuz you gotta green thumb like a motherfucker."

So believe me when I tell you human bondage is an especially frustrating undertaking. Not that I undertook anything, my dominion over this clinically depressed bondsman having been forced upon me. And let's be clear: I tried to "free" Hominy countless times. Simply telling him he was free had no effect. And once, I swear, I almost ditched him in the San Bernadino Mountains like an unwanted dog, but I saw a stray ostrich with a Pharcyde promotional bumper sticker affixed to its tail feathers and I lost my nerve. I even had Hampton draw up some manumission papers written in industrial-age jargon and paid some scrivener $200 to write out a contract on antique parchment paper that I found at a Beverly Hills stationery store, because apparently rich people still have use for it. What for? Who knows. Maybe, with the state of the banking system, they've gone back to the treasure map.

"To Whom It May Concern," the contract read. "With this deed I hereby emancipate, manumit, set free, permanently discharge, and dismiss my slave Hominy Jenkins, who's been in my service for the past three weeks. Said Hominy is of medium build, complexion, and intelligence. To all who read this, Hominy Jenkins is now a free man of color. Witness my hand on this day, October 17th, the year of 1838." The ruse didn't work. Hominy simply pulled down his pants, shit on my geraniums, and wiped his ass with his freedom, then handed it back to me.

"Medium intelligence?" he asked, raising a gray eyebrow. "One,

I know what year it is. Two, true freedom is having the right to be a slave." He hiked up his pants and slipped into his Metro-Goldwyn-Mayer plantationese. "I know taint nobody forcin' me, but dis here one slave you ain't never gwine be rid of. Freedom can kiss my postbellum black ass."

Slavery must have been profitable as hell for anybody to deal with all the mental anguish, but sometimes after a hot day of dehorning the goats and stringing barbed-wire fences, I'd be kicking back on the porch, watching the dusk scatter the smog red and heavy across the downtown sky, and Hominy would come outside with a pitcher of cold lemonade. There'd be something so satisfying about watching the condensation form and drip down the sides of the Tupperware as he slowly filled my glass, plop by painstaking ice cube plop, then fanned the horseflies and the heat from my face. In the cool air and ambient car stereo Tupac, I felt a refreshing hint of the dominion the landed Confederacy must have felt. Shit, if Hominy had always been so cooperative, I'd have fired on Fort Sumter, too.

On Thursdays, accidentally on purpose, Hominy would spill the refill in my lap. Sending me a not-so-subtle message, like a dog scratching at the screen door, that it was time for some action.

"Hominy."

"Yes, massa?" he'd say hopefully. Rubbing his hindquarters in preparation.

"Did you choose a counselor?"

"I looked on the Internet, and the therapists are all white. Standing in the forest or in front of a bookshelf, promising career and sexual fulfillment, and healthy relationships. How come you never see photos of them with their overachieving kids or fucking their partners to satisfaction? Where's the proof in the pudding?"

The wet patch on my pants would spread over my lap and toward my knees. "Okay, get in the truck," I'd say.

Oddly, Hominy didn't seem to mind that all the dominatrices

at Sticks and Stones, the BDSM club on the Westside I contracted to dole out my punishments for me, were white women. The Bastille room was his favorite torture chamber. There, naked save for a Union Civil War cap, Mistress Dorothy, a pale brunette whose pouty Maybelline red lips put Scarlett O'Hara's sneer to shame, strapped him to the wheel and whipped him silly. She'd clamp some contraption about his genitals and demand intel about Union Army troop movements and armament strength. Afterward Miss Dorothy would stick her head in the truck cab, plant a kiss on Hominy's cheek, and hand me the receipt. At two hundred bucks an hour plus "racial incidentals," the shit started to add up. The first five "coons," "jigaboos," "tar babies," and "Sambos" were free. After that, it was three dollars an epithet. And "nigger," in any of its varied forms, derivations, and pronunciations, was ten bucks a pop. Nonnegotiable. But after these sessions Hominy looked so happy it was almost worth it. Yet Hominy's happiness wasn't mine, it wasn't the city's, but I couldn't think of a way of restoring Dickens until one unusually warm spring evening returning home from Sticks and Stones.

Hominy and I found ourselves stuck on the 110 freeway, impatiently weaving from lane to lane. We were making good progress until we hit the stretch between the 405 and 105 interchanges and traffic began to slow. My father had a theory that poor people are the best drivers because they can't afford to carry car insurance and have to drive like they live, defensively. We were caught up in a slog of uninsured rust-bucket jalopies and compacts, all doing exactly fifty-five miles per hour, their trash bag windshields flapping in the wind. Hominy was beginning to come down from his masochistic high, the memories, if not the pain, of his session already beginning to fade away exit by exit. He poked at a bruise on his arm and asked himself where it came from. I snatched a joint from the glove compartment and offered him a medicinal hit.

"You know who was a pothead?" he said, refusing the doobage. "Little Scotty Beckett."

Scotty was a big-eyed Rascal who used to run with Spanky. Wore a floppy knit sweater and his baseball cap to the side, but the white boy was all punim and no pathos and he didn't last long. "Oh yeah? What about Spanky? Did he do drugs?"

"Spanky didn't do shit but fuck bitches. That's what Spanky did."

I rolled down the window. We still weren't moving very fast, and the stench of marijuana smoke hung guiltily in the air. The myth is that the Little Rascals, like a production of *Macbeth*, are cursed, that they all died horribly premature deaths.

GANG MEMBER	AGE	CAUSE OF DEATH
Alfalfa	42	Shot thirty times in the face (once for each freckle) in an argument over money
Buckwheat	49	Heart attack
Wheezer	19	Army training plane crash
Darla Hood	47	According to Hominy, he fucked her to death. In reality—hepatitis
Chubsy-Ubsy	21	Had something heavy on his heart. Unrequited love for Miss Crabtree and 300 lbs. of fat on a 5-foot frame
Froggy	16	Hit by truck
Pete the Pup	7	Swallowed alarm clock

Hominy squirmed in his seat, picking at the still-puffy red welts on his back, wondering why he was bleeding. Shit, maybe I was supposed to let him die. Maybe I should've just pushed him out of the car and onto the oily cracked asphalt of the Harbor Freeway. But what good would it do? Traffic came to a complete halt. A Jaguar, one of those ugly American-made models, was overturned in the fast lane. Its turtlenecked passenger unhurt, leaning against the median fence and reading a hardback novel you see only at airport bookstores. The rear-ended Honda sedan, with both its back end and its driver flattened and smoking, lay in the middle lane waiting to be carried to the junk- and graveyards, respectively. Jaguar model names sound like rockets: XJ–S, XJ8, E–Type. Hondas sound like cars designed by pacifists and humanitarian diplomats. The Accord, Civic, Insight. Hominy got out of the car to untangle the snarl. Waving his arms like the crazy man he was, he separated the cars by color, not that of the respective paint jobs, but by the hue of the motorists. "If you black, get back! White, to the right. Brown, go around. Yellow, follow the whites and let it mellow. Red, full speed ahead! Mulattos, full throttle!" If he couldn't categorize by sight, he asked the drivers what color they were. "Chicano? What color is that? You just can't make up a race, motherfucker. *Puto?* I got your *puto* right here, *pendejo!* You pick a lane, nigger, and stay in it! Get in where you fit in!"

With cops and flares arrived, and the traffic finally flowing freely, Hominy climbed back into the truck, dusting off his hands like he'd done something. "That's how you do shit. Sunshine Sammy taught me that. He used to say, 'Time waits on no man, but niggers wait on anybody with a twenty-five cent tip.'"

"Who the fuck is Sunshine Sammy?"

"Don't you worry about who Sunshine Sammy is. You new niggers got black presidents and golfers. I got Sunshine Sammy. The original Little Rascal, and by original I mean the very first one. And let me tell you, when Sunshine Sammy rescued the gang from an impossible predicament, now that was nonpartisan leadership."

Hominy slumped in his seat and clasped his hands behind his head and looked out the window and into his past. I flipped on the radio and let the Dodger game fill the silence. Hominy missed the good ol' days and Sunshine Sammy. I missed Vin Scully, the dulcet voice of objectivity, calling the play-by-play. For a baseball puritan like myself, the good ol' days were the days before the designated hitter, interleague play, steroids, and assholes in the outfield, baseball caps perched precariously atop their heads, flying off with every missed cut-off man and pop fly lost in the national pastime sun. They were me and Daddy, our mouths full of Dodger dogs and soda, two black bleacher and dharma bums sharing the June night heat with the moths, cursing a fifth-place team, and longing for the good ol' days of Garvey, Cey, Koufax, Dusty, Drysdale, and Lasorda. For Hominy any day when he could personify American primitivism was a good ol' day. It meant that he was still alive, and sometimes even the carnival coon in the dunk tank misses the attention. And this country, the latent high school homosexual that it is, the mulatto passing for white that it is, the Neanderthal incessantly plucking its unibrow that it is, needs people like him. It needs somebody to throw baseballs at, to fag-bash, to nigger-stomp, to invade, to embargo. Anything that, like baseball, keeps a country that's constantly preening in the mirror from actually looking in the mirror and remembering where the bodies are buried. That night the Dodgers lost their third straight. Hominy sat up in his seat and rubbed a porthole into the suddenly fogged-up windshield.

"We home yet?" he asked.

We were midway between the El Segundo and Rosecrans Avenue off-ramps, and it hit me: there used to be a sign that read DICKENS—NEXT EXIT. Hominy missed the good ol' days. I missed my father driving us back from the Pomona State Fair, elbowing me awake, the Dodger postgame on the radio as I rubbed the sleep from my eyes just in time to see that sign, DICKENS—NEXT EXIT, and know I was home. Shit, I missed that sign. And what are cities really, besides signs and arbitrary boundaries?

The green-and-white placard didn't cost much: a sheet of aluminum the size of a queen-sized bed, two six-foot metal poles, some traffic cones and flares, two reflective orange vests, two cans of spray paint, a couple of hard hats, and that night's sleep. Thanks to a downloaded copy of the *Manual of Uniform Traffic Control*

Devices, I had the design specifications for everything from the proper shade of green (Pantone 342) to the exact dimensions (60" x 36"), letter size (8"), and font (Highway Gothic). And after a long night of painting, cutting down the post to size, and stenciling SUNSHINE SAMMY CONSTRUCTION to the doors of the truck in removable paint, Hominy and I set back toward the freeway. Other than pouring and waiting for the cement foundation to dry, installing a traffic control device isn't all that different from planting a tree, and in the light of the high beams I set to work. Cleared the ivy, dug the holes, and planted the sign, while Hominy passed out in the front seat, listening to jazz on KLON.

As the sun rose over the El Segundo Boulevard overpass, the morning commute was starting in earnest. And amid the car honking, the rotors of the traffic helicopters beating overhead, and the grinding of truck gears, Hominy and I sat in the breakdown lane appreciating what we'd done. The sign was a dead ringer for any of the other "traffic control devices" one sees during the daily commute. It'd taken only a few hours, but I felt like Michelangelo staring at the Sistine Chapel after four years of hard labor, like Banksy after spending six days searching the Internet for ideas to steal and three minutes of sidewalk vandalism to execute them.

"Massa, signs are powerful things. It almost feels like Dickens exists out there in the smog somewhere."

"Hominy, what feels better, getting whipped or looking at that sign?"

Hominy thought a moment. "The whip feels good on the back, but the sign feels good in the heart."

When we arrived home that morning, I popped open a kitchen-table beer, sent Hominy home, grabbed the latest edition of *The Thomas Guide* from the bookshelf. At 4,084 square miles, much of Los Angeles County, like the ocean floor, remains in large part unexplored. Even though you needed an advanced degree in geomatics to understand its 800+ pages, *The Thomas Guide to Los Angeles County* is the spiral-bound Sacagawea for any intrepid explorer trying to navigate this urban oasis-less sprawl. Even in the days of GPS devices and search engines, it sits on the front seat of every taxicab, tow truck, and company car, and no Sureño worth their rolling "California stop" would ever be caught dead without one. I flipped the book open. Every year my father used to bring the new *Thomas Guide* home, and the first thing I'd do was turn to pages 704–5 and approximate the location of the crib, 205 Bernard Avenue, on the map. Finding my house in that giant tome grounded me somehow. Made me feel loved by the world. But 205 Bernard Avenue sat on a nameless peach-colored section of gridiron streets bordered by freeways on each side. I wanted to cry. It hurt knowing that Dickens had been exiled to the netherworld of invisible L.A. communities. Top-secret minority bastions like the Dons and the Avenues that've never had or needed *Thomas Guide* listings, official boundaries, or cheesy billboards announcing, "You are now entering . . ." or "You are now leaving . . ." because when the voice inside your head (the one you swear up and down isn't prejudice or racism) tells you to roll up the windows and lock the doors, you know you've entered the Jungle or Fruittown, and that when you start breathing again, you've exited. I dug up a blue marker, drew a crooked outline of my hometown as best as I could remember it, and scribbled DICKENS in big Dodger-blue letters across pages 704–5, and a little pictogram of the exit sign I'd just put up. If I ever raise the nerve, one day I'm going to erect two more signs. So if you find yourself hurtling southbound on the 110 freeway, speeding past two yellow-and-black blurs that read WATCH OUT FOR FALLING HOME PRICES and CAUTION—BLACK ON BLACK CRIME AHEAD, you'll know whom to thank for the roadside warnings.

THE DUM DUM
DONUT INTELLECTUALS

Seven

The Sunday after installing the roadside sign I wanted to make a formal announcement of my plan to reanimate the city of Dickens. And what better place to do so than the next meeting of the Dum Dum Donut Intellectuals, the closest approximation we had to a representative government.

One of the many sad ironies of African-American life is that every banal dysfunctional social gathering is called a "function." And black functions never start on time, so it's impossible to gauge how to arrive fashionably late without taking a chance of missing the event altogether. Not wanting to have to sit through the reading of the minutes, I waited until the Raiders game reached halftime. Since my father's death, the Dum Dum Donut Intellectuals had devolved into a group of star-struck, middle-class black out-of-towners and academics who met bimonthly to fawn over the semifamous Foy Cheshire. As much as black America treasures its fallen heroes, it was hard to tell if they were more impressed with his resiliency or that despite all he'd been through he still drove a vintage 1956 Mercedes 300SL. Nevertheless, they hovered around, hoping to impress him with their insight into an indigent black community that, if they'd just taken their racial blinders off for one second, they'd realize was no longer black but predominantly Latino.

The meetings consisted mostly of the members who showed up every other week arguing with the ones who came every other month about what exactly "bimonthly" means. I entered the donut shop just as the last copies of *The Ticker*, an update of statistics related to Dickens, were being passed around. Standing in the back near the blueberry fritters, I held the handout to my nose and inhaled the sweet smell of fresh mimeograph ink before giving it a cursory glance. *The Ticker* was a societal measure my father had designed to look like a Dow Jones stock report. Except that commodities and blue chips were replaced with social ills and pitfalls. Everything that was always up—unemployment, poverty, lawlessness, infant mortality—was up. Everything that's always down—graduation rates, literacy, life expectancy—was even further down.

Foy Cheshire stood underneath the clock. In ten years' time, other than gaining seventy-five pounds, he hadn't changed much. He wasn't much younger than Hominy, but he'd never grayed and his face bore only a few laugh lines. On the wall behind him were two framed poster-sized photos, one of a variety box of insanely puffy and succulent-looking donuts that looked nothing like the shrivelled-up, lumpy, so-called fresh pastries hardening before my eyes in the display case behind me, the other a color portrait of Pops, proudly wearing his APA tie clasp, his hair shaped to billowy perfection. I played the back. Judging from the serious mood in the room, there was a lot on the agenda and it'd be a while before the Dum Dums got to "ancilliary bidness."

Foy held two books, fanning them out in front of the group like a magician about to do a card trick. *Pick a culture, any culture.* He held one aloft, addressing his audience in an affected Southern Methodist drawl, even though he was from the Hollywood Hills by way of Grand Rapids. "One night, not long ago," Foy said, "I tried to read this book, *Huckleberry Finn*, to my grandchildren, but I couldn't get past page six because the book is fraught with the 'n-word.' And although they are the deepest-thinking, combat-ready eight- and ten-year-olds I know, I knew my babies weren't ready to comprehend *Huckleberry Finn* on its own merits. That's why I took the liberty to rewrite Mark Twain's masterpiece. Where the repugnant 'n-word' occurs, I replaced it with 'warrior' and the word 'slave' with 'dark-skinned volunteer.'"

"That's right!" shouted the crowd.

"I also improved Jim's diction, rejiggered the plotline a bit, and retitled the book *The Pejorative-Free Adventures and Intellectual and Spiritual Journeys of African-American Jim and His Young Protégé, White Brother Huckleberry Finn, as They Go in Search of the Lost Black Family Unit.*" Then Foy held up the copy of his revamped volume for examination. My eyesight isn't the best, but I could've sworn the cover featured Huckleberry Finn piloting the raft down the mighty Mississippi, while Captain African-American Jim stood at the helm, hands on narrow hips, sporting a cheesy goatee and a tartan Burberry sport coat exactly like the one Foy happened to be wearing.

I never much liked going to the meetings, but after my father died, unless there was an emergency on the farm, I showed up. Before Foy's appointment as lead thinker, there had been some talk of grooming me to step in as leader of the group. The Kim Jong-un of ghetto conceptualism. After all, I'd taken over the nigger-whispering duties. But I refused. Begging out by claiming I didn't know enough about black culture. That the only certainties I had about the African-American condition were that we had no concept of the phrases "too sweet" and "too salty." And in ten years, through countless California cruelties and slights against the blacks, the poor, the people of color, like Propositions 8 and 187, the disappearance of social welfare, David Cronenberg's *Crash*, and Dave Eggers's do-gooder condescension, I hadn't spoken a single word. During roll call Foy never called me by my proper name, but simply yelled, "The Sellout!" Looked me in the face with a sly and perfunctory smile, said, "Here," and placed a check mark next to my name.

Foy touched his fingertips together in front of his chest, the universal sign that the smartest person in the room is about to say something. He spoke loudly and quickly, his speech picking up in speed and intensity with every word. "I propose that we move to demand the inclusion of my politically respectful edition of *Huckleberry Finn* into every middle-school reading curriculum," he said. "Because it's a crime that generations of black folk come of age never having experienced this"—Foy snuck a peek at the original book's back cover—"this hilariously picturesque American classic."

"Is it 'black folk' or 'black folks'?" My having not spoken for the first time in years caught both of us off guard. But I came with the intention of saying something, so why not warm up the vocal cords. I took a bite out of the batch of Oreo cookies I'd boldly snuck in. "Which one is grammatically correct? I never know." Foy took a calming sip of cappuccino and ignored me. He and the rest of the non-Dickensian flock belonged to that scary subset of black lycanthropic thinkers I like to refer to as "wereniggers." By day, wereniggers are erudite and urbane, but with every lunar cycle, fiscal quarter, and tenure review their hackles rise, and they slip into their floor-length fur coats and mink stoles, grow fangs, and schlep down from their ivory towers and corporate boardrooms to prowl the inner cities, so that they can howl at the full moon over drinks and mediocre blues music. Now that his fame, if not his fortune, has waned, werenigger Foy Cheshire's foggy ghetto moor of choice is Dickens. Normally I try to avoid wereniggers at all costs. It's not the fear of being intellectually ripped to shreds that frightens me most, it's the cloying insistence on addressing everyone, especially people they can't stand, as Brother So-and-so and Sister This-and-that. I used to bring Hominy to the meetings to alleviate the boredom. Plus, he'd say the shit I was thinking. "Why you niggers talk so black, dropping the *g*'s in your gerunds in here, but on your little public television appearances you motherfuckers sound like Kelsey Grammer with a stick up his ass." But once he heard the widespread rumor that Foy Cheshire had used some of the millions in the royalties he'd earned over the years to purchase the rights to the most racist shorts in the *Our Gang* oeuvre, I had to ask Hominy to stop coming. He'd scream and stomp. Interrupt every motion with some histrionics. "Nigger, where are my *Little Rascal* movies!" Hominy swears his best work is on those reels. If the talk were true, it'd be impossible to forgive that self-righteous guardian of blackness for forever depriving the world of the best in American racial prejudice in Blu-ray and Dolby surround sound. But most everyone knows that, like alligators in the sewers, the lethality of Pop Rocks and soda, Foy Cheshire's ownership of the most racist *Little Rascal* films is nothing more than urban legend.

Always fast on his feet, Foy countered my insolence and Oreos with a bag of gourmet cannoli. We were both too good to eat the crap Dum Dum Donuts served up.

"This is serious. Brother Mark Twain uses the 'n-word' 219 times. That's .68 'n-words' per page in toto."

"If you ask me, Mark Twain didn't use the word 'nigger' enough," I mumbled. With my mouth filled with at least four of America's favorite cookies, I don't think anyone understood me. I wanted to say more. Like, why blame Mark Twain because you don't have the patience and courage to explain to your children that the "n-word" exists and that during the course of their sheltered little lives they may one day be called a "nigger" or, even worse, deign to call somebody else a "nigger." No one will ever refer to them as "little black euphemisms," so welcome to the American lexicon—Nigger! But I'd forgotten to order any milk to wash the cookies down with. And I never got the chance to explain to Foy and his close-minded ilk that Mark Twain's truth is that your average black nigger is morally and intellectually superior to the average white nigger, but no, those pompous Dum Dum niggers wanted to ban the word, disinvent the watermelon, snorting in the morning, washing your dick in the sink, and the eternal shame of having pubic hair the color and texture of unground pepper. That's the difference between most oppressed peoples of the world and American blacks. They vow never to forget, and we want everything expunged from our record, sealed and filed away for eternity. We want someone like Foy Cheshire to present our case to the world with a set of instructions that the jury will disregard centuries of ridicule and stereotype and pretend the woebegone niggers in front of you are starting from scratch.

Foy continued his sales pitch: "The 'n-word' is the most vile and despicable word in the English language. I don't believe anyone would argue that point."

"I can think of a more despicable word than 'nigger,'" I volunteered. Having finally swallowed my gooey chocolate-and-crème chaw, I closed one eye and held a half-bitten cookie so that the dark brown semicircle sat atop Foy's gigantic head like a well-coiffed Nabisco Afro that read OREO at its center.

"Like what?"

"Like any word that ends in —ess: Negress. Jewess. Poetess. Actress. Adultress. Factchecktress. I'd rather be called 'nigger' than 'giantess' any day of the week."

"Problematic," someone muttered, invoking the code word black thinkers use to characterize anything or anybody that makes them feel uncomfortable, impotent, and painfully aware that they don't have the answers to questions and assholes like me. "What the fuck you come here for, if you don't have anything productive to say?"

Foy raised his hands, asking for calm. "The Dum Dum Donut Intellectuals respect all input. And for those who don't know, this sellout is the son of our founder." Then he turned to me with a look of pity on his face. "Go on, Sellout. Say what you came to say."

Most times when someone presents before the Dum Dums you're required to use EmpowerPoint, a slide presentation "African-American software" package developed by Foy Cheshire. Not much different from the Microsoft product except that the fonts have names like Timbuktu, Harlem Renaissance, and Pittsburgh Courier. I opened the store's broom closet. Next to the mops and buckets, the old transparency projector was still there. Its glass top and lone sheet of transparency paper filthy as prison windows, but still usable.

I asked the assistant manager to dim the lights, then drew up and projected the following schematic onto the cork ceiling:

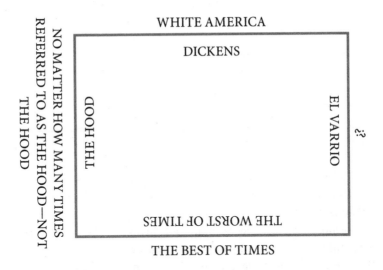

I explained that the boundary labels were to be spray-painted onto the sidewalks and that the lines of demarcation would be denoted by a configuration of mirrors and high-powered green pinpoint lasers, or if that proved to be cost prohibitive, I could simply circumnavigate the twelve miles of border with a three-inch strip of white paint. Hearing the words "circumnavigate" and "lines of demarcation" come out of my mouth made me realize that even though I was making this shit up on the spot, I was more serious about this than I thought I was. And yes, "I'm bringing back the city of Dickens."

Laughter. Waves and peals of deep black laughter of the kind kindhearted plantation owners long for in movies like *Gone with the Wind*. Laughter like you hear in basketball locker rooms, backstage at rap concerts, and in the backrooms of Yale University's all-white department of black studies after some fuzzy-hair-brained guest lecturer has dared to suggest that there's a connection between Franz Fanon, existential thought, string theory, and bebop. When the chorus of ridicule finally died down, Foy wiped away the tears of hilarity from his eyes, finished the last of the cannoli, scooted in behind me, and turned my father's photo toward the wall, thus saving Pops the embarrassment of having to witness his son desecrate the family intellect.

"You said you were going to bring back Dickens?" Foy asked, breaking the question-and-answer ice.

"Yes."

"We, and I think I speak for most of the group, have only one question: Why?"

Hurt that I expected everyone to care and no one did, I returned to my seat and spaced out after that. Half-listening to the usual diatribes about the dissolution of the black family and the need for black business. Waiting for Foy to say "and things of that nature," which is the "Roger. Over and out" of black intellectual communication.

". . . and things of that nature."

Finally. The meeting was over. And as the gathering broke up, I was twisting open my last Oreo cookie when, from out of nowhere, a callused black hand ganked it and popped it into a tight-lipped mouth.

"You bring enough for the whole race, nigger?"

With tufts of perm-straightened hair fastened to hot pink rollers stuffed underneath a see-through shower cap and giant hoop earrings dangling from both ears, the cookie snatcher looked more like a Blanche or a Madge than the notorious gangbanger known as King (pronounced "Kang") Cuz. And silently, very silently, I cursed Cuz as he slid his tongue over his metal-rimmed teeth, clearing tiny flecks of chocolaty goodness from his bridgework.

"That's what my teachers used to say to me if I was chewing gum and shit. 'You bring enough for the whole class?'"

"No doubt, nigger."

In all the time I've known Cuz, I've never had a real conversation with him beyond "No doubt, nigger." No one has, because even in his middle age, he's sensitive, and if you say the wrong thing, he'll show the world just how sensitive he is by crying at your funeral. So no one engages him in conversation; whenever he speaks to you, no matter what he says, man, woman, or child, you put as much bass in your voice as you possibly can and reply, "No doubt, nigger."

King Cuz has faithfully attended meetings of the Dum Dum Donut Intellectuals ever since my father nigger-whispered his mother off the Metro train tracks. Feet and hands bound in a jump rope, she had pitched herself onto the commuter rails screaming, "When a white bitch got problems, she's a damsel in distress! When a black bitch got problems, she's a welfare cheat and a burden on society. How come you never see any black damsels? Rapunzel, Rapunzel, let down your weave!" She was yelling so loud you could hear her suicidal protests over the ding-dong of the falling crossing gate and the blaring horn of the onrushing Blue Line. King Cuz was Curtis Baxter then, and I remember the windy wake of the passing train blowing young Curtis's tears sideways on his face as my dad cradled his mother in his arms. I remember the railroad tracks, rusty and ringing and still hot to the touch.

So you bring enough for the whole race?

Curtis grew up to become King Cuz. A gangster well respected for his brain and his derring-do. His set, the Rollin' Paper Chasers, was the first gang to have trained medics at their rumbles. A shoot-out would pop off at the swap meet and the stretcher-bearers would cart off the wounded to be treated in some field hospital set up behind the frontlines. You didn't know whether to be sad or impressed. It wasn't long after that innovation that he applied for membership to NATO. *Everybody else is in NATO. Why not the Crips? You going to tell me we wouldn't kick the shit out of Estonia?*

No doubt, nigger.

"I need to talk to you about a couple of things."

"No doubt, nigger."

"But not in here."

Cuz lifted me by the shirtsleeve and escorted me out the door and into the hazy Hound of the Baskervilles night. It's always a shock to have the day turn to dark without you, and we both paused to let the warm wet mist and the silence settle on our faces. Sometimes it's hard to tell what's more interminable, prejudice and discrimination or the goddamn meetings. Cuz made half a fist, examined his long, manicured nails, then raised one heavily teased eyebrow and smiled.

"First thing is 'bringing back Dickens.' Fuck what the rest of them niggers who ain't from the hood say, I'm thoroughly with that shit. It ain't but a couple of us in there, but the Dum Dums who from Dickens wasn't laughing. So set that off, cuz, because if you think about it, why can't black people have their own Chinese restaurants?"

"No doubt, nigger."

Then I did something I never thought I'd do. I engaged King Cuz in conversation, because I had to know, even if it cost me my life or, at the very least, what little cachet I had as the neighborhood's resident "quiet motherfucker."

"I have to ask you something, King Cuz."

"Call me Cuz, cuz."

"All right, Cuz. Why do you go to these meetings? Shouldn't you be out slanging and banging?"

"It used to be I'd go to listen to your father. Rest in peace, that nigger ran deep, for real. But now I go just in case these Dum Dum niggers get the notion to actually set foot in the hood, blowing the spot up and all. That way I can at least give the homies some Paul Revere–like advance notice. One if by Land Cruiser. Two if by C-class Mercedes. The bougies are coming! The bougies are coming!"

"Who's coming where?" It was Foy. Meeting over, he and the other wereniggers were piling into their cars. Making ready for a prowl on the town. Curtis "King Cuz" Baxter didn't bother to answer Foy. He simply spun on his Converse heels and pimp-walked into the blurry night. Listing hard to the right like a drunken seaman with an inner ear infection. He shouted back at me, "Think about them black Chinese restaurants. And get some pussy. You're too damn high-strung."

"Don't listen to that man, pussy is overrated."

As I unhitched and mounted my horse, Foy thumbed open two bottles of prescription pills and spilled three white tablets into his hand.

"Point zero zero one," he said, jiggling the tablets in his palm to make sure I'd see them. Zoloft and Lexapro.

"What, the dosage?"

"No, my fucking Nielsen ratings. Your dad used to think I was bipolar, but what I really am is by myself. Sounds like you are, too."

He pretended to offer me the pills before placing them gently on his tongue and washing them down with a swig from an expensive-looking silver flask. Since his cartoons had stopped airing, Foy had had a series of morning talk shows. Each successive failure slotted at a time earlier and earlier in the morning. Just as Bloods don't use the letter *C* because it's the first letter in Crip (Cap'n Crunch Cereal is Kap'n Krunch Kereal), Foy shows his gang affiliation by replacing the word "fact" with "black." And he has interviewed everyone from world leaders to dying musicians on programs titled *Black* and *Fiction, Blacktotum*. His latest installment was a nonsensical race forum on public access called *Just the Blacks, Ma'am*. It aired at five o'clock Sunday mornings. Ain't but two niggers in the world awake at five o'clock, and that's Foy Cheshire and his make-up artist.

It's hard to describe a man wearing probably close to $5,000 in a suit, shoes, and accessories as disheveled, but up close in the streetlight that's exactly what he was. All spit and no polish, his shirt wrinkled and losing its starch. The bottoms of his barely creased silk pants ringed brown with dirt and just starting to fray. His shoes were scuffed, and he reeked of crème de menthe. I once heard Mike Tyson say, "Only in America can you be bankrupt and live in a mansion."

Foy recapped his flask and jammed it into his pocket. Now that no one was looking, I waited for him to make the full werenigger transformation. Grow fangs and claws. I wondered if the hair on black werewolves was nappy. It had to be, right?

"I know what you up to."

"What am I up to?"

"You're about the same age your father was when he died. And you ain't said shit in a meeting for ten years. Why choose today to talk this nonsense about bringing Dickens back? Because you trying to reclaim the Dum Dums, take back what your father started."

"I don't think so. Any organization that holds lectures about the dangers of diabetes in a donut shop, you can keep."

Maybe I should've seen it then. My father had a checklist to determine whether or not someone was losing his mind. He said there were telltale signs of a mental breakdown that people often mistake for force of personality. Aloofness. Mood swings. Delusions of grandeur. Apart from Hominy, who, like one of those giant redwood slices you see at the science museum, was an open book, I only know how to tell if a tree is dying on the inside, not a person. The tree sort of withdraws into itself. The leaves become splotchy. Sometimes there are cankers and fissures in the bark. The branches might be bone-dry or soft and spongy to the touch. But the best way is to look at the roots. The roots are what anchors a tree to the ground, holds it in place on this spinning ball of shit, and if those are cracked and covered in spores and fungi, well . . . I remember looking at Foy's roots, a pair of expensive brown wingtips. They were scuffed and dusty. So, given the rumors about his wife filing for divorce, the bankruptcy, and his talk show's nonexistent ratings, maybe I should've known.

"I've got my eye on you," he said, sliding into his car. "The Dum Dum Donuts is all I have left. I will not let you fuck my shit up." Two goodbye beeps of his horn and he was gone. Swooping his Benz down El Cielo Boulevard, reaching Mach speed as he flew past Cuz, whose slow-footed strut was unmistakable even from a distance. It doesn't happen often, but once in a Crip blue moon, a member of the Dum Dum Donut Intellectuals says something ingenious like "black Chinese restaurants" and "pussy."

"No doubt, nigger," I said aloud.

And for the first time I meant it.

Eight

I went with the painted boundary. Not that the lasers cost so much, though the pointers that had the intensity I needed were a few hundred bucks apiece, it's that I found the painting to be meditative. I've always liked rote. The formulaic repetitiveness of filing and stuffing envelopes appeals to me in some fundamental life-affirming way. I would've made a good factory worker, supply-room clerk, or Hollywood scriptwriter. In school, whenever I had to do something like memorize the periodic table, my father would say the key to doing boring tasks is to think about not so much what you're doing but the importance of why you're doing it. Though when I asked him if slavery wouldn't have been less psychologically damaging if they'd thought of it as "gardening," I got a vicious beating that would've made Kunta Kinte wince.

I bought a shitload of white spray paint and a line-marking machine, the kind used to paint yardage markers and foul lines on ball fields, and before my morning chores, when the traffic was light, I'd haul my ass to the designated location, set up shop in the middle of the road, and paint the line. Paying no attention to the line's straightness or my attire, I laid down the border. It was a sign of the ineffectualness of the Dum Dum Donut think tank that no one had any idea what I was doing. Most folks who didn't know me mistook me for a performance artist or a crazy person. I was cool with the latter designation.

But after a few thousand yards of squiggly white lines, it became obvious to any Dickensian over the age of ten what I was doing. Unsolicited, groups of truant teens and homeless would stand guard over the line. Plucking leaves and debris out of the wet paint. Shooing away bicyclists and jaywalkers to prevent them from smearing the border. Sometimes, after retiring for the day, I'd return the next morning, only to find that someone else had taken up where I'd left off. Extended my line with a line of their own, often in a different color. Sometimes the line wouldn't be a line at all but drops of blood, or an uninterrupted string of graffiti signing off on my efforts, ___*AceBoonakatheWest sidecrazy63rdStGangsta*___, or, as in the case of the corner fronting the L.A. LGBTDL Crisis Center for Chicanos, Blacks, Non-Gays, and Anyone Else Who Feels Underserved, Unsupported, and Exploited by Hit Cable Television Shows, an arcing three-foot-wide, four-hundred-foot-long rainbow anchored with pots of gold condoms. Halfway down Victoria Boulevard where the El Harvard Bridge starts to cross the creek, someone bisected my line with *100 Smoots* in purple print. I still have no idea what that means, but I guess what I'm trying to say is that, with all the help, it didn't take long to finish painting the border. The police, many of whom knew me through my work and my watermelon, often escorted me from their patrol cars. Checking my boundary for accuracy against old editions of *The Thomas Guide*. I didn't mind Officer Mendez's good-natured teasing.

"What are you doing?"

"I'm looking for the lost city of Dickens."

"By painting a white line down the middle of a street that already has two yellow lines down the middle of it?"

"You love the mangy dog that shows up in your backyard as much as the puppy you got for your birthday."

"Then you should put up a flyer," she said, handing me a mock-up she'd hurriedly composed on the back of a wanted poster.

MISSING: HOMETOWN

Have you seen my city?
Description: Mostly Black and Brown. Some Samoan.
Friendly. Answers to the name of Dickens.

Reward Earned in Heaven.

If you have any information, please call this number 1-(800) DICKENS.

I appreciated the help and, using a wad of chewed gum, fastened the flyer to the nearest telephone post. For those looking to find the thing that you've lost, the decision of where to place your handbill is one of the toughest you'll ever make in life. I chose a space at the bottom of the pole between a circular for an Uncle Jam's Army concert at the Veterans Center. "Uncle Jam Wants You! To Serve and Funk in Los Afghanistan, California! Allah Ak-Open-Bar from 9–10 p.m.!" and a leaflet promoting a mysterious dream job that paid $1,000 a week, working from home. I hoped whoever posted that flyer had had a talk with human resources, because I seriously doubted they were making even $300 a week, and they definitely weren't working from home.

It took about six weeks to finish painting the border and the labels, and in the end I wasn't sure what I'd accomplished, but it was fun to see kids spend their Saturdays circumnavigating the city by carefully tracing their steps, walking heel-to-toe on the line, making sure they'd left not even an inch untrod upon. Sometimes I'd chance across an elderly member of the community standing in the middle of the street, unable to cross the single white line. Puzzled looks on their faces from asking themselves why they felt so strongly about the Dickens side of the line as opposed to the other side. When there was just as much uncurbed dog shit over there as here. When the grass, what little of it there was, sure in the fuck wasn't any greener. When the niggers were just as trifling, but for some reason they felt like they belonged on this side. And why was that? When it was just a line.

I have to confess that, in the days after I painted it, I, too, was hesitant to cross the line, because the jagged way it surrounded the remnants of the city reminded me of the chalk outline the police had needlessly drawn around my father's body. But I did like the line's artifice. The implication of solidarity and community it represented. And while I hadn't quite reestablished Dickens, I had managed to quarantine it. And community–cum–leper colony wasn't a bad start.

EXACT CHANGE, OR
ZEN AND THE ART
OF BUS RIDING AND
RELATIONSHIP REPAIR

Nine

Sometimes the smell wakes you up in the middle of the night. Chicago has the Hawk, and Dickens, despite its newly painted barrier, has the Stank, an eye-burning, colorless miasma of sulfur and shit birthed in the Wilmington oil refineries and the Long Beach sewage treatment plant. Carried inland by the prevailing winds, the Stank gathers up a steamy pungency as the fumes combine with the stench of the lounge lizards returning home from partying in Newport Beach, drenched in sweat, tequila shooter runoff, and gallons of overapplied Drakkar Noir cologne. They say the Stank drops the crime rate by 90 percent, but when the smell slaps you awake at three in the morning, the first thing you want to do is kill Guy Laroche.

It was a night about two weeks after I'd painted the border, the stench was especially strong, and I was unable to get back to sleep. I tried cleaning the stables, hoping the smell of fresh horse manure would remove the sting from my nostrils. It didn't work and I had to resort to covering my face with a dishrag soaked in vinegar to kill the fumes. Hominy walked in with my wet suit draped over one arm and a bowl in the other hand. He was dressed like a British manservant, complete with coat and tails and a vacillating BBC *Masterpiece Theatre* accent.

"What are you doing here?"

"I saw the lights and thought maybe Master would like the black hash and a little fresh air this evening."

"Hominy, it's four o'clock in the morning. Why aren't you in bed?"

"Same reason you aren't. It smells like a bum's asshole outside."

"Where'd you get the tux?"

"Back in the fifties every black actor had one. Show up for a casting call for butler or headwaiter and the studio would be like 'Boy, you just saved us fifty bucks. You're hired!'"

A little wake 'n' bake and some surfing wasn't a bad idea. I'd be too high to drive to the beach, but that would give me an excuse to see my girl for the first time in months. Catching some waves and a whiff of my baby? That'd be like killing two burdens with one stoner, so to speak. Hominy walked me into the living room, spun Daddy's recliner around, and patted the armrest.

"Sit."

The gas fireplace roared to life, and I stuck a punk into the flames, sparked the bowl, and took a long, smooth pull and was high before I could exhale. I must've left the back door open, because one of the newborn calves, shiny, black, barely a week old, and not yet used to the sounds and smells of Dickens, wandered in and stared me down with his big brown eyes. I blew a puff of hashish into his face, and together we could feel the stress leave our bodies. As the blackness peeled from our hides, the melanin fizzing and dissipating into nothingness like antacids dissolving in tap water.

They say a cigarette takes three minutes off your life, but good hashish makes dying seem so far away.

The distant staccato of gunfire sounded in the air. The last shoot-out of the night followed by the beating rotors of the police helicopter. The calf and I split a double of single malt to take the

edge off. Hominy pitched himself by the door. A parade of ambu-
lances sped down the street, and he handed me my surfboard like
a butler hands an English gentleman his coat. Feigned or not, sometimes I'm jealous of Hominy's obliviousness, because he, unlike
America, has turned the page. That's the problem with history, we
like to think it's a book—that we can turn the page and move the
fuck on. But history isn't the paper it's printed on. It's memory, and
memory is time, emotions, and song. History is the things that
stay with you.

"Master, I just thought you should know, my birthday's next
week."

I knew something was up. He was being too attentive. But
what do you get the slave who doesn't even want his freedom?

"Well, that's cool. We'll take a trip or something. In the meantime, could you do me a favor and put the calf out back?"

"I don't do farm animals."

Even when the air doesn't smell, when you walk the ghetto streets
in a spring suit, board tucked under one arm, no one really fucks
with you. Maybe once in a while a curious stick-up kid might
take the measure, look me up and down, and make a guess as to
how much the pawn shop would give him for an antique Town &
Country tri fin. Sometimes they stop me in front of the Laundromat,
stare in amazement at the homie wearing open-toe flip-flops, and
pinch my outer layer of black polyurethane skin.

"Check it out, cuz."

"S'up?"

"Where you keep your keys at?"

The 5:43 a.m. #125 westbound to El Segundo rolled in on time.
The pneumatic doors swung open with that strong, hissing efficiency
that I love, and the driver welcomed me aboard with a friendly
"Hurry up, motherfucker, you letting the stink in." Bus Operator

#632 thought we were broken up just because years ago she married that has-been gangster rapper (now semifamous television cop and malt liquor pitchman), MC Panache, had four kids, and had a restraining order requiring me to stay five hundred feet away from her and the children, because I would follow them home from school screaming, "Your daddy doesn't know his assonance from his elegy! And he calls himself a poet."

I took my usual seat, the one closest to the stairwell, kicked back, and stretched my feet into the aisle, wielding the board like a fiberglass African shield, deflecting the spitting barrage of pollyseed shells and insults as best I could.

"Fuck you."

"Fuck you."

Banished and hurt, I scuttled to the back of the bus, deposited my surfboard on the rear seat, and lay down on it like a heartbroken fakir sleeping on a bed of nails, trying to displace the emotional pain with the physical. The bus lumbered down Rosecrans, the unrequited love of my life, Marpessa Delissa Dawson, calling out stops like a Buddhist timekeeper, while a crazy man three rows in front of me recited the morning mantra: *I'm going to fuck that black bitch up. I'm going to fuck that black bitch up. I'm going to fuck that black bitch up. I'm going to fuck that black bitch up.*

There are more cars in Los Angeles County than in any other city in the world. But what no one ever talks about is that half those cars sit on cinder blocks in dirt patches passing for front yards from Lancaster to Long Beach. These not-so-mobile automobiles, along with the Hollywood sign, the Watts Towers, and Aaron Spelling's 56,500-square-foot estate, are the closest L.A. gets to approximating the ancient marvels of engineering like the Parthenon, Angkor Wat, the great pyramids, and the ancient shrines of Timbuktu. Those two- and four-door rusted pieces of antiquity stand impervious to the winds and acid rains of time, and like

Stonehenge, we have no idea what purpose these steel monuments serve. Are they testaments to the bitchin' and *firme* hot rods and lowriders that grace the covers of custom-car magazines? Maybe the hood ornaments and tail fins are aligned with the stars and the winter solstice. Maybe they're mausoleums, the resting places of backseat lovers and drivers. All I know is that each of these metallic carcasses means one less car on the road and one more rider on the bus of shame. Shame because L.A. is about space, and here one's self-worth comes from how one chooses to navigate that space. Walking is akin to begging in the streets. Taxicabs are for foreigners and prostitutes. Bicycles, skateboards, and Rollerblades are for health nuts and kids, people with nowhere to go. And all cars, from the luxury import to the classified-ad jalopy, are status symbols, because no matter how shoddy the upholstery, how bouncy the ride, how fucked-up the paint job, the car, any car, is better than riding the bus.

"Alameda!" Marpessa shouted, and a woman scurried aboard, toting one too many plastic shopping bags and pinning her purse tightly to her side with her elbow. She made her way down the aisle scanning for vacancies. I can spot an L.A. newcomer a mile away. They're the ones who board the bus smiling and greeting the other passengers, because they believe, despite all evidence to the contrary, that having to take mass transportation is only a temporary setback. They're the ones sitting under the Safe Sex ads, looking up quizzically from their Bret Easton Ellis novels, trying to figure out why the assholes surrounding them aren't all white and opulent like the assholes in the book. They're the ones who jump up and down like game show prizewinners when they discover that In-N-Out Burger has both a secret menu and a double-top-secret menu. "Mustard grilled patties? Get the fuck out of here!" They sign up for open mikes at the Laugh Factory. Jog along the boardwalk, trying to convince themselves that the double penetration scene they shot in Reseda last week is only a stepping-stone to bigger and better things. *La pornographie est la nouvelle nouvelle vague.*

Many parents brag about their kid's first words. Mommy. Daddy. I love you. Stop. No. That's inappropriate. My father, on the other hand, liked to boast about his first words to me. They weren't "Hello," or a prayer, but a sentiment found in the first chapter of every *Intro to Social Psych* textbook ever written: *We are all social scientists.* And I suppose my first field research was conducted on the bus.

When I was young, the municipal bus system was called the RTD. Officially, the acronym stood for Rapid Transit District, but to Angelenos who lived in hellholes like Watts, La Puente, and South Central, too young or too poor to drive, it stood for Rough Tough and Dangerous. My first scientific paper, written at age seven, was "Passenger Seating Tendencies by Race and Gender: Controlling for Class, Age, Crowdedness, and Body Odor." The conclusion was readily obvious. If forced to sit next to someone, people violated the personal space of women first and black people last. If you were a black male, then no one, including other black males, sat next to you unless they absolutely had to. Whereupon they'd reluctantly plop down next to me and invariably greet me with one of three security questions designed to assess my threat level.

1. Where do you live?
2. Did you see (insert sporting event or black-themed movie)?
3. I don't know where you from, homie. But you see this knife/gun/contagious skin rash? You don't fuck with me and I won't fuck with you, cool?

I could tell from the way they pulled her arms into the ground that the bags were getting heavy, that she was barely holding on to her groceries and dreams. Even though she was exhausted and growing more and more despondent with each bumpy rise and fall of the worn-out suspension, she preferred to stand rather than to sit next to me. They come to L.A. aspiring to be white. Even the ones who are biologically white aren't white white. Laguna Beach volleyball white. Bel Air white. Omakaze white. Spicolli white. Brett Easton Ellis white. Three first names white. Valet parking white. Brag about your Native American, Argentinian, Portuguese ancestry white. Pho white. Paparazzi white. I once got fired from a telemarketing job, now look at me, I'm famous white. Calabazas white. I love L.A. It's the only place where you can go skiing, to the beach and to the desert all in one day white.

She held on to her vision rather than sit next to me, not that I blamed her, because by the time the bus hit Figueroa Boulevard, there were a number of people on board whom I wouldn't have chosen to sit next to, either. Like the insane fucker who repeatedly pressed the "Stop Requested" button. "Stop this bus, goddammit! I want to get off! Where the fuck you going?" Even that early in the day, stopping a bus between designated stops was the same as asking the flight crew of an Apollo rocket to the moon to stop at the liquor store on the way—impossible.

"I said, Stop the motherfucking bus. I'm late for work, you fat fucking cow!"

Drivers, wardens, and concentration-camp commandants all have their own management style. Some like to sing to the passengers. Placating them with uplifting jazz age ditties like "Tea for Two" and "My Funny Valentine." Others like to hide, sit low in their seats, and let the inmates run the asylum and the aisles, seat belts unfastened in case the need for a quick getaway arises. Marpessa was no disciplinarian, but she wasn't a pushover either. Her average workday was filled with fights, purse snatchings, fare beaters, molestations, public intoxication, child endangerment, pandering, niggers constantly standing on the wrong side of the yellow line while the bus was in motion, and kicking game, to say nothing of the occasional attempted murder. Her union rep said a bus driver in this country is assaulted once every three days, and there were two things in the world Marpessa had long since decided she'd never be: a statistic and somebody's "fat cow." I don't know how she resolved the problem—with a kind word or the threatening wave of the metal nigger beater she kept behind her seat—because I fell asleep and didn't wake up until we reached El Segundo. Her call of "Last stop" echoing throughout the empty bus.

I know she hoped that I'd exit out the back, but even in that hideous Commie-gray Metro uniform, thirty pounds heavier, she was still unbearably cute. On the freeway you can't stop looking at a dog sticking its head out of a car window, and I couldn't take my eyes off her.

"Close your mouth, you're catching flies."

"You miss me?"

"Miss you? I haven't missed nobody since Mandela died."

"Is Mandela dead? Seems like he's going to live forever."

"Well, either way, there you go."

"See, you do miss me."

"I miss your fucking plums. I swear to God, sometimes I wake up in the middle of the night dreaming about your fucking plums and the juicy-ass pomegranates. I almost didn't break up with you because I kept thinking, Where am I going to get fucking canta-loupes that taste like a multiple orgasm?"

We'd rekindled our childhood friendship on the bus. I was seventeen, carless and clueless. She was twenty-one and fine enough to make that ill-fitting seaweed-brown RTD uniform look like haute-couture fashion. Except for the badge. No one, not even John Wayne, can pull off a badge. Back then she drove the #434—downtown to Zuma Beach. A route that once you got past the Santa Monica pier was mostly riderless, except for the burnouts, bums, and maids who serviced the Malibu estates and oceanfront bungalows. I surfed Venice and Santa Monica. Mostly Station 24. Sometimes 20. No real reason. The waves were shit. Crowded. Except that every now and then I'd see another surfer of color. As opposed to Hermosa, Redondo, and Newport, which were much closer to Dickens, but the breaks were dominated by straight-edge Jesus freaks who kissed their crucifixes before every set and listened to conservative talk radio after the sessions. Up the coast, along Marpessa's route, it was more laid-back. The Westside. AC/DC, Slayer, and KLOS–FM. The wave riders' crack- and hophead skeletons, tweaked on sunrise and the English Beat, cleansing their systems and their acne with cutbacks and bumpy floaters on the mushy breaks. But no matter where you surf, motherfuckers hog the sandbar.

The west end of Rosecrans Avenue, where the street dead-ends with the sand, is the 42nd Parallel between the kickback and uptight hemispheres of the L.A. County coastline. From Manhattan Beach down to Cabrillo, they called you nigger and expected you to run. El Porto north to Santa Monica, they called you nigger and expected you to fight. Malibu and beyond, they called the police. I started to take the bus farther and farther up the coast, so that I could spend more time chatting up Marpessa. We hadn't really seen each other since she started dating older boys and stopped hanging out at Hominy's. After two hours of swapping stories about slum life in Dickens and what Hominy was up to, I'd find myself miles from home, surfing with seals and dolphins at increasingly remote spots like Topanga, Las Tunas, Amarillo, Blocker, Escondido, and Zuma. Drifting onto private beachfronts where, soaking wet, the billionaire locals would stare at me as if I were a talking walrus with a willow-tree Afro when I'd walk through their sandy backyards, knock on the glass sliding doors, and ask to use the phone and the bathroom. But for some reason nonsurfing white folk trust a barefoot nigger carrying a board. Maybe they thought to themselves, His arms are too full to make off with the TV, and besides, where's he going to run to?

After a springtime's worth of weekend surfing, Marpessa trusted me enough to accompany me to my high school prom. With a graduating class of one, it was an intimate two-person affair, chaperoned and chauffeured by my father. We went dancing at Dillons, an under-twenty-one pagoda tower of a disco as segregated as anything else in L.A. The first floor—New Wave. Second floor—Top-40 soul. Third floor—watered-down reggae. Fourth floor—banda, salsa, merengue, and a touch of bachata in a vain attempt to steal Latino clientele from Florentine Gardens on Hollywood Boulevard. My father refused to go above the second floor. Me and Marpessa took the opportunity to ditch him, hiking up the smelly stairwell to the third floor, where we shimmied to Jimmy Cliff and the I-Threes, and camped out in back behind speakers, downing mai tais and standing as close to Kristy McNichol's crew as possible so that security wouldn't fuck with us, thinking we were the teenage movie star's token black friends. Then it was on to Coconut Teazers to see the Bangles, where Marpessa slurred whispered rumors that some guy named Prince was fucking the lead singer.

My ignorance of His Royal Badness almost got my ass kicked. And nearly postponed my first kiss until who knows when, but an early-morning Denny's Grand Slam Breakfast later, we were in the back of the pickup, speeding down the 10 freeway, doing eighty miles per hour in the fast lane, using the bags of feed and seed for pillows as we alternated wrestling with our tongues and thumbs. Played Who Can Hit the Softest. Kissed. Puked. Then kissed again. "Don't say 'French,'" she cautioned. "Say swap spit or bust a slob. Otherwise, you sound inexperienced."

My father, instead of keeping his eyes on the road, kept turning around, peering nosily through the little cab window, rolling his eyes at my breast-fondling technique, mocking the spastic way my head lolled uncontrollably when I kissed, and making the universal sign for "Fuck her already" by taking his hands off the wheel, forming a circular vagina with one hand, and sticking his index finger into it over and over again. For a man whose only evidence that he'd ever had sex with someone not enrolled in his class is possibly me, he sure was talking a lot of shit.

Between the bus and rides, the back of the pickup, the trips on horseback to the Baldwin Theater, it's crazy how much of our relationship was spent in motion. Marpessa put her feet on the steering wheel and covered her face in a tattered copy of Kafka's *The Trial*. Though I can't say for sure, I'd like to think she was hiding a smile. Most couples have songs they call their own. We had books. Authors. Artists. Silent movies. On weekends we used to lie naked in the hayloft, flicking chicken feathers off one another's back and leafing through *L.A. Weekly*. There'd be a retrospective of Gerhard Richter, David Hammons, Elizabeth Murray, or Basquiat at LACMA, and we'd tap the ad and say, "Hey, they're exhibiting our oil on canvas." We'd spend hours picking through the used-film bins at Amoeba Records on Sunset, hold up a copy of Erich Maria Remarque's *All Quiet on the Western Front*, and say, "Hey, they're digitally remastering our movie," then dry-hump in the Hong Kong movie section. But Kafka was our genius. We'd take turns reading *Amerika* and *Parables* out loud. Sometimes we'd read the books in incomprehensible German and do free-association translations. Sometimes we'd set the text to music and break-dance to the *The Metamorphosis*, slow-dance to *Letters to Milena*.

"Remember how you used to say I reminded you of Kafka?"

"Just because you burned some of your shitty poems doesn't mean I thought you were anything like Kafka. People tried to stop Kafka from destroying his work, I struck the matches for you."

Touché. The doors opened and the salty smell of the ocean, oil deposits, and seagull droppings wafted into the bus. I hesitated at the bottom stair, fumbling with the board like I was having trouble getting it through the doors.

"How's Hominy?"

"He's all right. Tried to kill himself a while back."

"He's so fucking crazy."

"Yeah. Still is. You know, his birthday is coming up. I got an idea you can help me with." Marpessa leaned back and rested her book on a second-trimester-sized paunch.

"Are you pregnant?"

"Bonbon, don't play yourself."

Mad as she was at me, I couldn't stop smiling, because I couldn't remember the last time she'd called me Bonbon. While not the roughest sobriquet, it's the closest thing I've ever had to a street name. When I was young I had a reputation for being extremely lucky. I never suffered from the typical ghetto maladies. I was never baby-shook. Never contracted rickets, ringworm, sickle-cell trait, lockjaw, early-onset diabetes, or the "'itis." Hoodlums would jump my friends but leave me alone. The cops somehow never got around to putting my name on a scare card or my neck in a choke hold. I never had to live in the car for a week. No one ever mistook me for that punk who shot, raped, snitched on, impregnated, molested, welched, disrespected, neglected, or fucked over someone's peoples. Rabbit's Foot, Starchild, Four-Leaf-Lucky-Motherfucker, none of the nicknames stuck until, at eleven years old, I was involuntarily entered by my father in the citywide spelling bee sponsored by the now-defunct *Dickens Bulletin*, a paper so black the newsprint/ink color scheme was reversed, as in Honky City Council Approves Budget Increase . . . The finals pitted me against Nakeshia Raymond. Her word was "omphaloskepsis." Mine was "bonbon." And after that, up until the night my father died, it was *Bonbon, pick my numbers. Bonbon, blow on my dice. Bonbon, take my civil service exam for me. Bonbon, kiss my baby.* Yeah, since Pops got popped, people tend to keep their distance.

"Bonbon . . ." Marpessa squeezed her hands together to stop them from shaking. "I'm sorry about the way I treated you earlier. This fucking job . . ."

Sometimes I think that there's no such thing as measurable intelligence and that, if there is, it definitely isn't a predictor of anything, especially for colored people. Maybe morons can't become brain surgeons, but a genius can be either a cardiologist or a postal clerk. Or a bus driver. A bus driver who made some fucked-up choices. Never put down the books, but after our brief relationship fell for an abusive old-school, then wannabe gangster rapper who dragged her out by her half-done hair in the mornings and, while she was still in her footy pajamas, forced her to case jewelry stores in the Valley. I never could figure why the places didn't call the police immediately upon seeing a young African-American female suspect walk dead into the middle of the store exactly ten minutes after opening time, stare directly at the security guards and the cameras, while counting her steps out loud as she paced off the distance between the diamond rings and brooches.

Eyes blackened, she'd show up at my place, skulking in the shadows like a film noir villainess wanted for overacting and underappreciating her self-worth. College wasn't for her, because to her mind the workplace turns black women into indispensable, well-paid number threes and fours, but never ones or twos. Sometimes getting pregnant early in life is a good thing. It slaps you to attention. Straightens your posture. Marpessa stood at the back door, eating a peach she'd pulled off the tree. The blood from her nose and lip mingled with the nectar, dripped down her chin and onto her shirt and once spotless sneakers, the sun behind her turning the edges of her frizzy undone hair into a flaming corona of split ends and shame. She wouldn't come inside, she'd only say, "My water broke," which of course broke my heart. A maniacal drive and an epidural later, Martin Luther King, Jr., Hospital, aka Killer King, got one right. A child, middle name Bonbon, a milk-guzzling, nipple-gnawing terror who serves as your incentive to apply for a Class B driver's license, reminds you that next to Kafka, Gwendolyn Brooks, Eisenstein, and Tolstoy your favorite thing is to drive. Is to keep moving, to guide your bus and your life gently and slowly into the terminus and take a well-deserved respite.

"So you going to help out with Hominy?"

"Just get the fuck off the bus."

With a push of the ignition button, the bus growled to life. Marpessa was next to go; she shut the door in my face, but slowly.

"You know, it was me that painted that line around Dickens."

"I heard some shit about that. But why?"

"I'm bringing the city back. Bringing you back, too!"

"Good luck with that."

Bouncing up and down Ocean Avenue in the back of a shit box pickup truck with some shaggy, aboriginal, blond-haired white boys, damn near as dark as you, their sun-baked faces peeling like the old "Local Motion" bumper stickers affixed to the tailgate, sometimes you feel more like a surfer than you do when you're bellied atop your board staring into the misty horizon waiting for the next set. Kind enough to offer you a ride, you return the favor with smoke. Puffing and passing, and trying to keep your stick from getting dinged up with every California pothole hit and high-as-hell, whoa-dude-is-it-me-or-are-the-caution-lights-getting-shorter? sudden stop.

"Incredible bud, dude. Where'd you get this shit?"

"I know some Dutch coffee shop owners."

Ten

That wintery day in the segregated state of Alabama, when Rosa Parks refused to give up her bus seat to a white man, she became known as the "Mother of the Modern-Day Civil Rights Movement." Decades later on, a seasonally indeterminate afternoon in a supposedly unsegregated section of Los Angeles, California, Hominy Jenkins couldn't wait to give up his seat to a white person. Grandfather of the post-racial civil rights movement known as "The Standstill," he sat in the front of the bus, on the edge of his aisle seat, giving each new rider the once-over. Unfortunately for him, Dickens is a community as black as Asian hair, as brown as James, and after forty-five minutes of standing-room-only, all-minority ridership, the closest he got to a white person was the dreadlocked woman who got on at Poinsettia Avenue toting a rolled-up yoga mat.

"Happy birthday, Hominy," she said gaily, standing over him, her face dripping Bikram sweat onto his shirtsleeve.

"How does everyone know it's my birthday?"

"It says so on the front of bus. Big bright lights: Bus #125 Happy Birthday, Hominy!—Yowza, like a motherfucker!"

"Oh."

"Did you get anything good for your birthday?"

Hominy pointed to the blue-and-white cigarette-box-sized signs stickered under the windows that lined the front third of the bus.

PRIORITY SEATING FOR SENIORS, DISABLED,
AND WHITES
Personas Mayores, Incapacitadas y Güeros Tienen
Prioridad de Asiento.

"That's my birthday present."

Dickens used to celebrate Hominy's birthday as a collective. Not that there were parades and key-to-the-city accolades, but people would congregate outside his home chanting "Yowza!" and armed with eggs, peashooters, and meringue pies. They'd take turns ringing the doorbell. And when he answered, they'd shout, "Happy birthday, Hominy!" and hurl pastries and chicken ovum at his shiny black face. Ecstatic, he'd wipe himself clean, change clothes, and prepare himself for the next celebratory band of well-wishers, but when the city disappeared, so did the birthday tradition. It became just me knocking on his door and asking Hominy what he wanted for his birthday this year. His answer was always the same: "I don't know. Just get me some racism and I'll be straight." Then he'd look to see if I was hiding a rotten tomato or a sack of flour behind my back. *Some boys come round here and smush 'matoes in yo face?* Usually I'd buy him some black Americana tchotchke. Two porcelain banjo-playing pickaninnies picking tunes underneath the Wisteria Tree, an Obama sock monkey, or a pair of eyeglasses that invariably slide down the bridges of African-American and Asian noses.

But when I'd noticed that Hominy and Rodney Glen King shared the same birthday, April 2, it dawned on me that if places like Sedona, Arizona, have energy vortexes, mystical holy lands where visitors experience rejuvenation and spiritual awakenings,

Los Angeles must have racism vortexes. Spots where visitors experience deep feelings of melancholy and ethnic worthlessness. Places like the breakdown lane on the Foothill Freeway, where Rodney King's life, and in a sense America and its haughty notions of fair play, began their downward spirals. Racial vortices like the intersection of Florence and Normandie, where misbegotten trucker Reginald Denny caught a cinder block, a forty-ounce, and fucking centuries of frustration to the face. Chavez Ravine, where a generations-old Mexican-American neighborhood was torn down, its residents forcibly removed, beaten, and left uncompensated to make room for a baseball stadium with ample parking and the Dodger Dog. Seventh Street, between Mesa and Centre, is the vortex where in 1942 a long line of buses idled as Japanese-Americans began the first step toward mass incarceration. And where would Hominy be most happy but on the #125 bus rolling through Dickens, a racial vortex unto itself. His seat on the right-hand side, three rows from the front door, the spinning epicenter of racism.

The signs were such good replicas, most people didn't notice the difference, and even after you "read" them, your comprehension tricked you into thinking the signs said what they'd always said, PRIORITY SEATING FOR SENIORS AND THE DISABLED, and although it was the first, the yogi's complaint wouldn't be the only one Marpessa fielded that day. Once the black cat was out of the bag, all shift long the passengers bitched and moaned. Pointed to the stickers and shook their heads, not so much from disbelief that the city had the nerve to reinstitute public segregation, but that it had taken so long to do so. The complimentary slices of Baskin-Robbins Oreo Cookie Cake, the airplane jiggers of J&B Brandy, and her blasé disclaimer, "It's Los Angeles, the most racist city in the world, what the fuck you going do?" only went so far in assuaging their anger.

"That's some bullshit!" a man shouted before asking for more cake and drink. "And to be perfectly frank, I'm *offended*."

"What does that mean, I'm offended?" I asked the unrequited love of my life, talking to her through the panoramic rearview mirror. It hadn't been hard to convince Marpessa to convert the #125 bus into a rolling party center, she loved Hominy as much as I did. And a promised first edition of Baldwin's *Giovanni's Room* didn't hurt either. "It's not even an emotion. What does being offended say about how you feel? No great theater director ever said to an actor, 'Okay, this scene calls for some real emotion, now go out there and give me lots of offendedness!'"

Marpessa worked the stick shift knob with her fingerless leather-gloved hand with such forceful dexterity I found myself fidgeting in my seat.

"That's saying a lot coming from a callow farm boy who's never been offended in his life because his head's too high in the clouds."

"That's because if I ever were to be offended, I wouldn't know what to do. If I'm sad, I cry. If I'm happy, I laugh. If I'm offended, what do I do, state in a clear and sober voice that I'm offended, then walk away in a huff so that I can write a letter to the mayor?"

"You're a sick fuck, and those damn signs you made have fucking set black people back five hundred years."

"And another thing, how come you never hear anyone say, 'Wow, you've pushed black people ahead five hundred years'? How come no one ever says that?"

"You know what you are? A fucking race pervert. Crawling through people's backyards and smelling their dirty laundry, while you jack off cross-dressed as a fucking white man. It's the goddamn twenty-first century, people died so I could get this job, and I let your sick ass talk me into driving a segregated bus."

"Correction. It's the twenty-sixth century, because as of today I've set black people five hundred years ahead of everybody else on the planet. And besides, look how happy Hominy is."

Marpessa glanced up at the mirror and snuck a peek at the birthday boy.

"He doesn't look happy. He looks constipated."

She was right, Hominy didn't necessarily look happy, but neither do motorcycle daredevils standing atop fifty-foot-high jump ramps, revving their engines and staring out at the desert expanse and precipitous drop that is Gila Monster Canyon. Yet, as he stood on the lookout for one of his Caucasian betters, gripping the seatback in front of him, nervously scanning his surroundings like some suicidal gazelle looking over the Serengeti for a jungle cat to whom he could sacrifice himself, one has to understand that death-defying feats are their own reward, and of course, when a rare white lioness boarded the bus at Avalon Boulevard and dropped her exact change in the fare box coin by carefully counted-out coin, Hominy, the skittish nigger-gazelle, was looking in the wrong direction, oblivious to the signals from the rest of the herd that a predator was on board. The hushed silence. The raised eyebrows. The wrinkled noses. When he finally did catch the woman's scent, it was almost too late. She hovered over him, stalking her prey from behind an elephantine man dressed from head to toe in basketball gear and reading a sports magazine. Eventually, the aging early-warning system inside Hominy's nappy head screamed, "Look out! A white bitch!" and he snapped to "Yes, ma'am" attention. And without being asked or ordered, Hominy relinquished his seat in a manner so obsequious, so unctuously Negro, that the act was less an offer of his place than a bequeathal. Because to him that seat, as hard and plastic and orange-brown as it was, was her birthright, and his gesture was a tribute, a long-overdue payment to the gods of white superiority. If he could have figured out a way to stand up on bended knee, he would have.

If a smile is just a frown turned upside down, then the look of contentment on Hominy's face as he shuffled to the back of the bus was a pout turned inside out. I think that in part it's why no one protested his actions. We recognized the face he was wearing as a mask from our own collections. The happy mask we carry in our back pockets, and like bank robbers whip out when we want to steal some privacy or make an emotional getaway. It took all my self-control not to beg the woman to do me the honor of sitting in my seat. Sometimes I think that inert, cigar-store Indian wooden smirk is the result of natural selection. That it's "survival of the witless," and we're the black moths in that classic evolution photo, clinging to the dark, soot-covered tree, invisible to our predators and yet somehow still vulnerable. The job of the swarthy moth is to keep the white moth occupied. Glued to the tree with bad poetry, jazz, and corny stand-up routines about the difference between white moths and black moths. "Why do white moths always be flying toward lights, slamming into screen doors, and shit? You never see black moths do that. Stupid fluttering motherfuckers." Anything to keep the white moth next to us and thereby reducing our chances of being targets for birds of prey, the volunteer army, or Cirque de Soleil. It always bothered me that in those photos, the white moth was invariably higher up the tree trunk. What were those textbooks trying to imply? That despite supposedly being more at risk, the white moth was still higher up the evolutionary and social ladder? Regardless, I suppose that black moth wore the same face Hominy did, that subservient countenance inherent in all black lepidoptera and people. That autonomic eager-to-please response that's triggered anytime you're approached in a store and asked, "Do you work here?" The face worn every moment you're on the job and not in the bathroom stall, the face flashed to the white person who saunters by and patronizingly pats you on the shoulder and says, "You're doing a fine job. Keep up the good work." The face that feigns acknowledgment that the better man got the promotion, even though deep down you and they both know that you really are the better man and that the best man is the woman on the second floor.

So when Hominy, the stoop-shouldered epitome of obsequiousness, stood up and made that face, everyone on board felt like they, too, had a white person next to them baring their forearms and wanting to compare tans after they've returned from a Caribbean vacation. Felt like Asians being asked, "No, where are you from originally?" Like Latinos being asked for proof of residency and big-chested women being asked, "So are those real?"

It wasn't until Marpessa noticed that the unknown white woman completed the three-hour round-trip from El Segundo Plaza to Norwalk and back again that she began to get suspicious, but by then it was too late. The bus was nearly empty and her shift was almost over.

"You know her, don't you?"

"No, I don't."

"And I don't believe you." Marpessa popped her gum and picked up the in-dash microphone, filling the bus with amplified derision. "Miss. Excuse me, would the lady with the strawberry-blond hair who was preternaturally comfortable with a literal busload of niggers and Mexicans (and by 'Mexicans' I mean all people. Central, South, North, and whatever Americas have you, native-born and otherwise), please approach the front of the bus. Thank you."

The dusk lowered itself onto El Porto Harbor, and as the white woman sauntered down the aisle, the sunlight decanted itself through the front windshield and into the bus in blinding streaks of overlapping purple and orange hues, lighting her up like a beauty pageant winner. I hadn't noticed how pretty she was. Too pretty. It wouldn't be hard to argue that Hominy gave up his seat, not because she was white, but because she was so fucking fine, and that notion had me reassessing the entire civil rights movement. Maybe race had nothing to do with it. Maybe Rosa Parks didn't give up her seat because she knew the guy to be unapologetically gassy or one of those annoying people who insists on asking what you're reading, then without prompting tells you what he's reading, what he wants to read, what he regrets having read, what he tells people he's read but really hasn't read. So like those high school white girls who have after-school sex with the burly black athlete in the wood shop, and then cry rape when their fathers find out, maybe Rosa Parks, after the arrest, the endless church rallies, and all the press, had to cry racism, because what was she going to say: "I refused to move because the man asked me what I was reading"? Negroes would've lynched her.

Marpessa looked at me, then at her lone white passenger, then back at me, and stopped the bus in the middle of a busy intersection, flinging open the doors with all the civil servant courtesy she could muster. "Everybody who I don't know personally, get the fuck off the bus." "Everybody" being a lazy skateboarder and two kids who'd spent the past hour necking like twisted rubber bands in the back, who quickly found themselves in the middle of Rosecrans Avenue holding free transfer tickets that flapped uselessly in the sea breeze. Miss Freedom Rider was about to join them when Marpessa blocked her passage like Governor Wallace blocked the entrance to the University of Alabama in 1963.

In the name of the greatest people that have ever trod this earth, I draw the line in the dust and toss the gauntlet before the feet of tyranny, and I say segregation now, segregation tomorrow, segregation forever.

"What's your name?" Marpessa asked as she cajoled the bus northbound onto Las Mesas.

"Laura Jane."

"Well, Laura Jane, I don't know how you know this fertilizer-smelling fool right here, but I hope you like to party."

Unlike those expensive, staid, day-trip excursions to Catalina Island, the impromptu four-wheel birthday party cruise up the Pacific Coast Highway was free and jumping like a motherfucker. Our highway-next-to-the-ocean-liner had all the amenities: Open bar. Stomped-on aluminum can, whisk-broom shuffleboard. Casino gambling, which consisted of pitching pennies, dominoes. A coin-flip game called Get Like Me, and a disco lounge. Captain Marpessa womaned the helm, drinking and cursing like a pissed-off pirate. I filled in as First Mate, Purser, Deck Hand, Bartender, and DJ. We'd picked up some more passengers on the way when the bus pulled into the Jack in the Box drive-thru across the street from Malibu pier, cranking Whodini's "Five Minutes of Funk," and when we ordered fifty tacos and a shitload of sauce, the entire night shift quit on the spot and climbed aboard, aprons, paper hats, and all. If I had pen and paper and the bus had a bathroom, I would've posted another sign—ALL EMPLOYEES MUST WASH THEIR HANDS AND THEIR MINDS BEFORE RETURNING TO THEIR LIVES.

After night falls, once past Pepperdine University, where the highway narrows into a two-lane hill that stretches like a skate ramp to the stars, there isn't much light. Just the occasional flash of oncoming high beams, and, if you're lucky, a lonely bonfire on the sand, and the sheets of moonlight give the Pacific Ocean a glassy black obsidian sheen. It was on this same stretch of winding road that I first courted Marpessa. I bussed her on the cheek. She didn't flinch, which I interpreted as a good sign.

Although the bus cruise was bumping, Hominy had spent most of the ride standing in the middle of the dance floor, stubbornly holding on to the overhead bar and, by proxy, the history of American discrimination, but around Puerco Beach, Laura Jane had managed to coax him out of his ancient mindset by grinding her pelvic bone rhythmically against his backside and playing with his ears. "Freaking," we used to call it, and she pranced around Hominy, her hands overhead, caressing the beat. When the song ended, she shouldered her way toward the bow, the fuzz on her upper lip beaded with sweat. Goddamn, she was fine.

"Wicked party."

The radio buzzed to life, and a dispatcher said the word "whereabouts" in a concerned voice. Marpessa turned down the music, said something I couldn't hear, then blew a kiss into the receiver and switched off the radio. If New York is the City That Never Sleeps, then Los Angeles is the City That's Always Passed Out on the Couch. Once past Leo Carrillo, PCH begins to smooth out, and when the moon disappears behind the Santa Monica Mountains, painting the night sky pitch-black, if you listen closely you can hear two faint pops in fairly quick succession. The first is the sound of four million living-room television sets flickering off in unison, and the second is the sound of four million bedroom ones being powered on. Moviemakers and photographers often speak of the uniqueness of L.A. sunlight, the ways it pours itself across the sky, golden and sweet, like Vermeer, Monet, and breakfast honey all rolled into one. But the L.A. moonlight, or lack thereof rather, is just as special. When night falls, I mean really falls, the temperature drops twenty degrees and a total amniotic blackness blankets and comforts you like a lover making the bed while you're still in it, and that brief moment between television sets popping off and back on is the calm before the after-hours strip clubs in Inglewood open, before the cacophony of New Year's Eve gunshots rings out, before Santa Monica, Hollywood, Whittier, and Crenshaw Boulevards come slowly cruising to life, is when Angelenos take time to pause and reflect. To give thanks to the late-night joints in Koreatown. To Mariachi Square. To chili burgers and pastrami dip sandwiches. To Marpessa, peering through the windshield and squinting at the stars, driving by dead reckoning rather than simply following the road. The tires ground assuredly over the asphalt, the bus rolling through the stratosphere, and when she heard the second pop, Marpessa gave the go-ahead for more music, and before long, Hominy and the rest of the Jack in the Box ballet were again pirouetting in the aisle, singing out loud to Tom Petty.

"Where'd he find you?" Marpessa asked Laura Jane, her eyes still fixed on the Milky Way.

"He hired me."

"You a prostitute?"

"Damn near. Actress. Part-time submissive to pay the bills."

"Parts must be hard to come by if you have to do this shit." Marpessa cut her eyes at Laura Jane, bit her bottom lip, and turned her attention back to the celestial night.

"Have I ever seen you in anything?"

"I do mostly television commercials, but it's tough. Whenever I'm up for a part, the producers look at me like you just did and say, 'Not suburban enough,' which in the industry is code for 'too Jewish.'"

Sensing that Marpessa hadn't quite cleared her chakras during her L.A. moment of silence, Laura Jane pressed her pretty face cheek-to-cheek with Marpessa's jealous mug and together they studied themselves in the rearview mirror, looking like a pair of mismatched conjoined twins attached at the head. One middle-aged and black, the other young and white, sharing the same brain but not the same thought process. "Makes me wish I was black," the white twin said, smiling and running her hands over her darker sister's burning cheeks. "Black people get all the jobs."

Marpessa must've put the bus on autopilot, because her hands were off the steering wheel and around Laura Jane's neck. Not choking her, but pointedly straightening the collar of her dress, letting her evil twin know she was ready to pounce as soon as her side of the brain gave the okay. "Look, I doubt that black people 'get *all* the jobs.' But even if they do, it's because Madison Avenue knows niggers spend a dollar and twenty cents of every dollar they earn on the crap they see on television. Let's take the standard luxury car commercial . . ."

Laura Jane nodded as if she were really listening, slyly slipping her arms around Marpessa and onto the steering wheel.

For a second we veered across the double yellow lines, but she made a deft correction and gently guided the bus back into the passing lane.

"Luxury cars. You were saying?"

"The subtle message of the luxury car commercial is 'We here at Mercedes-Benz, BMW, Lexus, Cadillac, or whatever the fuck, are an equal-opportunity opportunist. See this handsome African-American male model behind the wheel? We'd like you, o holy, highly sought after white male consumer between the ages of thirty and forty-five, sitting in your recliner, we'd like you to spend your money and join our happy, carefree, prejudice-free world. A world where black men drive sitting straight up in their seats and not sunk so low and to the side you can see only the tops of their gleaming ball-peen heads.'"

"And what's so wrong with that?"

"But the subliminal message is 'Look, you lazy, fat, susceptible-to-marketing, poor excuse for a white man. You've indulged this thirty-second fantasy of a nigger dandy commuting from his Tudor castle in an aerodynamically designed piece of precision German engineering, so you'd better get your act together, bro, and stop letting these rack-and-pinion-steering, moon-roof, manufacturer's-suggested-retail-price-paying monkeys show you up and steal your piece of the American dream!'"

At mention of the American dream, Laura Jane stiffened and returned the conn to Marpessa. "I'm offended," she said.

"Because I used the word 'nigger'?"

"No, because you're a beautiful woman who just happens to be black, and you're far too smart not to know that it isn't race that's the problem but class."

Laura Jane planted a loud, wet smack on Marpessa's forehead, and spun on her Louboutin heels to go back to work. I grabbed my love's arm in mid swing, saving Laura Jane from a rabbit punch she never saw coming.

"You know why white people don't ever just happen to be white? Because they all think they've just happened to have been touched by God, that's why!"

I thumbed the lipstick print off Marpessa's angry forehead.

"And tell that class oppression garbage to the fucking Indians and the dodo birds. Talking about I should 'know better.' She's Jewish. *She* should know better."

"She didn't say she was Jewish. She said people *think* she looks Jewish."

"You are a fucking sellout. That's why I fucking dumped your ass. You never stick up for yourself. You're probably on her side."

Godard approached filmmaking as criticism, the same way Marpessa approached bus driving, but in any case, I thought Laura Jane had a point. Whatever Jewish people supposedly look like, from Barbra Streisand to the nominally Jewish-ish Whoopie Goldberg, you never see people in commercials that look "Jewish," just as you never see black people that come off as "urban" and hence "scary," or handsome Asian men, or dark-skinned Latinos. I'm sure those groups spend a disproportionate amount of their incomes on shit they don't need. And, of course, in the idyllic world of television advertisement, homosexuals are mythical beings, but you see more ads featuring unicorns and leprechauns than you do gay men and women. And maybe nonthreatening African-American actors are overrepresented on television. Their master's degrees from the Yale School of Drama and Shakespearean training having gone to waste, as they stand around barbecue pits delivering lines like "Prithee, homeboy. Forsooth, thou knowest that Budweiser is the King of Beers. Uneasy lies the frothy head that wears the crown." But if you really think about it, the only thing you absolutely never see in car commercials isn't Jewish people, homosexuals, or urban Negroes, it's traffic.

The bus slowed as Marpessa leaned into a left turn that took us off the highway and down a hidden, winding service road.

We crept past a limestone outcropping, a set of rickety wooden coastal access stairs, and through an unused parking lot. From there, she downshifted, threw the bus in gear, and dune-buggied the vehicle directly onto the sand, where she parallel-parked with the horizon and, since the tide was up, in about a foot and a half of seawater.

"Don't worry, these things are like all-terrain vehicles and damn near amphibious. Between the mudslides and L.A.'s shitty sewage system, a bus has to be able to slog through anything. If we'd used Metro buses to land on the beaches of Normandy on D-day, World War II would've ended two years earlier."

The doors, both back and front, flew open, and the Pacific lapped lovingly at the bottom stairs, turning the bus into one of those Bora-Bora hotel rooms that sit on pylons fifty yards out to sea. I half expected to see a Jack in the Box service rep pull up on a Jet Ski delivering towels and a second round of sourdough burgers and vanilla shakes.

Al Green was singing about love and happiness. Laura Jane stripped naked. In the dim interior light her thin, smooth, pale skin was as iridescent as the nacre interior of an abalone shell. She strutted passed us. "I played a mermaid in a tuna commercial once. However, I have to say there was no black talent on that shoot. How come there aren't any African-American mermaids?"

"Because black women hate to get their hair wet."

"Oh." And with that, using the bus's aluminum latticework like a stripper working the pole, she flung herself into the water. Followed by the Jack in the Box crew, also naked, except for their paper hats.

Hominy sidled up to the front and looked longingly at the water.

"Master, are we still in Dickens?"

"No, Hominy, we aren't."

"Well, where is Dickens, then? Out there past the water?"

"Dickens exists in our heads. Real cities have borders. And signs. And sister cities."

"Will we have all that soon?"

"I hope so."

"And, massa, when we going to get my movies from Foy Cheshire?"

"Soon as we reestablish Dickens. We'll see if he has them. I promise."

Hominy paused at the doorway and, fully clothed, tested the water with the toe of his brogans.

"You know how to swim?"

"Uh-huh. Don't you remember 'Gon' Deep Sea Fishin'?'"

I'd forgotten about that macabre *Little Rascals* classic. The gang plays hooky from school and ends up on a fishing trawl sent out to catch a shark that's been terrorizing the waterfront. Since Pete the Pup has eaten the bait, they smear little Hominy in cod-liver oil, prick his finger, and hook his belt loop to the end of a fishing rod, lower him into the water, and use him as shark chum. While underwater he has to suck the air out of a school of puffer fish to keep from drowning. An electric eel repeatedly zaps him in the groin. The episode ends with a giant octopus showing its appreciation for the Little Rascals, ridding the sea of the fanged menace (turns out Alfalfa's singing voice is so shrill he can carry a shark-repellant note underwater) by spraying the boys in black ink. When the dinge-colored bunch return home to a jetty full of concerned parents, Hominy and Buckwheat's doo-ragged mammy blurts out, "Buckwheat, I dun tol' yo' pappy, I ain't takin' care uh nun ob hiz odder chil'ren!"

Marpessa fell asleep in my lap, and I stared out into the ocean, listening to the breaking surf and the peals of laughter. But mostly I was transfixed by Laura Jane's shimmering pink coral nakedness backstroking through the ocean, nipples pointing to the stars, pubic hair sashaying in the clear water like a ginger tuft of silken sea grass. A scissor kick, a teasing glimpse, and she was underwater. Marpessa socked me hard in the ribs. It took all my willpower not to give her the satisfaction of rubbing out the pain.

"Look at you, fiending after some white bitch like every other L.A. nigger."

"White babes don't do nothing for me. You know that."

"Bullshit, your fucking hard-on woke me up."

"Aversion therapy."

"What's that?"

I balked at telling her about my father locking my head into the tachistoscope and for three hours flashing split-second images of the forbidden fruit of his era, pinups and *Playboy* centerfolds, in my face. Bettie Page, Betty Grable, Barbra Streisand, Twiggy, Jayne Mansfield, Marilyn, Sophia Loren; then he'd force ipecac and okra smoothies down my throat. I'd vomit my guts out while he blasted Buffy Sainte-Marie and Linda Ronstadt on the stereo. The visual stimuli worked, but the auditory stuff didn't take. To this day, whenever I'm feeling down and troubled, I crank Rickie Lee Jones, Joni Mitchell, and Carole King from the stereo, all of who were shouting-out California way before Biggie, Tupac, or any of the Ice Coons. But if you look carefully, and the light is just right, you can see the afterimages of Barbi Benton's naked centerfold burned into my pupils as if they were discount plasma TVs.

"It's nothing. I just don't like white girls is all."

Marpessa sat up and nestled her head into the crook of my neck. "Bonbon?" She smelled like she always did—of baby powder and designer shampoo. It was all she needed. "When did you fall in love with me?"

"*The Color of Burnt Toast,*" I said, naming the bestselling memoir about the guy from Detroit with a "crazy" white mother who didn't want her biracial children to be traumatized by the word "black," so she raised them as brown, called them beigeoloids, celebrated Brown History Month, and, until he was ten years old, grew up believing that the reason he was so dark was because his absentee father was the lightning-scorched magnolia tree in the housing project courtyard. "You let my father convince you to join the Dum Dum Donuts book club. Everybody else loved the book, but during the question-and-answer session you went off on dude. 'I'm so fucking tired of black women always being described by their skin tones! Honey-colored this! Dark-chocolate that! My paternal grandmother was mocha-tinged, café-au-lait, graham-fucking-cracker brown! How come they never describe the white characters in relation to foodstuffs and hot liquids? Why aren't there any yogurt-colored, egg-shell-toned, string-cheese-skinned, low-fat-milk white protagonists in these racist, no-third-act-having books? That's why black literature sucks!'"

"I said 'Black literature sucks'?"

"Yup, and I was head over heels."

"Shit, white people got complexions, too."

A surprisingly strong swell rocked the bus from side to side. In the glow of the headlights I spotted an outsider forming to the left. I kicked off my sneakers and socks, tore off my shirt, and swam out to meet it. Marpessa stood in the doorway, shin-deep in the rising tide, her hands cupped around her mouth so that she could be heard above the crashing waves and the howl of a steadily increasing south-by-southwest wind. "Don't you want to know when I fell in love with you?"

As if she were ever in love with me.

"I fell in love with you every time we went out to eat! I'd say to myself, 'Thank God, a black man who doesn't insist on sitting facing the door! Finally, a nigger who doesn't have to pretend that he's a big man! That has to be on guard at all times because somebody might be after him because he's so fucking bad!' How could I not fall in love with you?"

The key to bodysurfing a good wave is timing. Wait for the exact moment the tide drops the pit of your stomach into your groin. Swim two strokes ahead of the curl, and as soon as the current makes you feel weightless, make two more hard strokes, lift your chin, throw one arm tight to your side and the other straight out in front, palm down, and slightly bent at the elbow, then just ride to shore.

City Lites: An Interlude

I never understood the concept of the sister city, but I'd always been fascinated by it. The way that these twin towns, as they're sometimes known, choose and court each other seems more incestuous than adoptive. Some unions, like that of Tel Aviv and Berlin, Paris and Algiers, Honolulu and Hiroshima, are designed to signal an end to hostilities and the beginning of peace and prosperity; arranged marriages in which the cities learn to love one another over time. Others are shotgun weddings, because one city, (e.g., Atlanta) impregnated the other (e.g., Lagos) on a first date that spun violently out of control centuries ago. Some cities marry up for money and prestige; others marry down to piss off their mother countries. *Guess who's coming to dinner? Kabul!* Every now and then, two cities meet and fall in love out of mutual respect and a love for hiking, thunderstorms, and classic rock 'n' roll. Think Amsterdam and Istanbul. Buenos Aires and Seoul. But in the modern age, where your average town is too busy trying to balance budgets and keep the infrastructure from crumbling, most cities have a hard time finding a soul mate, so they turn to Sister City Global, an international matchmaking organization that finds love partners for lonely municipalities. It was two days after Hominy's birthday party and although I—and the rest of Dickens—was still hungover, when Ms. Susan Silverman, City Match Consultant, called about my application, I couldn't have been more excited.

"Hello. We're happy to have processed your application for International Municipal Sisterhood, but we can't seem to find Dickens on the map. It's near Los Angeles, right?"

"We used to be an official city, but now it's kind of occupied territory. Like Guam, American Samoa, or the Sea of Tranquillity."

"So you're near the ocean?"

"Yes, an ocean of sorrow."

"Well, it doesn't matter that you're not a recognized city, Sister City Global has paired communities before. For instance, Harlem, New York's sister city is Florence, Italy, because of their respective renaissances. Dickens hasn't had a renaissance, has it?"

"No, we haven't even had a single Day of Enlightenment."

"That's too bad, but I do wish I'd known you were a coastal community, because that makes a difference. But as it were, I ran your demographics through Urbana, our matchmaking computer, and it came back with three prospective sisters."

I grabbed my atlas and tried to guess who would be the lucky ladies. I knew better than to expect Rome, Nairobi, Cairo, or Kyoto. But figured second-tier hotties like Naples, Leipzig, and Canberra were definitely in play.

"Let's see your three sister cities in order of compatibility . . . Juárez, Chernobyl, and Kinshasa."

While I didn't quite understand how Chernobyl had made the cut, especially since it's not even a city, at least Juárez and Kinshasa were two major municipalities with global profiles, if not besmirched reputations. But beggars can't be choosy. "We'll accept all three!" I shouted into the phone.

"That's all well and good, but I'm afraid all three have rejected Dickens."

"What? Why? On what grounds?"

"Juárez (aka the City That Never Stops Bleeding) feels that

Dickens is too violent. Chernobyl, while tempted, felt that, in the end, Dickens's proximity to the Los Angeles River and sewage treatment plants was a problem. And questioned the attitudes of a citizenry so laissez-faire about such rampant pollution. And Kinshasa, of the Democratic Republic of the Congo . . ."

"Don't tell me Kinshasa, the poorest city in the poorest country in the world, a place where the average per capita income is one goat bell, two bootleg Michael Jackson cassette tapes, and three sips of potable water per year, thinks we're too poor to associate with."

"No, they think Dickens is too black. I believe 'Them backward American niggers ain't ready!' is how they put it."

Too embarrassed to tell Hominy that my efforts to find Dickens a sister city had failed, I stalled him with little black lies. "Gdansk is showing some interest. And we're getting feelers from Minsk, Kirkuk, Newark, and Nyack." Eventually I ran out of cities that ended in *k* or any other letter, and in a show of disappointment, Hominy turned over a plastic milk crate, placed it in the driveway, and placed himself on the auction block. Shirt off, breasts drooping, standing next to a sign hammered into the lawn: FOR SALE—PRE-OWNED NEGRO SLAVE—ONLY BEATEN ON THURSDAYS—GOOD CONVERSATION PIECE.

He stayed there for over a week. Leaning on the horn wouldn't budge him from his perch, so whenever I needed to use the car, I'd have to yell, "Look out, man, Quakers!" or "Here comes Frederick Douglass and those damn abolitionists. Run for your lives!" which would send him ducking into the cornstalks for cover. But the day I needed to drive out to meet my apple tree connection he was being especially stubborn.

"Hominy, can you get your ass out of the way?"

"I refuse to toil fo' no massa who can't manage a simple task such as finding a sister city. And today, this here field nigger refuses to move."

"Field nigger? Not that I want you to, but you don't do a lick of work. You spend all your time in the Jacuzzi. Field nigger, my ass, you're a goddamn hot-tub-sauna-banana-daiquiri nigger. Now move!"

In the end I decided on three sister cities, each, like Dickens, a real municipality that disappeared under dubious circumstances. The first was Thebes. Not the ancient Egyptian city, but the immense silent movie set from Cecil B. DeMille's *The Ten Commandments*. Built to scale and since 1923 buried under the massive Nipomo Dunes along the beaches of Guadalupe, California, its massive wooden gates, hypostyle temples, and papier-mâché sphinxes served as home to Ramses and a phalanx of centurion and legionnaire extras. Maybe one day an offshore storm will uncover it and dust it off, so that Moses can lead the Israelites back into Egypt and Dickens into the future.

Next the thriving invisible city of Dickens formed sisterhoods with two more municipalities, Döllersheim, Austria, and the Lost City of White Male Privilege. Döllersheim, a long-since-vaporized village in northern Austria, just a grenade's throw from the Czech border, was the birthplace of Hitler's grandfather on his *mutter*'s side. Legend has it that, right before the war, the Führer, in an effort to erase his medical history (one testicle, nose job, syphilis diagnosis, and ugly baby picture at a time), his original surname (Schicklgruber-Bush), and his Jewish bloodline, had his crack troops prove their crackness by bombing the town back into the First Reich. As a historical erasure it was quite an effective tactic, because no one knows anything definitive about Hitler other than he was the quintessential asshole, humorless, and a frustrated artist, though you could say that about almost anyone.

There was a bit of a silent bidding war from ghost towns around the world for the honor of being Dickens's third sister city. The abandoned Varosha district, a once-vibrant high-rise section of Famagusta, Cyprus, evacuated during the Turkish invasion and never demolished or repopulated, made an exciting pitch. We also received a stunning bid from Bokor Hill Station, the unsettled French resort settlement whose rococo ruins continue to this day to rot in the Cambodian jungle. After an impressive presentation, Krakatoa, East of Java, was a frontrunner. War-torn and evacuated towns like Oradour-sur-Vayres in France, Paoua and Goroumo in the Central African Republic, all made strong pushes for civic sisterhood. But in the end we found it impossible to ignore the impassioned pleas of the Lost City of White Male Privilege, a controversial municipality whose very existence is often denied by many (mostly privileged white males). Others state categorically that the walls of the locale have been irreparably breached by hip-hop and Roberto Bolaño's prose. That the popularity of the spicy tuna roll and a black American president were to white male domination what the smallpox blankets were to Native American existence. Those inclined to believe in free will and the free market argue that the Lost City of White Male Privilege was responsible for its own demise, that the constant stream of contradictory religious and secular edicts from on high confused the highly impressionable white male. Reduced him to a state of such severe social and psychic anxiety that he stopped fucking. Stopped voting. Stopped reading. And, most important, stopped thinking that he was the end-all, be-all, or at least knew enough to pretend not to be so in public. But in any case, it became impossible to walk the streets of the Lost City of White Male Privilege, feeding your ego by reciting mythological truisms like "We built this country!" when all around you brown men were constantly hammering and nailing, cooking world-class French meals, and repairing your cars. You couldn't shout "America, love it or leave it!" when deep down inside you longed to live in Toronto. A city you told others was "so cosmopolitan," by which you really meant "not too cosmopolitan." How could you call or think someone a "nigger" when your own kids, lily-white and proper, called you "nigger" when you refused them the keys to the car? When everyday "niggers" were doing things that they aren't supposed to able to do, like swimming in the Olympics and landscaping their yards. My goodness, if this nonsense keeps up, one day a nigger is going to, God forbid, direct a good movie. But not to worry, Lost City of White Male Privilege, real or imagined, me and Hominy had your backs and were proud to make you a sister city of Dickens, aka the Last Bastion of Blackness.

TOO MANY MEXICANS

Eleven

"Too many Mexicans," Charisma Molina muttered. Speaking through her perfect French manicure so she wouldn't be overheard. It wasn't the first time I'd heard the racist sentiment expressed in public. Ever since the Native Americans trod up and down El Camino Real in their moccasins, seeking the source of those annoying fucking bells that rang at daybreak every Sunday morning, scaring away the bighorn sheep and ruining many a mescaline-tripping spirit walk, Californians have been cursing the Mexicans. The Indians, who were looking for peace and quiet, ended up finding Jesus, forced labor, the whip, and the rhythm method. "Too many Mexicans," they'd whisper to themselves in the wheat fields and back pews when nobody was looking.

White people, the type who never used to have anything to say to black people except "We have no vacancies," "You missed a spot," and "Rebound the basketball," finally have something to say to us. And on hot 104-degree San Fernando Valley days, when we're carrying their groceries to their cars or stuffing their mailboxes with bills, they turn and say, "Too many Mexicans," a tacit agreement between aggrieved strangers that it's neither the heat nor the humidity, but that the blame lies with our little brown brothers to the south and the north and next door, and at the Grove, and everywhere else in Califas.

For black people "too many Mexicans" is the excuse we, the historically most documented workers in history, give ourselves for attending racist rallies protesting the undocumented workers seeking better living conditions. "Too many Mexicans" is an oral rationalization to remain stuck in our ways. We like to dream over tea about relocating, finding better living conditions, while riffling through the real estate classifieds.

"What about Glendale, baby?"

"Too many Mexicans."

"Downey?"

"Too many Mexicans."

"Bellflower?"

"Too many Mexicans."

Too many Mexicans. It's a bromide for every unlicensed contractor tired of being underbid and refusing to blame their lack of employment on shoddy workmanship, nepotistic hiring practices, and a long list of shitty online references. Mexicans are to blame for everything. Someone in California sneezes, you don't say "Gesundheit" but "Too many Mexicans." Your horse in the fifth comes up lame in the backstretch at Santa Anita? *Too many Mexicans.* The donkey on the button rivers a third queen at Commerce Casino? *Too many Mexicans.* It's a constant California refrain, but when Charisma Molina, assistant principal of Chaff Middle School and best friend to Marpessa (my girlfriend, no matter what the fuck she says), said it, it was both the first time I'd ever heard a Mexican-American say it and, though I didn't know it then, the first time I'd heard anyone mean it. Literally.

Unlike the Little Rascals, whenever I played hooky from school, I never went fishin'—I went to school. I'd sneak out of the house while my dad had fallen asleep during Blackology class and jet over to Chaff to watch the kids play hand- and kickball through the chain-link fence. If I was lucky, I'd catch a glimpse of Marpessa, Charisma, and their homegirls holding court at the rear gate, sassy as a brass big band, hula-hooping their hips, chanting, *Ah beep beep, walking down street, ten times a week . . . "Ungawa! Ungawa!" That means black power! . . . I'm soul sister number nine, sock it to me one more time . . .*

For the kids at Chaff, the annual Career Day, held about two weeks before the summer break, was enough to make most of them at least contemplate career suicide before they'd even taken an aptitude test or written a résumé. Held outdoors on the schoolyard blacktop, the assemblage of coal miners, driving-range golf-ball retrievers, basket weavers, ditch diggers, book-binders, traumatized firefighters, and the world's last astronaut never does much to inspire. Every year it was the same old thing. We'd carry on about how indispensable and fulfilling our jobs were, but no one ever had answers for the questions from the back row. If you're so fucking important and the world can't run with-out you, then why are you here boring us to tears? Why do you look so unhappy? How come there aren't any female firemen? How come nurses move so motherfucking slow? The only question ever answered to the children's satisfaction was directed to the last as-tronaut, an elderly black gentleman, so feeble he moved like he was experiencing weightlessness here on Earth. How do astronauts go to the bathroom? *Well, I don't know about now, but in my day they taped a plastic bag to your ass.*

Nobody wants to be a farmer, but about a month after Hom-iny's birthday celebration, Charisma asked me to do something different. We sat on my front porch puffing gage, while she goaded me by saying she was tired of watching the Lopezes, or the "Stetson Mexicans next door," as she called them, their horses draped and saddled in glitzy *vaquero* finery, embarrass me year after year with their brocaded, crushed-velvet cowboy suits and fancy rope tricks. "Nobody cares about the subtle differences between manure and fertilizer or sustainable disease management in the butternut squash. These kids have short attention spans. You have to grab them immediately and never let go. I can't imagine anything worse than last year, when your presentation was so fucking boring the kids threw your own organic tomatoes at you."

"That's why I'm not coming. I don't need the abuse."

Charisma closed one eye and peered into the bowl, then handed it back to me.

"This shit's cashed."

"You want some more?"

Charisma nodded her head.

"I do, and I also want to know what the fuck this weed's called, and why does the stock market and all the shit I read in my graduate English lit seminar suddenly make sense to me?"

"I call it Perspicacity."

"Well, that's how good this shit is, I know what 'perspicacity,' a word I've never heard, means."

A dog barked. A cock crowed. A cow mooed. The din of the Harbor Freeway went E-I-E-I-O. Charisma flung back her long straight black hair from her face and took a hit that illuminated the mysteries of the Internet, *Ulysses*, Jean Toomer's *Cane*, and the American fascination with cooking shows. She also understood how to get me to participate in Career Day.

"Marpessa's going to be there."

I didn't need any more smoke to know that I'd never stop loving that woman.

With a bank of storm clouds rolling in from the west, it looked like rain. But nothing could dissuade Charisma from making sure her students would have the benefit of discovering the tens of career opportunities available to indigent minority youth in today's America. After the garbage men, parole officers, DJs, and hype men had their say, it was time for some action. Marpessa, representing the transportation industry, who hadn't even so much as looked my way the entire day, put on a stunt-driving demonstration that would've made the *Fast and Furious* movie franchise proud as she expertly slalomed her thirteen-ton bus between traffic cones, spun tire-smoke-billowing donuts over the four-square courts, and, after hitting a makeshift ramp constructed of lunch benches and tables, circled the schoolyard on two wheels. When the fancy driving was over, she invited the children for a tour of her bus. Loud and head-slappingly happy when they boarded, after ten minutes or so they filed off the bus in a quiet, orderly manner, somberly thanking Marpessa as they exited. One educator, a young white man, the sole white teacher in the school, was sobbing into his hands. After one last mournful look at the bus, he wandered away from the rest of the group and sank against the ball box, trying to get his shit together. I could never have imagined that an explanation of the transfer system and fare hikes could be so depressing. A light rain began to fall.

Charisma announced it was time for the more pastoral portions of the program. Nestor Lopez was up. From Jalisco, by way of Las Cruces, the Lopezes were the first Mexican family to integrate the Farms. I was about seven when they moved in. My father used to complain about the music and all the cockfighting. The only homeschool lesson in Mexican-American history I'd ever received was "Don't you ever fight a Mexican. Because if you fight a Mexican, you have to kill a Mexican," but Nestor, even though he was four years older than me and I might one day have to kill him over an unreturned Hot Wheels car or some shit, was crazy cool. On Sunday afternoons, when he came home from catechism, we'd watch *charro* movies and shaky videotapes of ersatz small-town rodeos. We'd drink porcelain cups of hot and cinnamony *ponche* his mom had made for us, and spend the rest of the afternoon recoiling from macabre videos with titles like *300 porrazos sangrientos, 101 muertes del jaripeo, 1,000 litros de sangre,* and *Si chingas al toro, te llevas los cuernos.* And yet, even though I saw most of the action through the cracks of my fingers, I've never been able to erase the images of those hard-luck cowboys riding bulls with no hands, no rodeo clowns, no medics, and no fear, as massive *toros destructores* bucked them into hatless invertebrate rag dolls. We'd bellow in vicarious pain as the incredibly pointy bullhorns punctured their rhinestoned shirts and aortas. High-five when a fallen rider's jawbone and skull got stomped into the blood-caked dirt. In time, as black and Latin boys are wont to do, we drifted apart. Socialized victims of prison gang edicts that had nothing to do with us but stipulated the separation of niggers and spics. Now, other than the occasional block party, I see Nestor only on Career Day, when, to the accompaniment of the *William Tell Overture*, he comes tearing out from behind the defunct metal shop, trick-riding and bronco-busting his ass off.

I've never been able to figure exactly what career path Nestor represents—"show-off," I suppose—but at the end of his rodeo sideshow, he doffed his ball-and-tasseled sombrero to the raucous applause of the crowd and stared me down with a "top that" sneer as he paraded past, doing a no-hand headstand in the saddle. Charisma then introduced me to a collective yawn so loud it could be heard throughout Dickens.

"What's that sound, an airplane taking off?"

"No, it's the nigger farmer. Must be Career Day at the middle school again."

I led a jittery brown-eyed calf onto home plate of a baseball diamond backstopped with a rickety chain-link fence. Some of the braver children ignored their rumbling stomachs and vitamin deficiencies to break rank and approach the animal. Cautiously, afraid they might catch a disease or fall in love, they petted the calf, speaking the syntax of the damned.

"His skin soft."

"Them eyes look like Milk Duds. I wants to eat them shits."

"Way this cow nigger be licking his lips, mooin' and droolin' 'n' shit, remind me of your retarted mother."

"Fuck you. You retarted!"

"All y'all retarted. Don't you know cows human, too?"

The irony of mispronouncing "retarded" notwithstanding, I knew that I was a hit, or at least the calf was. Charisma folded her tongue between her teeth and split the air with a sharp football-coach whistle. The same whistle she used to warn me and Marpessa that my father was making his way up the walkway. Two hundred kids quieted instantly and turned their attention deficit disorders toward me.

"Hello, everybody," I said, spitting on the ground, because that's what farmers do. "Like you guys, I'm from Dickens . . ."

"Where?" a bunch of students shouted. I might as well have said I was from Atlantis. The children weren't from "no Dickens." And they stood, throwing up gang signs and telling me where they were from: Southside Joslyn Park Crip Gang. Varrio Trescientos y Cinco. Bedrock Stoner Avenue Bloods.

In retaliation I tossed up the closest thing the agricultural world has to a gang sign and slid my hand across my throat—the universal sign for Cut the Engine—and announced, "Well, I'm from the Farms, which like all those places you've named, whether you know it or not, is in Dickens, and Assistant Principal Molina asked me to demonstrate what the average day for a farmer is like, and since today is this calf's eight-week anniversary, I thought I'd talk about castration. There are three methods of castration . . ."

"What's 'castration,' maestro?"

"It's a way of preventing male animals from fathering any children."

"Don't they got cow rubbers?"

"That's not a bad idea, but cows don't have hands and, like the Republican Party, any regard for a female's reproductive rights, so this is a way to control the population. It also makes them more docile. Anyone know what 'docile' means?"

After passing it under her runny nose, a skinny chalk-colored girl raised a hand so disgustingly ashy, so white and dry-skinned, that it could only be black.

"It means bitchlike," she said, volunteering to assist me by stepping to the calf and flicking his downy ears with her fingers.

"Yes, I guess you could say that it does."

At either the mention of "bitch" or the misguided notion they were going to learn something about sex, the children closed in and tightened the circle. The ones who weren't in the first two rows were ducking and scooting around for better vantage points. A few kids climbed to the top of the backstop's rafters and peered down on the procedure like med students in an operating theater. I body-slammed the calf on its side and kneeled down on his neck and rib cage, then directed my unlotioned cowhand to grab and spread his hind legs until the little dogie's genitals were exposed to the elements. Seeing that I had their attention, I noticed Charisma checking on her still-whimpering employee, then tiptoeing back aboard Marpessa's bus. "As I was saying, there are three methods of castration: surgical, elastic, and bloodless. In elastic you place a rubber band right here, preventing any blood flow going to the testicles. That way they'll eventually shrivel up and fall off." I grabbed the animal at the base of his scrotum and squeezed so hard the calf and the schoolchildren jumped in unison. "For bloodless castration, you crush the spermatic cords here and here." Two firm pinches of his vas deferens glans sent the calf into whimpering convulsions of pain and embarrassment, and the students into spasms of sadistic laughter. I whipped out a jackknife and held it up high, twisting my hand in the air, expecting the blade to glint dramatically in the sunlight, but it was too cloudy. "For surgery . . ."

"I want to do it." It was the little black girl, her clear brown eyes fixed on the calf's scrotum and bulging with scientific curiosity.

"I think you need a permission slip from your parents."

"What parents? I live at El Nido," she said, referring to the group home on Wilmington, which in the neighborhood was tantamount to name-dropping Sing Sing in a James Cagney movie.

"What's your name?"

"Sheila. Sheila Clark."

Sheila and I changed places, clambering over and under one another without taking any weight off the hapless calf. When I got to the back end, I handed her the knife and the emasculator, which, like the garden shears they resembled, and any other good tool, does exactly what its name says it's going to do. Two pints of blood, a surprisingly deft removal of the top half of the scrotum, an artful yank of the testes into the open air, an audible crunching severing of the spermatic cord, a schoolyard full of shrieking pupils, teachers, and one permanently sexually frustrated calf later, I was finishing up my lecture for the benefit of Sheila Clark and three other grade-schoolers intrigued enough to wade into the spreading pool of blood to get a better look at the wound, while I wrestled with the still squirming calf. "When the bull is lying here helpless on his side, we in the farming industry like to call this the 'recumbent position,' and now isn't a bad time to inflict other painful procedures on the animal, like dehorning, vaccinations, branding, and marking the ears . . ."

The rain fell harder. The drops, big and warm, kicked up small clouds of dust as they pelted the hard, dry pavement. In the middle of the schoolyard the janitorial staff was hurriedly unloading a Dumpster. They tossed the broken wooden desks, cracked blackboards, and shards of a termite-ridden handball wall into a big pile, then stuffed the crevices with newspaper. Normally Career Day ended with a giant marshmallow roast. The skies were getting even darker. I had the feeling the kids would be disappointed. In the growing wetness the teachers, save for the crybaby staring into the flat basketball as if his world had come to an end, and other careerists tried to round up the kids, snatching them off the broken-down swings, rusted-out monkey bar and jungle gym sets, while Nestor galloped around the frightened herd, steering them away from the gates. Marpessa had started the bus, and Charisma climbed out just as the calf started to recover from the shock. I looked for my assistant, Sheila Clark, but she was too busy holding up the pair of bloody testicles by their stringy entrails, dangling them in the air and slamming them into one other like a pair of twenty-five-cent vending machine clacker balls to be of any use.

As I slipped the animal into a headlock, turning on my back and digging my boot heels into his crotch to keep him from kicking me in the face, Marpessa U-turned the bus around and headed out the side gate and onto Shenandoah Street without so much as a goodbye wave. Fuck her. Charisma stood over me smiling, reading the hurt in my eyes.

"You two were so meant for each other."

"Do me a favor? In my bag there's some antiseptic and a little jar of goop that says *Fliegenschutz*." Assistant Principal Molina did what she's always done since she was a little girl: she got her hands dirty, spraying the writhing animal with disinfectant and slathering on the sticky Fliegenschutz over the gaping wound where his testicles used to be.

When she finished, the white teacher, his face streaked with tears, tapped his boss on the shoulder, and like a television cop handing in his badge and gun, he solemnly removed the shiny new Teach for America button fastened to his sweater vest, placed it in Charisma's palm, and walked off into the squall.

"What was that about?"

"When we were on the bus, your skinny farmhand, Sheila here, stood up, pointed to the PRIORITY SEATING FOR WHITES sign, and told young Mr. Edmunds he could have her seat. And that idiot takes her up on her offer, sits down, realizes what he's done, and fucking loses it."

"Wait, the signs are still up?"

"You don't know?"

"Know what?"

"You talk a lot of shit about the hood, but you don't know what's going on in the hood. Ever since you put those signs up,

Marpessa's bus has been the safest place in the city. She'd forgotten all about them, too, until her shift supervisor pointed out she hadn't had an incident report since Hominy's birthday party. But then she started thinking about it. How people were treating each other with respect. Saying hello when they got on, thank you when they got off. There's no gang fighting. Crip, Blood, or cholo, they press the Stop Request button one time and one fucking time only. You know where the kids go do their homework? Not home, not the library, but the bus. That's how safe it is."

"Crime is cyclical."

"It's the signs. People grouse at first, but the racism takes them back. Makes them humble. Makes them realize how far we've come and, more important, how far we have to go. On that bus it's like the specter of segregation has brought Dickens together."

"What about that crybaby teacher?"

"Mr. Edmunds is a good math specialist, but obviously he can't teach the kids anything about themselves, so fuck him."

More or less healed, the calf scrambled to its feet. Sheila, his little emasculator, leaned teasingly in his face, holding his testes from her earlobes like costume jewelry. One last goodbye sniff of his manhood and he ambled off to commiserate with the ball-less tetherball poles that stood bent and useless next to the cafeteria. Charisma rubbed her tired eyes. "Now, if I get these little mother-fuckers to behave in school like they do on the bus, we'd be on to something."

Led by Nestor Lopez, who was ten lengths ahead of the pack, galloping in for his reward money, Sheila's classmates were being shepherded over the concrete plains, marched through the drizzle and past the rows of thatch tarpaper-roofed bungalows, windows glassed with newsprint and colored construction paper. Buildings in such disrepair they made the one-room African schoolhouses on late-night television fundraisers damn near look like college lecture halls in comparison. It was a modern-day Trail of Tears. The kids were circled around the mound of broken school furniture. Their excitement undeterred despite the crackle of the raindrops on the giant bags of marshmallows and the steadily darkening pile of wood and damp newsprint. Behind them was the school's auditorium, the roof of which had collapsed in the Northridge quake of '94 and had never been rebuilt. Charisma ran her hand down the length of Nestor's Rose Parade saddle bells. The jingle-jangle made the kids smile. Just then Sheila Clark, tearfully rubbing her shoulder, ran up. "Ms. Molina, that white boy stole one of my balls!" she wailed, pointing at the chubby Latino kid, three shades darker than her, vainly trying to superball the testis against the wet ground. Charisma gently stroked Sheila's braided head, soothing her feelings. That was a new one on me. Black kids referring to their Latino peers as white. When I was their age, back when we used to scream "Not it!" before games of Kick the Can and Red Light, Green Light, back before the violence, the poverty, and the infighting had reduced our indigenous land rights from all of Dickens to isolated city blocks of gang turf, everyone in Dickens, regardless of race, was black and you determined someone's degree of blackness not by skin color or hair texture but by whether they said "For all intents and purposes" or "For all intensive purposes." Marpessa used to say that despite the fall of straight black hair that cascaded down to her butt and her *horchata* complexion, she didn't know Charisma wasn't black until the day Charisma's mother stopped by to pick her up from school. Her walk and talk so different from her daughter's. Stunned, she turned to her best friend. "You Mexican?" Thinking her homegirl was tripping, Charisma blanched, about to exclaim, "I ain't Mexican," when, as if seeing her for the first time, she took a good look at her own mother in the after-school context of the surrounding black faces and rhythms, and was like "Oh fuck, I *am* Mexican! *¡Hijo de puta!*" That was a long time ago.

Before lighting the bonfire, Assistant Principal Molina addressed her troops. It was obvious in the seriousness in her face and the tone of her voice that she was a general at the end of her rope. Resigned to the fate that the black and brown troops she was sending out into the world didn't have much of a chance. *Cada día de carreras profesionales yo pienso la misma cosa. De estos doscientos cincuenta niños, ¿cuántos terminarán la escuela secundaria? ¿Cuarenta pinche por ciento? Órale, y de esos cien con suerte, ¿cuántos irán a la universidad?* ¿Online, junior, clown college, *o lo que sea?* About five, *más o menos. ¿Y cuántos graduarán?* Two, maybe. *Qué lástima. Estamos chingados.*

And although like most black males raised in Los Angeles, I'm bilingual only to the extent that I can sexually harass women of all ethnicities in their native languages, I understood the gist of the message. Those kids were fucked.

I was surprised how many of the children carried lighters, but no matter how many attempts were made to start the bonfire, the water-soaked wood wouldn't catch. Charisma ordered a group of students to the storage shed. They returned bearing cardboard boxes, the contents of which they dumped on the ground. Soon there was a pyramid of books about five feet wide and three feet high and rising.

"Well, what the fuck are you waiting for?"

She didn't have to ask twice. The books caught like kindling, and the flames of a good-sized bonfire licked the sky as the students happily roasted marshmallows on number two pencils.

I pulled Charisma aside. I couldn't believe she was burning books. "I thought school supplies were in short supply."

"Those aren't books. Those came from Foy Cheshire. He has a whole curriculum called 'Fire the Canon!' featuring such rewritten classics as *Uncle Tom's Condo* and *The Point Guard in the Rye* that he's pushing on the school board. Look, we've tried everything: smaller classrooms, longer hours, bilingual, monolingual, and sublingual educations, Ebonics, phonics, and hypnotics. Color schemes designed to promote the optimum learning environment. But no matter what warm-to-medium-cool hues you paint the walls, when it all comes down to it, it's white teachers talking white methodology and drinking white wine and some wannabe white administrator threatening to put your school into receivership because he knows Foy Cheshire. Nothing works. But I'll be damned if the Chaff Middle School will hand out copies of *The Dopeman Cometh* to its students."

I kicked a partially burned tome away from the fire. The cover was charred but still readable, *The Great Blacksby*, page one of which was:

Real talk. When I was young, dumb, and full of cum, my omnipresent, good to my mother, non-stereotypical African-American daddy dropped some knowledge on me that I been trippin' off of ever since.

Using my lighter, I finished torching the book myself and held its flaming pages under the marshmallow on a wooden ruler that Sheila had kindly offered me. She had fashioned a leash from a jump rope and was stroking the calf on the head, while the Latino was trying to surgically reattach his testicles with Elmer's glue and a paper clip, until Charisma grabbed him by the neck and stood him up.

"You kids have a good Career Day?"

"I want to be a veterinarian!" Sheila answered.

"That's gay," countered her Latino nemesis, who was juggling the gonads with one hand.

"Juggling is gay!"

"Calling people who call you 'gay' just because you called them 'gay' is gay!"

"Okay, that's enough." Charisma scolded. "My God, is there anything you kids don't think is gay?"

The fat boy thought for a long moment. "You know what's not gay . . . being gay."

Laughing through her tears, Charisma collapsed on a beige fiberglass bench as the three o'clock bell rang; it'd been a long day. I sidled in next to her. The clouds finally caved in and the drizzle turned into a steady downpour. The students and faculty ran to their cars, the bus stop, and the waiting arms of their parents, while we sat there in the shower like good Southern Californians, umbrellaless and listening to the raindrops sizzle in the slowly dying fire.

"Charisma, I thought of a way to get the kids to behave and respect each other like they do on the bus."

"How?"

"Segregate the school." As soon as I said it, I realized that segregation would be the key to bringing Dickens back. The communal feeling of the bus would spread to the school and then permeate the rest of the city. Apartheid united black South Africa, why couldn't it do the same for Dickens?

"By race? You want to segregate the school by color?"

Charisma looked at me like I was one of her students. Not stupid, but clueless. But if you asked me, Chaff Middle School had already been segregated and re-segregated many times over, maybe not by color, but certainly by reading level and behavior problem. The English as a Second Language speakers were on a different learning track than the English When and Only If I Feel Like It speakers. During Black History Month, my father used to watch the nightly television footage of the Freedom buses burning, the dogs snarling and snapping, and say to me, "You can't force integration, boy. The people who want to integrate will integrate." I've never figured out to what extent, if at all, I agree or disagree with him, but it's an observation that's stayed with me. Made me realize that for many people integration is a finite concept. Here, in America, "integration" can be a cover-up. "I'm not racist. My prom date, second cousin, my president is black (or whatever)." The problem is that we don't know whether integration is a natural or an unnatural state. Is integration, forced or otherwise, social entropy or social order? No one's ever defined the concept. Charisma was giving segregation some thought, though, as she slowly rotated the last of the marshmallows in the flame. I knew what she was thinking. She was thinking about how her middle-school alma mater was now 75 percent Latino, when in her day it was 80 percent black. Thinking about listening to her mother, Sally Molina, tell stories about growing up in segregated small-town Arizona in the 1940s and '50s. Having to sit on the hot side of the church, the farthest away from Jesus and the fire exits. Having to go to the Mexican schools and bury her parents and her baby brother at the Mexican cemetery outside of town on Highway 60. How when the family moved to Los Angeles in 1954, the racial discrimination was more or less the same. Except that unlike the black Angelenos, they could at least use the public beaches.

"You want to segregate the school by race?"

"Yeah."

"If you think you can do it, go ahead. But I'm telling you, there's too many Mexicans."

I can't speak for the children, but driving home, the newly castrated calf in the front seat of the pickup, his head out the window catching raindrops on his tongue, I left Career Day as inspired as I'd ever been and with renewed focus. What was it Charisma said, "It's like the specter of segregation has brought the city of Dickens back together again." I decided to give my new career as City Planner in Charge of Restoration and Segregation another six months. If things didn't work out, I could always fall back on being black.

Twelve

It rained buckets that summer after Career Day. The white boys at the beach called it "bummer," as in the "Bummer of '42." The weather reports were nothing but nonstop references to record rainfall and continuous cloud cover. Every day, at around nine thirty, a low-pressure system settled over the coastline and it'd pour off and on until early evening. Some folks won't surf in the rain, even more refuse go out after a storm, worried about contracting hepatitis from the sludge and all the polluted runoff that flows into the Pacific after a heavy downpour. Personally, I like catching waves in the rain, fewer fuckers in the lineup, no windsurfers. Stay away from the arroyos near Malibu and Rincon, which tend to overflow with septic waste, and you'll be fine. So that summer I didn't worry about fecal matter and microbes. I agonized over my satsumas and segregation. How do you grow the world's most water-sensitive citrus tree under monsoon conditions? How do you racially segregate an already segregated school?

Hominy, the race reactionary, was no help. He loved the idea of bringing back segregated education, because he thought the idea would make Dickens more attractive to white resettlement. That the city would return to being the thriving white suburb of his youth. Cars with tail fins. Straw hats and sock hops. Episcopalians and ice cream socials. It would be the opposite of white flight, he said. "The Ku Klux influx." But when I'd ask him how, he'd just shrug and, like a conservative senator without any ideas, filibuster me with unrelated stories about the good ol' days. "Once, in an episode called 'Pop Quisling,' Stymie tried to avoid taking a history test he hadn't studied for by setting his desk on fire, but of course he ended up burning down the entire school and the gang had to take the test on top of a fire truck 'cause Miss Crabtree didn't play that shit." Then there was the guilt that comes along with being a segregationist. I stayed up nights trying to convince Funshine Bear, whose fur over the years had mottled and turned from sun-ray yellow to toe-jam brown, that the reintroduction of segregation would be a good thing. That like Paris has the Eiffel Tower, St. Louis the Arch, and New York an insanely huge income disparity, Dickens would have segregated schools. If nothing else, the Chamber of Commerce brochure would look attractive. *Welcome to the Glorious City of Dickens: The Urban Paradise on the Banks of the Los Angeles River. Home to Roving Bands of Youth Groups, a Retired Movie Star, and Segregated Schools!*

Lots of people claim to get their best ideas in water. The shower. Floating in the pool. Waiting for a wave. Something about negative ions, white noise, and being in isolation. So you'd think that surfing in the rain would be the equivalent of a one-man brainstorm—but not me. I get my good ideas not while surfing but while driving home from surfing. So sitting in traffic, after a nice rainy-day July session, reeking of sewage and seaweed, I watched the remedial rich kids pour out of summer school at Intersection Academy, a prestigious oceanfront private "learning fulcrum." As they crossed the street to their waiting limousines and luxury cars, they'd flash me "hang loose" and gang signs, stick their shaggy heads into my cab, and say, "Bro, you got any weed? Hang ten, African-American waverider!"

Despite the steady downpour, the students never seemed to get wet. Mostly because valets and scullery maids chased after their rambunctious wards holding umbrellas over their heads, but some kids were just too white to get wet. Try to imagine Winston Churchill, Colin Powell, and Condoleezza Rice, or the Lone Ranger, soaked from head to toe and you'll get the idea.

For a hot second, when I was eight, Pops flirted with enrolling my intellectually lazy ass in a fancy prep school. He stood over me while I was shin-deep in the rice paddy, planting stalks into the mud. He muttered something about choosing between Jews in Santa Monica and Gentiles in Holmby Hills, then began citing research that black kids who go to school with white kids of any religion "do better," while also positing some not-so-credible research that black people were "better off" during segregation. I don't remember his definition of "better off" or why I didn't go to Interchange or Haverford-Meadowbrook. The commute, maybe. Too expensive. But watching those kids, the sons and daughters of music and movie industry moguls, file out of that state-of-the-art building, it dawned on me that, as the sole student of Daddy's K thru Forever Home School, I had been the beneficiary of a most segregated education, one with thankfully little exposure to infinity pools, homemade foie gras, and American ballet. And while I was no closer to figuring out how to save my satsuma crop, I did have an idea how to racially segregate what, for all intents and purposes and Latinos, was an all-black school. I drove home, my father's voice swimming in my head.

When I got back home, Hominy was waiting for me out in the yard, standing under a large green-and-white golf umbrella, his bare feet making a deep hammer-toed impression in the wet grass. Ever since I'd agreed to segregate the middle school, he'd become a much better worker. He was no fucking John Henry by any stretch, but if he took an interest in something on the farm, he'd at least show some self-initiative. Lately he'd been very protective of the satsuma tree. Sometimes he'd stand next to it for hours, shooing away birds and bugs. The satsumas reminded him of the camaraderie of studio life. Thumb-wrestling with Wheezer. Slapping Fatty Arbuckle upside the head. Truth or Dare games where the loser would have to streak through the Laurel and Hardy set. It was during a long break between shots on "I See Paris, I See France" that Hominy discovered the satsuma mandarin. Most of the gang had gathered around the craft services table, downing cupcakes and cream soda. But there were some southern theater owners on the set that day, and the studio, wanting to make nice with a caste system that refused to show their movies because they featured colored and white kids playing together, asked Hominy and Buckwheat to eat with some Japanese extras who, during the immigration roundup of '36, had been drafted to play Mexican bandits. The extras offered them some nonunion soba noodles and satsumas imported from the Land of the Rising Sun. The black boys found the fruit's perfectly balanced bittersweet flavor to be the only thing that removed the nasty taste of comic-relief watermelon from their mouths. Eventually, he and Buckwheat had riders put in their contracts: only satsumas were allowed on set. No clementines, tangerines, or tangelos. Because nothing restored one's dignity like a sweet juicy satsuma orange after a hard day of cooning.

Hominy still thinks I tend the tree to suit his needs, he doesn't know that I planted it the same day me and Marpessa officially split. I'd finished freshman year midterms and driven home, flying west on CA-91, spurred on by what I thought would be the awaiting congratulatory fuck and not a note pinned through the sow's ear that simply read, *Naw, nigger.*

He pulled desperately on the sleeve of my wetsuit. "Massa, you told me to tell you when the satsumas were the size of Ping-Pong balls." Like a golf caddy who refuses to give up on an employer's woeful round, Hominy held the umbrella over my head. Handed me the refractometer and urged me into the backyard, where we tramped through the mud to the waterlogged tree. "Please, massa, hurry. I don't think they going to make it."

Most citrus fruits require frequent watering, but the inverse is true for satsumas. They turn water into piss, and no matter how much pruning I did, that year's crop hung heavy and mean on the branches. If I couldn't figure out a way to decrease the water intake, the yield would be shit and I'd have wasted ten years and fifty pounds of imported Japanese fertilizer. I clipped a mandarin off the nearest tree. Snipping it a quarter inch above the navel, I dug my thumb into the bumpy flesh, ripping it open and squeezing a few drops into the refractometer, the small, overpriced, Japanese-made machine that measures the percentage of sucrose in the juice.

"What's it say?" he asked desperately.

"Two point three."

"What's that on the sweetness scale?"

"Somewhere between Eva Braun and a South African salt mine."

I never nigger-whispered to my plants. I don't believe that plants are sentient beings, but after Hominy went home I talked to those trees for an hour. Read them poetry and sang them the blues.

Thirteen

I've experienced direct discrimination based on race only once in my life. One day I foolishly said to my father that there was no racism in America. Only equal opportunity that black people kick aside because we don't want to take responsibility for ourselves. Later that very same day, in the middle of the night, he snatched me up out of bed, and together we took an ill-prepared cross-country trip into deepest, whitest America. After three days of non-stop driving, we ended up in a nameless Mississippi town that was nothing more than a dusty intersection of searing heat, crows, cotton fields, and, judging by the excited look of anticipation on my father's face, unadulterated racism.

"There it is," he said, pointing toward a run-down general store so out of date the pinball machine blinking happily in the window took only dimes and displayed a mind-numbing high current score of 5,637. I looked around for the racism. Out front, three burly white men with those sun-baked crow's-foot visages that make age an indeterminate number sat on wooden Coca-Cola crates, loudly talking shit about an upcoming stock-car race. We pulled into the gas station across the street. A bell rang, startling both the black attendant and me. Reluctantly, he broke away from the video chess game he was playing with a friend on the television.

"Fill 'er up, please."

"Sure thing. Check the oil?" My father nodded, never taking his eyes off the store. The attendant, Clyde, if the name fancily stitched in red cursive on the white patch on his blue coveralls was to be trusted, jumped to his duties. He checked the oil, the tire pressure, and slid his grease rag over the front and back windshields. I don't think I'd ever seen service with a smile before. And whatever was in that spray bottle, the windows had never been so clean. When the tank was full, my father asked Clyde, "You think me and the boy could sit here a mite?"

"Sure, go ahead."

A *mite*? I hung my head in embarrassment. I hate when people get all folksy around black people they think they're superior to. What was next? Fixin'? Sho' 'nuff? A chorus of "Who Let the Dogs Out"?

"Dad, what are we doing here?" I mumbled, my mouth full of the saltine crackers I'd been stuffing down my gullet since Memphis. Anything to take my mind off the heat, the endless cotton fields, and the thought of how bad slavery must have been for someone to convince themselves that Canada wasn't that far away. Although he never spoke about it, like his runaway ancestors, my father, too, fled to Canada, dodging the draft and the Vietnam War. If black people ever do get slave reparations, I know plenty of motherfuckers who owe Canada some rent money and back taxes.

"Dad, what are we doing here?"

"We're reckless eyeballing," he said, removing a pair of 500x General Patton binoculars from a fancy leather case, placing the black metal monstrosities to his eyes, and turning toward me, his eyes big as billiard balls through the thick lenses. "And I do mean reckless!"

Thanks to years of my father's black vernacular pop quizzes and an Ishmael Reed book he kept on top of the toilet for years, I knew that "reckless eyeballing" was the act of a black male deigning

to look at a southern white female. And there was my dad staring
through his binoculars at a storefront no more than thirty feet
away, the Mississippi sun glinting off the massive spectacles like
two halogen beacons. A woman stepped out onto the porch, an
apron tied around her gingham dress, a wicker broom in her hand.
Shielding her eyes from the glare, she began to sweep. The white
men sat open-legged and open-mouthed, aghast at the sheer fucking nigger audacity.

"Look at those tits!" my father shouted, loud enough for the
entire cracker county to hear. Her chest wasn't all that, but I
imagine that through the portable equivalent of the Hubble Space
Telescope her B-cup breasts looked like the *Hindenburg* and the
Goodyear blimp, respectively. "Now, boy, now!"

"Now what?"

"Go out there and whistle at the white woman."

He shoved me out the door, and kicking up a blinding cloud of
red delta dust, I crossed a two-lane highway covered with so much
rock-hard clay I couldn't tell if the road had ever been paved.
Obligingly, I stood in front of the white lady and began to whistle.
Or at least tried to. What my father didn't know is that I didn't
know how to whistle. Whistling is one of the few things you learn
at public school. I was homeschooled, so my lunch hours were spent
standing in the backyard cotton patch reciting all the Negro Re-
construction congressmen from memory: Blanche Bruce, Hiram
Rhodes, John R. Lynch, Josiah T. Walls . . . so although it sounds
simple, I didn't know how to just put my lips together and blow. And
for that matter, I can't split my fingers into the Vulcan high-sign,
burp the alphabet on command, or flip someone the bird without
folding down the non-insulting fingers with my free hand. Having a
mouthful of crackers didn't help either, and the end result was an ar-
rhythmic spewing of pre-chewed oats all over her pretty pink apron.

"What's this crazy fool doing?" the white men asked each
other between eye rolls and tobacco expectorations. The most taci-

turn member of the trio stood up and straightened out his *No Nig-gers in NASCAR* T-shirt. Slowly removing the toothpick from his mouth, he said, "It's the 'Boléro.' The little nigger is whistling 'Boléro.'"

I jumped up and down and pumped his hand in excitement. He was right, of course, I was trying to re-create Ravel's masterpiece. I may not know how to whistle, but I could always carry a tune.

"The 'Boléro'? Why, you stupid motherfucker!"

It was Pops. Storming out of the car and moving so fast his dust cloud kicked up its own dust cloud. He wasn't happy, because apparently not only did I not know how to whistle, I didn't know *what* to whistle. "You're supposed to wolf whistle! Like this . . ." Recklessly eyeballing her the whole way, he pursed his lips and let go a wolf whistle so lecherous and libidinous it curled both the white woman's pretty painted toes and the dainty red ribbon in her blond hair. Now it was her turn. And my father stood there, lustful and black, as she just as defiantly not only recklessly eye-balled him back but recklessly rubbed his dick through his pants. Kneading his crotch like pizza dough for all she was worth.

Dad quickly whispered something in her ear, handed me a five-dollar bill, said I'll be back, and together they hurried into the car and tore out down some dirt road. Leaving me to be lynched for his crimes.

"Is there a black buck Rebecca ain't fucked from here to Natchez?"

"Well, least she knows what she likes. Your dumb peckerwood ass still ain't decided whether you like men or not."

"I'm bisexual. I likes both."

"Ain't no such thing. You either is or you ain't. Man crush on Dale Earnhardt, my ass."

While the good old boys argued the merits and manifestations of sexuality, I, thankful to be alive, went inside the store for a soda. They carried only one brand and one size, Coca-Cola in the classic seven-ounce bottle. I twisted one open and watched the effervescent sprites of carbon dioxide dance in the sun rays. I can't tell you how good that Coke tasted, but there's an old joke that I never understood until that bubbling brown elixir slid soothingly down my throat.

Bubba the redneck, a nigger, and a Mexican are sitting at the same bus stop when BAM! a genie appears out of nowhere in a cloud of smoke. "You each get one wish," says the genie, adjusting his turban and his ruby rings. So the nigger says, "I wish for all my black brothers and sisters to be in Africa, where the land will nourish us and all Africans can prosper." The genie waved his hands, and BAM! all the blacks left America and went to Africa. The Mexican then said, "*Órale*, that sounds good to me. I want all my Mexican peoples to be in Me-hee-co where we can live well and have yobs and drink from glorious pools of tequila." BAM! They all went to Mexico and left America. Then the genie turns to Bubba the redneck and says, "And what is it you desire, Sahib? Your wish is my command." Bubba looks at the genie and says, "So you're telling me that all the Mexicans are in Mexico and all the niggers are in Africa?"

"Yes, Sahib."

"Well, it's kinda hot today, I guess I'll have a Coke."

That's how good that Coke was.

"That'll cost seven cents. Just leave it on the counter, boy. Your new mommy be back in no time."

Ten sodas and seventy cents later, neither my new mother nor my old father had returned and I had to take a wicked piss. The fellows at the gas station were still playing chess, the attendant's cursor hovering hesitatingly over a cornered piece as if his next decision decided the fate of the world. The attendant slammed a knight onto a square. "You ain't fooling nobody with that Sicilian gambit chicanery. Your diagonals is vulnerable as shit."

My bladder about to burst, I asked black Kasparov where the bathroom was located.

"Restrooms are for customers only."

"But my dad just purchased some gas . . ."

"And your father can shit here until his heart's content. You, on the other hand, are drinking the white man's Coke like his ice is colder than ours."

I pointed to the row of seven-ounce sodas in the cooler. "How much?"

"Dollar-fifty."

"But they're seven cents across the street."

"Buy black or piss off. Literally."

Feeling sorry for me, and winning on points, black Bobby Fischer pointed into the distance at an old bus station.

"See that abandoned bus station next to the cotton gin?"

I sprinted down the road. Although the building was no longer operational, balls of cottonseed still blew in the wind like itchy snowflakes. I made my way to the back, past the gin, the empty pallets, a rusted forklift, and the ghost of Eli Whitney. The filthy one-toilet bathroom buzzed with flies. The floors and the seat were flypaper sticky. Glazed to a dull matte yellow by four generations of good ol' boys with bottomless bladders, pissing countless gallons of drunk-on-the-job clear urine. The acrid stink of unflushed racism and shit shriveled my face and put goosebumps on my arms. Slowly I backed out. Underneath the faded WHITES ONLY stenciled on the grimy lavatory door, I ran my finger through the grit and wrote THANK GOD, then peed on an anthill. Because apparently the rest of the planet was "Colored Only."

Fourteen

At first glance the Dons, the hilly neighborhood about ten miles north of Dickens that Marpessa moved to after she married MC Panache, looks like any well-to-do African-American enclave. The tree-lined streets are twisting. The houses are fronted with immaculate Japanese-style gardens. The wind chimes somehow coerce the air currents into Stevie Wonder songs. American flags and campaign signs supporting crooked politicians are displayed proudly in the front yard. When we were dating, sometimes after a night out, me and Marpessa would cruise the neighborhood, wheeling Daddy's pickup truck through streets with Spanish names like Don Lugo, Don Marino, and Don Felipe. We used to refer to the modern but smallish homes with their pools, plate-glass windows, stone facades, and weatherproofed balconies overlooking downtown Los Angeles as "Brady Bunch houses." As in "The motherfucking Wilcoxes came up, dude. Them niggers kicking it in a Brady Bunch house off Don Quixote." We hoped one day to live in one of these homes and have a barrel of children. The worst thing that could happen to us was that we'd falsely accuse our oldest son of smoking, a poorly thrown football would break our daughter's nose, and our slightly slutty maid would constantly throw herself at the mailman. Then we'd die and go into worldwide syndication like all good American families.

For ten years, ever since our breakup, I'd periodically park outside her crib, wait until the lights went out, then through the binoculars and a sliver of open bay window curtain, I'd take in the life I should've been living, a life of sushi and Scrabble, kids studying in the living room and playing with the dog. After the children went to bed, I'd watch *Nosferatu* and *Metropolis* with her, crying like a baby because the way Paulette Goddard and Charlie Chaplin in *Modern Times* circle around each like two dogs in heat reminded me of us. Sometimes I'd sneak up to the porch and, in the screen door, leave a snapshot of the growing satsuma tree on her porch with *Our son, Kazuo, says hello* written on the back.

There isn't much you can do about segregating a school when school isn't in session, and that summer I spent more time outside her house than for legal reasons I care to admit, until one warm August night, the forty-foot Metro bus parked in Marpessa's driveway forced me to abort my stalker protocol. Like their white-collar comrades, it's not unusual for black blue-collar employees like Marpessa to take their work home with them. Regardless of your income level, the old adage of having to be twice as good as the white man, half as good as the Chinese guy, and four times as good as the last Negro the supervisor hired before you still holds true. Nevertheless, I was surprised as hell to see the #125 bus sitting in her driveway, its back end blocking the sidewalk, its right-side tires ruining a once-perfect lawn.

Tree photo in hand, I crept past the gardenias and the Westec security sign. Rising to my tippy-toes, I peered into a side window, cupping my hands around my eyes. Even in the cool of the midnight air, the vehicle was still warm and thick with the scent of gasoline and the sweat of the working class. It'd been four months since Hominy's birthday party and the PRIORITY SEATING FOR SENIORS, DISABLED, AND WHITES signs were still up. I wondered aloud how she got away with them.

"She says it's an art project, nigger."

The barrel of the snub-nosed .38 boring into my cheekbone

was cold and impersonal, but the voice behind the gun was the exact opposite, warm and friendly. Familiar. "Dude, if I hadn't recognized the smell of cow shit on your ass, you'd be dead as good black music."

Stevie Dawson, Marpessa's younger brother, spun me around and, gun in hand, gave me a bear hug. Behind him stood a red-eyed Cuz, a tipsy grin happily cutting across his mug. His boy Stevie was out of jail. I was glad to see him, too; it'd been at least ten years. Stevie's rep was even more dastardly than Cuz's. Gang-unaffiliated only because he was too crazy for the Crip sets and too mean for the Bloods. Stevie hates nicknames, because he feels real bad motherfuckers don't need one. And although there are a few hardheads around the way who answer to their Christian names, when niggers say Stevie, it's like a Chinese homophone. If you've been around, you know exactly who they mean. In California you get three strikes. If you're convicted of two felonies, the next guilty verdict, no matter how minor, can mean life in prison. Somewhere along the line the catcher must have dropped Stevie's third strike, because the system had sent him back to the plate.

"How did you get out?"

"Panache sprung him," Cuz answered, offering me a sip of Tanqueray that was almost as nasty as its diet grapefruit soda chaser.

"What, he performed one of his shitty benefit concerts and snuck you out in a speaker?"

"Power of the pen. Between his TV cop gig and the beer commercials, Panache knows some big-time white people. Letters were written, and here I am. Conditionally paroled like a motherfucker."

"What conditions?"

"The condition that I don't get caught. What else?"

One of the dogs began to bark. The kitchen curtains parted, spilling light onto the driveway. I flinched, even though we were out of sight.

"No need to be scared. Panache ain't here."

"I know. He's never here."

"And how you know that, you been stalking my sister again?"

"Who's out there?" It was Marpessa, saving me from further embarrassment. I mouthed to Stevie that I wasn't there.

"It's just me and Cuz."

"Well, bring your asses inside before something happens."

"All right, we'll be in in a second."

The first time I met Stevie, back when he and his sister lived in Dickens, there was a limousine parked in front of their house. Except for prom night, you don't see many limos in the ghetto. And that black stretch Cadillac—crammed from mini bar to back window with roughnecks, light and dark, tall and short, smart and stupid—held Stevie's boys. Boys who over the years disappeared in ones and twos and, on really bloody days—threes. Bank robberies. Food truck holdups. Assassinations. Panache and King Cuz were the only homies he had left. And though Stevie and Panache really liked each other, it was a relationship that profited both parties. Panache wasn't no punk, but Stevie gave him real street cred in the rap scene, and for Stevie, Panache's success reminded him that all things are possible if one can get the right white people on your side. Back then Panache fancied himself a pimp. Sure, he had women doing shit for him, but what nigger didn't? I remember Panache in the living room staring Marpessa down, rapping what would become his first gold record, while Stevie DJ'd for him.

> Three in the afternoon, Mormons at my pad
> Need new croaker sacks and feelin' bad
> Promising salvation to a nigger like me
> Brigham Young must be stupid and high on PCP

If Stevie had a Latin motto, it'd be *Cogito, ergo Boogieum.* I think, therefore I jam.

•

"How come Marpessa's bus is parked here?" I asked him.

"Nigger, how come *you* here?" he barked back.

"I wanted to leave this for your sister." I showed him the photo of the satsuma tree, which he snatched from my hand. I wanted to ask him if he'd received all the fruit I'd sent him over the years: the papayas, kiwis, apples, and blueberries, but I could tell from the suppleness of his skin, the whiteness of his eyes, the sheen in his ponytail, and the relaxed way he leaned on my shoulder that he had.

"She told me about you leaving these pictures."

"Is she mad?"

Stevie shrugged and continued to stare at the Polaroid. "The bus here because they lost Rosa Parks's bus."

"Who lost Rosa Parks's bus?"

"White people. Who the fuck else? Supposedly, every February when schoolkids visit the Rosa Parks Museum, or wherever the fuck the bus is at, the bus they tell the kids is the birthplace of the civil rights movement is a phony. Just some old Birmingham city bus they found in some junkyard. That's what my sister says, anyway."

"I don't know."

Cuz took two deep swallows of gin. "What you mean, 'You don't know'? You think that after Rosa Parks bitch-slapped white America, some white rednecks going to go out of their way to save the original bus? That'd be like the Celtics hanging Magic Johnson's jersey in the rafters of the Boston Garden. No fucking way.

"Anyway, she thinks what you did with the bus, with the stickers and shit, is special. That it makes niggers think. In her way, she's proud of you."

"Really?"

I looked at the bus. Tried to see it in a different light. As something more than forty sheet-metal feet of trivial rights iconography dripping transmission fluid onto the driveway. Tried to picture it hanging from the ceiling of the Smithsonian, a tour guide pointing up to it and saying, "This is the very bus from which Hominy Jenkins, the last Little Rascal, asserted that the rights of African-Americans were neither God-given nor constitutional, but immaterial."

Stevie held the photo under his nose, took a deep breath, and asked, "When these oranges going to be ready?"

I wanted to point to the greenish-orange balls and brag about how I'd figured out that if I covered the ground around the tree with white waterproof sheeting, not only would I be able to keep moisture from seeping into the soil, the whiteness would reflect the sunlight back into the tree and improve the color of the fruit. But all I could manage was "Soon. They'll be ripe soon."

Stevie took one last sniff of the picture, and then passed it under King Cuz's cavernous nostrils.

"Smell that citrus, nigger? That's what freedom smells like."

Then he grabbed me by the shoulders. "And what's this I hear about black Chinese restaurants?"

Fifteen

It was the smell that brung 'em. At about six in the morning, I found the first boy curled up in my driveway, breathing heavily, pressing his nose under the gate like a horny dog. He looked happy. He wasn't in the way, so I left him alone and went to milk the cows. Los Angeles, for whatever reason, is chock-full of autistic children and I thought he was one of the afflicted. But later in the day he had company. By noontime, nearly every child on the block had crammed into my front yard. They spent the last day of summer vacation playing Uno on the grass and trying to see who could hit the softest. They plucked needles from the cacti and stuck each other in the behind, they popped my rose petals and scratched their names into the driveway with rock salt. Even the Lopez kids, Lori, Dori, Jerry, and Charlie, who lived next door and had two pristine acres of backyard and a decent-sized pool to play in, were circled around little brother Billy, laughing hysterically as he noshed on a peanut butter sandwich. Then a little girl I didn't recognize staggered over to the elm tree and drowned a column of ants in vomit.

"Okay, what the fuck?"

"The Stank," Billy said, after swallowing a mouthful of a peanut butter—and judging from what appeared to be bug legs on his tongue—and flies sandwich. I didn't smell anything, so Billy dragged me out into the street. It wasn't hard to see why the young girl retched; the stench was overwhelming. The Stank had rolled in overnight and settled over the neighborhood like some celestial flatulence. Jesus. But why hadn't I noticed it earlier? I stood in the middle of Bernard Avenue, the kids beckoning me over, waving frantically like World War I soldiers urging a wounded comrade out of the mustard gas and back into the relative safety of the trenches. As soon as I reached the curb, it hit me, the refreshing pungency of citrus. No wonder the kids refused to stray from my property, the satsuma tree was perfuming the grounds like some ten-foot-tall air freshener.

Billy yanked my pant leg. "When those oranges going to be ready?"

I wanted to tell him tomorrow, but I was too busy pushing the little girl aside so I could throw up on the elm, gagging not from the smell but because Billy had two red fly eyes stuck in his teeth.

The next morning, the first day of school, the neighbor kids and their parents were gathered at the driveway gate. The youngsters, shiny and clean in brand-new school clothes, pawed at the wooden fence, trying to catch glimpses of the farm animals through the wooden slats. The adults, some still in their pajamas, yawned, looked at their watches, and adjusted their bathrobe belts as they placed milk money—twenty-five cents for a pint of my unpasteurized—in their children's hands. I sympathized with the parents, because after being up all night in the lingering remnants of the Stank, building an imaginary all-white school, I was tired, too.

It's hard to determine when satsumas are ripe. Color isn't a very good indicator. Neither is rind texture. Smell is good, but the best way to tell is simply to taste them. However, I trust the refractometer more than my taste buds.

"What's the reading, massa?"

"Sixteen point eight."

"Is that good?"

I tossed Hominy an orange. When satsumas are ready to eat, the skin is so supple, they damn near peel themselves. He popped a wedge into his satchel mouth and pretended to faint dead away in a pratfall so well executed the rooster stopped crowing for fear the old man was dead.

"Oh shit."

The kids thought he was hurt. I did, too, until he flashed a wide "Yes sir, boss. Dat's good eatin'!" smile as bright and warm as the rising sun. He stood up in sections, then soft-shoed and somersaulted his way to the fence, showing that there was some of both the old vaudevillian and the stunt coon still left in him. "I sees white people!" he exclaimed in faux horror.

"Let them in, Hominy."

Hominy opened the gate partway, as if he were peering through a Chitlin' Circuit curtain: "A little black boy is in the kitchen watching his mother fry up some chicken. Seeing the flour, he dabs some on his face. 'Look at me, Ma,' he says, 'I'm white!' 'What'd you say?' says his mama, and the boy says, 'Look at me, I'm white!' WHAP! His mama slaps the shit out of him. 'Don't you ever say that!' she says, then tells him to go tell his father what he said to her. Crying hard as Niagara Falls, the boy goes up to his father. 'What's wrong, son?' 'M-M-Mommy sl-sl-slapped me!' 'Why she do that, son?' his father asks. 'B-b-because I-I said I was w-w-white.' 'What?' BLAAAAM! His father slaps him even harder than his mama did. 'Now go tell your grandmother what you said! She'll teach you!' So the boy's crying and shaking and all confused. He approaches his grandmother. 'Why, baby, what's wrong?' she asks. And the boy says, 'Th-th-they sl-slapped me.' 'Why, baby—why they'd do that?' He tells her his story and when he gets to the end, PIE-YOW! His grandmamma slaps him so hard she almost knocks him down. 'Don't you ever say that,' she says. 'Now what did you learn?' The boy starts rubbing his cheek and says, 'I learned that I've been white for only ten minutes and I hate you niggers already!'"

The kids couldn't tell whether he was joking or just ranting, but they laughed anyway, each finding something funny in his expressions, his inflections, the cognitive dissonance in hearing the word "nigger" coming from the mouth of a man as old as the slur itself. Most of them had never seen his work. They just knew he was a star. That's the beauty of minstrelsy—its timelessness. The soothing foreverness in the languid bojangle of his limbs, the rhythm of his juba, the sublime profundity of his jive as he ushered the kids into the farm, retelling his joke in Spanish to an uncaptive audience running past him, cups and thermoses in hand, scattering the damn chickens.

Un negrito está en la cocina mirando a su mamá freír un poco de pollo . . . ¡Aprendí que he sido blanco por solo diez minutos y ya los odio a ustedes mayates!

They say breakfast is the most important meal of the day, and for some of those kids it might be their only meal, so in addition to the milk, I offered, children and adults alike, a fresh satsuma mandarin. I used to hand out candy canes and horsy rides on the first day of school. Mount them three to a saddle and pony the little shits to campus. Not anymore. Not when two years ago, the sixth-grader Cipriano "Candy" Martínez, a half-Salvadoran, half-black boy who lived over on Prescott Place, tried to Lone Ranger and Hi-yo, Silver! Away! his ass out of an abusive household. Following the steaming piles of horseshit, I had to go all the way to Panorama City to track him down.

I picked up two kids straying near the stalls by their elbows and hoisted them into the air.

"Stay away from the fucking horses!"

"What about the orange tree, mister?"

Unable to resist the enticing smell of the satsumas and hold off until recess or the soap operas for their midday snacks, my customers were huddled under the mandarin tree, guiltily standing in piles of peeled skin, their lips wet with fructose.

"Take as many as you want," I said.

My father used to say, "Give a nigger an inch and he'll take an ell." I never knew what an "ell" was, but in this case it meant the stripping of my precious satsuma tree bare. Hominy, holding his lumpy stomach in both hands because he was five months' pregnant with about twenty citrus fruit babies, ambled up to me.

"These greedy niggers gon to take all your oranges, massa!"

"That's all right, I only need a couple."

And to prove my point, a plump blue-ribbon satsuma, trying its best to escape the feeding frenzy, rolled right up to my feet.

An ebullient Hominy, with sun on his face and the sweet taste of satsumas on his minstrel-pink tongue, pied-pipered the children to their dooms. Followed by their doting, overprotective parents and me, the biggest rat of them all, bringing up the rear. Kristina Davis, a tall little girl, whose lanky bones and white teeth owed their growth and strength to years of consumption of my unpasteurized milk, sidled up to me and clasped my hand with a solid grip.

"Where's your mother?" I asked.

Kristina put her fingers to her lips and inhaled.

In neighborhoods like Dickens, before concerned parents with secret service earpieces stuffed into their auditory canals marshaled your every move, you used to learn more on your way to and from school than you did in school. My father was aware of this, and to further my extracurricular education, every so often he'd drop me off in a strange neighborhood and make me walk to the local place of learning. It was a lesson in social orienteering, except that I didn't have a map, a compass, a mess kit, or a slang-to-slang dictionary. Thankfully, for the most part, in L.A. County you can gauge the threat level of a community by the color of its street signs. In Los Angeles proper the signs are a hollowed-out metallic midnight blue. If a bird's nest constructed of pine needles was tucked inside the sign, it meant evergreen trees and a nearby golf course. Mostly white public-school kids whose parents lived above their means in upper-middle-class neighborhoods like Cheviot Hills, Silver Lake, and the Palisades. Bullet holes and a stolen car wrapped around the post signified kids about my hair texture, allowance level, and clothing style in neighborhoods like Watts, Boyle Heights, and Highland Park. Sky blue signified kick-back cool bedroom communities like Santa Monica, Rancho Palos Verdes, and Manhattan Beach. Chill dudes commuting to school by any means necessary from skateboard to hang glider, the good-bye lipstick prints from their trophy-wife mothers still on their cheeks. Carson, Hawthorne, Culver City, South Gate, and Torrance are all designated by a working-class cactus green; there the little homies are independent, familiar, and multilingual. Fluent in Hispanic, black, and Samoan gang signs. In Hermosa Beach, La Mirada, and Duarte the street signs are the bland brown of cheap blended malt whiskey. The boys and girls mope their way to school, depressed and drowsy, past the hacienda-style tract housing. The sparkling white signs denote Beverly Hills, of course. Exceedingly wide hilly streets lined with rich kids unthreatened by my appearance. Assuming that if I was there I belonged. Asking me about the tension of my tennis racquets. Schooling me on the blues, the history of hip-hop, Rastafarianism, the Coptic Church, jazz, gospel, and the myriad of ways in which a sweet potato can be prepared.

I wanted to release Kristina into the wild. Urge her to take the most circuitous route to school possible. Let her run unchaperoned under the jet-black street signs of Dickens and take an honors class in snail trails. Audit a seminar in watching your friend walk into Bob's Big Boy and steal the breakfast tips from the counter. Formulate an independent study on the poetics of the rainbows in sprinkler water and the call of the early-bird-purple-sequined halter-top-prostitute caterwauling to potential johns on Long Beach

Boulevard. I was about to let Kristina loose, but we'd reached the school just as the nine o'clock bell rang.

"Hurry up, you're going to be late."

"Everybody's already late," she said, running off to join her friends.

Everyone was late. Students, staff, faculty, parents, legal guardians, all were congregated in front of Chaff Middle School, ignoring the bell and taking the measure of their newly minted crosstown rivals from across the street.

The Wheaton Academy Charter Magnet School of the Arts, Science, Humanities, Business, Fashion, and Everything Else was a sleek, state-of-the-art plate-glass building that looked more like a death star than a place of learning. Its student body was white and larger-than-life. None of this was real, of course, as the Wheaton Academy was a phony construction site. A vacant lot now, surrounded by a plywood fence painted blue, with small rectangle cutouts through which passersby could watch building that would never take place. The school was nothing more than a five-by-five watercolor artist's rendition of the Center of Marine Sciences at the University of Eastern Maine that I downloaded, had blown up, mounted under plastic, and attached to a gate bolted with a chain lock. The pupils were ballet dancers, platform divers, violinists, fencers, volleyball players, and pottery makers whose black-and-white photos I hijacked from the Intersection Academy and Haverford-Meadowbrook websites, had enlarged, and pasted onto the fence. If anyone had been paying attention, they would've noticed that in reality the Wheaton Academy would be ten times the size of the lot it was supposed to be built upon. But if the red letters stenciled underneath the drawing were to be believed, then by all indications the Wheaton Academy was indeed "Coming Soon!"

Not soon enough for Dickens, of course, whose concerned but suspicious parents, eager for their children to join the ranks of the giant Anglo kids, whose metal braces brightened not only their impossibly white smiles but their futures. An overzealous mother, pointing demonstrably at a studious child and an attentive teacher poring over the results of a spectrograph pointed at the stars, asked Charisma the question on everyone's mind.

"Assistant Principal Molina, what my kids have to do to go to that school? Take a test?"

"Of sorts."

"What that mean?"

"What do those students in the photo all have in common?"

"They white."

"Well, there's your answer. Your child can pass that test, they're in. But you didn't hear it from me. All right, the show's over. Anybody who's ready to learn, let's go, because I'm locking the doors behind me. *Vámonos*, people."

By the time the 9:49 westbound arrived at Rosecrans and Long Beach in a noxious but punctual cloud of exhaust fumes, the crowd had long since dissipated, and I sat at the bus stop next to Hominy, smoking a doobie and cradling my last two satsuma mandarins. Marpessa opened the bus doors, a sinister look somewhere between disregard and disgust stitched onto her face like an angry black woman Halloween mask. A look that might scare off her co-workers and the niggers on the corner, but not me. I tossed her the oranges, and she sped off without even a thank you.

After five hundred feet or so, the #125 bus, its brakes invariably as worn out as a bum's shoes, slammed to an ear-splitting halt, reversed, and made a sharp right turn. The only real fights Marpessa and I ever had were about whether three rights made a left. She insisted they did. I believed that after three pointless right turns, you might be traveling left but you'd be one block behind your original starting point. By the time the bus made its way back to me, having proved, if nothing else, that a couple of illegal U-turns puts you right back where you started from, the 9:49 was now the 9:57.

The doors opened, Marpessa still at the wheel. This time her face was slathered with satsuma juice and an irrepressible smile. I always liked the sound of seat belts unbuckling. That emancipating click and whir of the belt recoiling to wherever it goes never ceases to give me pleasure. Marpessa brushed away the peels in her lap and stepped off the bus.

"Okay, Bonbon, you win," she said, plucking the joint from my mouth and marching her perfectly plump behind back onto the bus, apologizing for the delay but not the smell as she buckled in and slipped into traffic, blowing smoke out of the narrow driver's-side window, her pink fingernails coolly flicking ashes onto the street. She didn't know it, but she was smoking Aphasia. So I knew that between us bygones would be bygones. Or as we say in Dickens, "It be like that sometimes . . . *Is exsisto amo ut interdum.*"

Sixteen

Later that day, like any good social pyromaniac worth their accelerant, I returned to the scene of the crime. The only arson investigator on site was Foy Cheshire. It was the first time in twenty-some-odd years I'd ever seen him venture outside Dum Dum Donuts, his feet on actual Dickens terra firma. And there he stood in front of the blue clapboards of the would-be Wheaton Academy, his Mercedes half-parked on the sidewalk, taking photographs with an expensive-looking camera. From atop my horse, on the Chaff side of the street, I watched him snap a picture, then jot something down in his notebook. Above me a student opened a second-story window, looked up from a school-issued microscope so old Leeuwenhoek would've called it antiquated, and stuck her processed head into the air to gaze out at the Godzilla-sized child prodigy of the Wheaton Academy peering into an electron microscope so advanced it'd make Cal Tech envious.

From the other side of the street Foy spotted me. He cupped his hands around his mouth and called out, the traffic speeding loudly up and down Rosecrans Avenue forcing me to play peek-a-boo with both his image and his words.

"You see this shit, Sellout? You know who did this?"

"Yeah, I know!"

"Damn right, you know. Only the forces of evil would stick an all-white school in the middle of the ghetto."

"Like who, the North Koreans or somebody?"

"What the North Koreans care about Foy Cheshire? This is without doubt a CIA conspiracy, or maybe even bigger, like a secret HBO documentary about me! Some nefarious shit is afoot! Which if you'd been to a meeting in the past couple of months . . . Did you know some racist asshole put a sign on a public bus . . ."

It used to be that when some fools did a drive-by, an oncoming car slowing down for no apparent reason was fair warning. The throaty belch of a V-6 engine losing rpm and slipping into first gear was the urban equivalent of the crack of a hunter snapping a twig and startling his prey. But with these new hybrid, silent-running, energy-saving automobiles, you don't hear shit. By the time you realize what's going on, a bullet has slammed into the back quarter panel of your iridium-silver Benz and your assailants have already quietly sped off, yelling, "Take your black ass back to white America, nigger!" while getting fifty-five miles to the gallon. I thought I recognized the laugh that belonged to the thin black arm holding the familiar-looking revolver that looked a lot like the gun Marpessa's brother, Stevie, had held to my head two weeks prior. And the stealth gangsterism of an electric car drive-by had all the earmarks of King Cuz's battlefield generalship. As I made my way across the street to see if Foy was okay, I definitely recognized the scent of the orange that one of the assailants had thrown upside Foy's head—that was one of my satsumas.

"Foy, you okay?"

"Don't touch me! This is war, and I know whose side you're on!"

I backed away as Foy dusted himself off, muttering about conspiracies and defiantly marching toward his car like he was leaving the Philippines under siege. The gull-wing door to his classic sports car opened up, and before getting in, Foy paused to put on his aviator sunglasses and, in his best General BlackArthur, announced, "I shall return, motherfucker. Believe that shit!"

Behind us, the student on the second floor closed her window and returned to her microscope, blinking rapidly as she readjusted the focus, moved the slide around, and scribbled her findings in her notebook. Unlike Foy and me, she was resigned to her situation, because she knows that in Dickens it be like that sometimes, even when it doesn't have to be.

APPLES AND ORANGES

Seventeen

I'm frigid. Not in the sense that I don't have any sexual desire, but in the obnoxious way men in the free-love seventies projected their own sexual inadequacies onto women by referring to them as "frigid" and "dead fish." I'm the deadest of fish. I fuck like an overturned guppy. A plate of day-old sashimi has more "motion of the ocean" than I do. So on the day of the shooting and drive-by orange-ing, when Marpessa stuck a tongue suspiciously tangy with satsuma tartness into my mouth and ground her pudenda into my pelvic bone, I lay there on my bed—motionless. My hands covering my face in shame, because fucking me is like fucking Tutankhamen's sarcophagus. If my sexual ineptitude was a problem, she never let on. She simply boxed my ears and worked my beached-whale carcass over like a Saturday-night wrestler looking for revenge in a grudge match I didn't want to end.

"Does this mean we're back together?"

"It means I'm thinking about it."

"Can you think about it a little faster, and maybe a little more to the right? Yeah, that's it."

Marpessa's the only person to ever diagnose me. Not even my father could figure me out. I'd make a mistake, like, say, mis-identify Mary McLeod Bethune for Gwendolyn Brooks, it'd be

"Nigger, I have no fucking idea what the fuck is wrong is with you!" Followed by all 943 pages of the *BDSM IV* (*Black Diagnostic and Statistical Manual of Mental Disorders*, fourth edition) flying at my head.

Marpessa sorted me out, though. I was eighteen. Two weeks from finishing up my first semester of college. We were in the guesthouse. She—thumbing through the bloodstained *BDSM IV*. Me—in my usual postcoital position, rolled up into a ball like a frightened teenage armadillo, and crying my eyes out for no earthly reason.

"Here, I finally figured out what's wrong with you," she said, snuggling up to me. "This is what you have, Attachment Disorder." Why do people have to tap the page when they know they're right? A quick read-aloud will suffice. You don't have to rub it in with all the smug finger tapping.

"Attachment Disorder—Markedly disturbed and developmentally inappropriate social relatedness in most contexts, scenes, and happenings. Beginning before age five and continuing into adulthood as evidenced by either 1. and/or 2.:

1. *persistent failure to initiate or respond in a developmentally appropriate fashion to most social interactions (e.g., the child or adult responds to caregivers and black lovers with a mixture of approach, avoidance, and resistance to comforting. May exhibit frozen watchfulness).* Hoi Polloi Translation—The nigger flinches or jumps whenever you touch him. Runs hot and cold, and has no friends to speak of. And when he isn't staring at you like you just got off the banana boat, he's crying like a little bitch.

2. *diffuse attachments as manifested by indiscriminate sociability with marked inability to exhibit appropriate selective attachments to black people and things (e.g., ex-*

cessive familiarity with relative strangers or lack of se-
lectivity in choice of attachment figures). Hoi Polloi
Translation—The nigger fucking white hos out there at
UC Riverside.

It was a miracle we lasted as long as we did.

I stared at her blurry silhouette for a long time before she
poked her head from behind the chessboard-patterned shower
curtain. I'd forgotten how brown she was. How good she looked,
her stringy hair clumped to the side of her face. Sometimes the
sweetest kisses are the shortest. We could discuss the clean-shaven
pubes later.

"Bonbon, what's the time frame?"

"For us, from now until. For the segregation thing, I'm thinking I want to be done by Hood Day. That gives me another six
months."

Marpessa pulled me in and handed me a tube of apricot scrub
that hadn't been opened since the last time she showered off here.
I rubbed the exfoliant into her back and scratched a message into
the grainy, supposedly skin-softening swirls. She always could read
my writing.

"Because between that nigger Foy and the rest of world, this
shit's going to catch up with you sooner or later. Forget the racial
segregation, you know motherfuckers wasn't too keen on Dickens
even when it did exist."

"You were in that car today, weren't you?"

"Shit, when Cuz and my brother picked me up from work and
we drove back here, soon as we crossed that white line you painted,
it was like, you know, when you enter a banging-ass house party
and shit's bumping, and you get that thump in your chest and you
be like, if I were to die right now, I wouldn't *give a fuck*. It was like
that. Crossing the threshold."

"You threw that fucking orange. I knew it."

"Hit that stupid motherfucker square in the face."

Marpessa pressed the crack of her shapely rear end into my groin. She had to get back to the kids, we wouldn't have much time, and knowing me, we wouldn't need much time.

Despite that initial scratch of her seventeen-year itch, Marpessa insisted we start slow. Since she worked weekends and put in crazy overtime, we had to date on Mondays and Tuesdays. Our nights on the town were trips to the mall, coffee shop poetry readings, and, most bothersome for me, open-mike nights at the Plethora Comedy Club. Marpessa hated my Wheaton-Chaff segregation joke and insisted that I improve my sense of humor by learning to tell a joke. When I protested, she'd say, "Look, now you ain't the only black man in the world that can't fuck, but I refuse to go out with the only one with absolutely no sense of humor."

From the music clubs to the jailhouses to the fact that you can find Korean taco trucks only in white neighborhoods, L.A. is a mind-numbingly racially segregated city. But the epicenter of social apartheid is the stand-up comedy scene. The city of Dickens's paltry contribution to the long-running tradition of black funnymen is an open-mike night, sponsored by the Dum Dum Donut Intellectuals, that on the second Tuesday of the month transforms the shop into a twenty-table club called the Comedy Act and Forum for the Freedom of Afro-American Witticism and Mannerisms That Showcase the Plethora of Afro-American Humorists for Whom . . . there's more, but I've never managed to finish reading the temporary marquee they hang over the giant donut sign that hovers over the parking lot. I just call the place the Plethora for short, because despite Marpessa's insistence that I had no sense of humor, there were a plethora of unfunny black guys who, like every black sports analyst trying to sound intelligent, use and misuse the word "plethora" at every opportunity.

As in:

Q: How many white boys does it take to screw in a light-
   bulb?
A: A plethora! Because they stole it from a black man!
   Lewis Latimer, a black man who invented the light-
   bulb and a plethora of other smart-ass shit!

And believe me, jokes like that would get a plethora of applause.
Every black male, I don't care what shade or political persuasion
he is, secretly thinks he can do one of three things better than anyone in the world: play basketball, rap, or tell jokes.

If Marpessa thinks that I'm not funny, she never heard my father. Back in the heyday of black stand-up comedy, he also dragged
me to the Tuesday-night open mikes. In the history of American
black people, there have been only two with the complete inability
to tell a joke: Martin Luther King, Jr., and my father. Even at the
Plethora the "comedians" would occasionally lapse into unin-
tentional humor. "I'm auditioning for a role in Tom Cruise's newest movie. Tom Cruise plays a retarded judge . . ." The problem
with open-mike night at the Plethora was that there was no time
limit, because "time" is a white concept, which was fitting, because
the problem with my father's comedy was that he had no sense of
timing. At least Dr. King had the good sense to never try to tell a
joke. Daddy told his jokes the same way he'd ordered pizza, written poetry, and written his doctoral thesis—in APA format. Following the standards of the American Psychological Association,
he'd toddle onstage and open up with the oral equivalent of a Title
Page. Stating his name and the title of the joke. Yes, his jokes had
titles. "This joke is called 'Racial and Religious Differences in
Drinking Establishment Patronage.'" Then he'd deliver the Ab-
stract of the joke. So instead of simply saying, "A rabbi, a priest,
and a black guy walk into a bar," he'd say, "The subjects of this joke
are three males, two of whom are clergymen, one of the Jewish
faith, the other an ordained Catholic minister. The religion of the

African-American respondent is undetermined, as is his educational level. The setting for the joke is a licensed establishment where alcohol is served. No, wait. It's a plane. I'm sorry, my mistake. They are going parachuting." Finally, he'd clear his throat, stand too close to the mike, and deliver what he liked to call "The Main Body" of the joke. Comedy is war. When a comedian's routine works, they've killed; if the bits fall flat, they refer to it as dying. My father didn't die onstage. He martyred himself for that other unrecognized completely unfunny black man who, just as there must be extraterrestrial life, is out there somewhere. I've seen self-immolations that were funnier than my father's routine, but there were no gongs to ring or oversized canes with which to pull him offstage. He'd just ignore the booing and segue from the punch line to the Conclusion. The Results of the joke were a smattering of coughing. A chorus of vocalized disapproval and a plethora of yawning found to be significant. He'd end with the joke's Reference Section:

"Jolson, Al (1918). 'Sambo and Mammy Cleared for Takeoff on Runaway 5,' *Ziegfeld Follies*.

"Williams, Bert (1917). 'If Niggers Could Fly,' The Circuitous Chitterling Tour.

"The Unknown Minstrel (circa 1899). 'Dem Vaudeville Peckerwoods Sho' Am Stealing My Shit,' The Semi-Freemason Hall, Cleveland, Ohio.

"And don't forget to tip your waitress."

Even though she'd be exhausted from a long day transporting the masses, Marpessa would make sure we arrived early, volunteering me for comic duty by putting my name at the top of the sign-up sheet. I can't tell you how much I dreaded hearing the emcee introduce me. "Now put your hands together for Bonbon."

I would stand on that stage feeling as if I were having an out-of-body experience. Staring out into the audience and seeing myself in the front row prepping rotten tomatoes, eggs, and spoiled lettuce heads to throw at the droll motherfucker telling every ripped-off, antiquated Richard Pryor joke he could remember from his father's record collection. But every Tuesday night Marpessa forced me to take the stage, saying that she would continue withholding sex until I made her laugh. Usually after my so-called routine, I'd return to the table to find her fast asleep, unable to tell if she was exhausted from work or from boredom. One night I finally managed to tell an original joke, that in homage to my father had a title, albeit a rather long one:

Why All That Abbott and Costello Vaudeville Mess Doesn't Work in the Black Community

Who's on first?
I don't know, your mama.

Marpessa cracked the fuck up, rolling in the thin space between the folding chairs that passed for an aisle. I knew the sex drought would end that night.

They say never laugh at your own jokes, but all the best comics do, and as soon as the open mike was closed, I sprinted outside and hopped aboard bus #125, which was parked right outside the club, because Marpessa was using it as the family car, afraid to let the rolling memorial out of her sight. Before she could even think about releasing the parking brake, I was already lying naked on the backseat ready for a tinted-window quickie. Marpessa reached under the driver's seat, pulled out a large cardboard box, dragged it down the aisle, and dumped the contents in my lap. Burying my aching erection in two inches of report cards, computer printouts, and progress reports.

"What the fuck's all this?" I asked. Sifting through the paperwork so my dick could get some air.

"I'm acting as Charisma's go-between. It's early yet. It's only been six weeks, but she thinks the segregated schooling is already working. Grades are up and behavioral problems are down, but she wants you to confirm those results with some statistical analysis."

"Goddamn it, Marpessa! It's going to take just as long to put all this shit back in the box as it will to do the math."

Marpessa grabbed the base of my penis and squeezed.

"Bonbon, are you ashamed of my being a bus driver?"

"What? Where's this coming from?"

"Nowhere."

No amount of my amateur ear nuzzling was able to erase the wistful look on her face or make her nipples erect. Bored at my attempts at foreplay, she slipped a progress report into my pee hole and twisted my dickhead around so that I could read it like it was the Early Bird dinner menu. A sixth-grader named Michael Gallegos was taking subjects I didn't understand and getting grades I couldn't decipher. But according to the teacher's comments, he was showing marked improvement in something called number sense and operations.

"What the hell kind of grade is a 'PR'?"

"PR means shows proficiency."

Charisma had intuitively grasped the psychological subtleties of my plan even as it was just starting to make sense to me. She understood the colored person's desire for the domineering white presence, which the Wheaton Academy represented. Because she knew that even in these times of racial equality, when someone whiter than us, richer than us, blacker than us, Chineser than us, better than us, whatever than us, comes around throwing their equality in our faces, it brings out our need to impress, to behave, to tuck in our shirts, do our homework, show up on time, make our free throws, teach, and prove our self-worth in hopes that we won't be fired, arrested, or trucked away and shot. In essence, Wheaton Academy is saying to her students what Booker T. Washington, the Great Educator and founder of the Tuskegee Institute, once told his uneducated people: "Cast down your buckets where you are." While I'll never understand why it had to be a bucket, why the shortsighted Booker T. couldn't recommend that we cast down our books, slide rules, or laptops, I did sympathize with his and Charisma's need for an on-call Caucasian panopticon. Believe me, it's no coincidence that Jesus, the commissioners of the NBA and NFL, and the voices on your GPS (even the Japanese one) are white.

There are no greater anaphrodisiacs than racism and a report card in one's urethra, and when a half-naked Marpessa clambered on top of me, both she and my penis laid their sleepy heads down in the vicinity of my belly button, she still clutching my phallus, having gone to wherever it is bus drivers go to dream. Flight school probably, because in Marpessa's dreams buses can fly. They arrive on time and never break down. They use rainbows for bridges and clouds for docking bays, and wheelchair riders roll and yaw alongside like fighters protecting a bomber wing. When she reaches cruising altitude, she clears flocks of seagulls and niggers migrating south for the rest of their lives with a horn that doesn't beep but plays Roxy Music, Bon Iver, Sunny Levine, and Nico's "These Days." And all her passengers make a living wage. And Booker T. Washington is a regular rider who, when he boards the bus, tells her, "When you see Bonbon, the Cosmic Sellout and your one true love, cast down your panties where you are."

Eighteen

Come November, about six weeks after the shooting, I was making good progress with Marpessa, but less headway on what were, since I was now having sex on a semiregular basis, the two more immediate goals in my life, segregating Dickens and raising a successful potato crop in Southern California. I knew why I couldn't get the potatoes to grow, because the climate's too warm. But when it came to thinking of good ideas for separating the races by race, all of a sudden I had racism block, and Hood Day was only a few months away. Maybe I was like every other contemporary artist, I had only one good book, one album, one despicable act of large-scale self-hatred in me.

Hominy and I were in the row I'd dedicated to the tubers. Me on my hands and knees, checking the compost mixture, the soil density, and shoving russet seed potatoes in the ground, while he brainstormed suggestions for citywide discrimination and fucked up the one job he had, which was to lay the garden hose with the holes I punctured into it face up.

"Massa, what if we gave everybody we don't like a badge and assigned them to camps?"

"That's been done."

"Okay, how about this? Designate people into three groups:

black, colored, and godlike. Institute some curfew laws and a pass system . . ."

"Old hat, kaffir boy."

"This'll work in Dickens, cause everybody—Mexican, Samoan, or black—is basically a shade of brown." He dropped the hose on the wrong side of the trench and dug into his pocket. "Now, at the bottom we'll have the Untouchables. These are the people who are completely useless. Clippers fans, traffic cops, and people who have dirty jobs where they work with human and animal waste, like yourself."

"So if I'm an Untouchable, and you're my slave, what does that make you?"

"As a talented artist and thespian. I'z a Brahmin. After I die, I get nirvana. You come back exactly to where you are now, wallowing in cow shit."

I appreciated the help, but as Hominy rattled on about the varnas and delineating his version of the Indian caste system as it might apply to Dickens, I began to figure out what my mental block was. I was feeling guilty. Realizing I was the *Arschloch* at the Wannsee Conference, the Afrikaner parliamentarian in Johannesburg in '48, the wannabe hipster on the Grammy committee who in an effort to make the award more inclusive comes up with meaningless categories like Best R&B Performance by Duo or Group with Vocals and Best Rock Instrumental by a Soloist Who Knows How to Program But Can't Play Any Instruments. I was the fool who, as topics like railroad car allotments, bantu stands, and alternative music were raised, was too cowardly to stand up and say, "Do you motherfuckers realize how ridiculous we sound right now?"

With the potatoes planted, the compost spread, and the hose finally in the correct furrow, it was time to test my makeshift irrigation system. I opened the water spigot and watched one hundred feet of unpunctured green garden hose swell as it wound its way through the string beans, past the Spanish onions, and around the cabbage, until six jets of water squirted into the sky, arcing high over but not onto the potatoes, turning a small barren patch of land near the back fence into a mini flood plain. Either the holes were too small or the water pressure was too high; in any case, there'd be no homegrown spuds this year. Next week's forecast was for 80 degrees. Way too warm to get any kind of root vegetables started.

"Massa, you not going to turn it off? You wastin' water."

"I know."

"Well, then maybe next time you plant the potatoes in the dirt where the water's landing."

"I can't. That's where my dad's buried."

Motherfuckers don't believe I buried him in the backyard. But I did. Had my lawyer, Hampton Fiske, backdate some forms and planted him in the far corner where the stagnant pond used to be. Nothing ever grows over that square of land. Not before he died or since. There's no headstone. Before Marpessa's satsuma tree I tried to plant an apple tree for a cenotaph. Dad used to like apples. He ate them all the time. People who didn't know him thought he was really healthy, because you'd rarely see him in public without a Macintosh and a can of V-8. Pops loved the Braeburns and the Galas, but the Honeycrisps were his favorites. Offer him a bland-ass Red Delicious and he'd look at you like you were talking bad about his mama. I regret that I never checked the pocket of his sports coat when he died. I'm certain there was an apple in there. He always brought one to nibble on after the meetings were over. If I had to guess, I'd say it was a Golden Russet, those keep well during winter. We never grew apple trees, though. Much as he complained about the pretentious white people on the Westside, I think he secretly liked to drive over to Gelson's whenever they had Opalescents on sale for $4.50/lb., or to the Farmers Market if some Enterprises were in. I drove all the way to Santa Paula looking for a tree to plant. Something special. Since the late 1890s, Cornell

University has been breeding the world's best apples. The school used to be chill. If you asked nicely and paid the shipping and handling, they'd send you a box of late-season Jonagolds just to spread the gospel. But in recent years, for whatever reason, Cornell has taken to licensing the new varietals to local farmers, and unless you own a farm in upstate New York, you're shit out of luck and have to make do with the occasional imported Florina. So now the university orchards in Geneva, New York, are to the black market apple trade what Medellín, Colombia, is to cocaine. My connect was Oscar Zocalo, my lab partner at Riverside, who was doing his postgrad at Cornell. We met in the airport parking lot during an air show. Yahoos flying biplanes, putting Sopwith Camels and Curtisses through their paces. Oscar insisted we do the "deal" car window to car window, crime-movie-style. The sample was so delicious that I scooped up the excess juice running down my chin and rubbed it into my gums. I don't know if this is irony or not, but the best fucking apples taste like peaches. I drove home with a ready-for-ground Velvet Scrumptious tree, the crack of the apple world, insane yield, perfect snap, chock-full of vitamin C. I planted the tree about two feet from where I buried Daddy. I thought it would be nice if he had some shade. Two days later it was dead. And the apples tasted like mentholated cigarettes, liver and onions, and cheap fucking rum.

I was standing on my father's grave, in the mud, underneath the water spray meant for the potatoes. From there I could see the whole farm from front to back. The rows of fruit trees. Separated by color. Light to dark. Lemons. Apricots. Pomegranates. Plums. Satsumas. Figs. Pineapples. Avocados. The fields, which rotate from corn to wheat, then to Japanese rice, if I feel like paying the water bill. The greenhouse sits in the middle. Backed by leafy processions of cabbage, lettuce, legumes, and cucumbers. The grapes on vines along the south fence, tomatoes on the northern, then the white blanket of cotton. Cotton that I haven't touched since my father died. What was it Hominy said to me when I first started popping off about bringing back Dickens? *You heard the saying, you can't see the forest for the trees? Well, you can't see the niggers for the plantation.* Who was I kidding? I'm a farmer, and farmers are natural segregationists. We separate the wheat from the chaff. I'm not Rudolf Hess, P. W. Botha, Capitol Records, or present-day U.S. of A. Those motherfuckers segregate because they want to hold on to power. I'm a farmer: we segregate in an effort to give every tree, every plant, every poor Mexican, every poor nigger, a chance for equal access to sunlight and water; we make sure every living organism has room to breathe.

"Hominy!"

"Yes, massa?"

"What day is it?"

"Sunday. Why, you going down to Dum Dum's?"

"Yeah."

"Then ask that bitch-nigger where my fucking *Little Rascals* movies at!"

Nineteen

Attendance was light, maybe ten people. Foy, unshaven and draped in a wrinkled suit, stood in the corner twitching and blinking uncontrollably. Foy had been in the news lately. His out-of-wedlock children so numerous, they'd filed a class-action suit against him for the emotional distress he'd caused by sticking his face in front of a camera or microphone at every opportunity. At this point it was only the smooth Euclidean planar perfection of his box cut and his Rolodex that was holding both him and the Dum Dum Donut Intellectuals together. Hard to lose faith in a man who even at the worst of times can keep his hair on point and call upon friends like Jon McJones, a black conservative who'd recently added the "Mc" to his slave name. McJones read from his latest book, *Mick, Please: The Black Irish Journey from Ghetto to Gaelic*. The author was a good get for Foy, and with the free Bushmills, there should have been more people, but there was no doubt the Dum Dum Donut Intellectuals were dying. Maybe the notion of a cabal of stupid black thinkers had finally outlived its usefulness. "I'm in Sligo, a small artist hamlet on the northern coast of the Emerald Isle," McJones was reading. His lisp and faux-white enunciation made me want to punch him in the face. "The all-Ireland hurling championship is on the telly. Kilkenny versus Galway. Men with sticks chasing a small white ball. A round-shouldered bloke in a fisherman's sweater stands behind me gently tapping the butt end of a shillelagh into the palm of his hand. I've never felt more at home."

I copped a seat near King Cuz, who was playing the back as usual, munching on a maple bar and leafing through a stray issue of *Lowrider* magazine. When Foy Cheshire spotted me, he tapped his Patek Philippe like I was a deacon walking in late to church. Something wasn't right about Foy. He kept interrupting McJones with meaningless questions.

"So hurling, that's also college slang for vomiting, am I right?"

Seeing as he wasn't using it, I borrowed Cuz's copy of *The Ticker*. In the fiscal quarter since the Wheaton Academy's inception, employment in Dickens was up an eighth. Housing prices had risen three-eighths. Even graduation rates were up a quarter. Finally, black people were in the black. And though it was still early in the social experiment and the sample size was relatively small, the numbers didn't lie. For the past three months, since the Wheaton Academy went up, the students at Chaff Middle School were performing considerably better. Not that anyone was going to be skipping any grades or putting in an appearance on *Who Wants to Be a Millionaire* anytime soon, but on average, the scores on the state proficiency exams were approaching, if not mastery, a promising competency. And as near as I could make out from the state guidelines, the improvement was such that, in all likelihood, the school would not be going into receivership, at least not anytime soon.

After the reading was over, Foy strode to the front of the room, clapping like an enthusiastic child at his first puppet show. "I'd like to thank Mr. McJones for that stimulating reading, but before we get into this afternoon's subject matter, I have an announcement. The first is that my latest public-access show, *Black Checker*, has been canceled. The second is that, as many of you may know, a new battle has begun, and the enemy dreadnought is right here offshore in the form of the Wheaton Academy, which is an all-white school. Now, I have friends in high places, and they all deny the existence of the Wheaton Academy. But fret not, I have developed a secret weapon." Foy dumped the contents of his attaché case onto the nearest table, a new book. Two people immediately got up and left. I wanted to join them, but remembered I was there for a reason, and part of me was insanely curious as to what American classic Foy would bastardize next. Before passing it around the room, Foy coyly showed the book to Jon McJones, who shot back a look that said, "Nigger, you sure you want to unleash this shit on the world?" When it reached the back, King Cuz handed it off to me without even looking at it, and as soon as I read the title, I didn't want to let go. *The Adventures of Tom Soarer.* It dawned on me that Foy's written works were Black Folk(s) Art and were going to be worth something one day. I was beginning to regret the book burning thing and that I hadn't started a collection, because I'd spent the past ten years looking down my broad black nose at probably now-impossible-to-find first-and-only-edition titles like *The Old Black Man and the Inflatable Winnie the Pooh Swimming Pool, Measured Expectations, Middlemarch Middle of April, I'll Have Your Money—I Swear.* On the cover of *Tom Soarer,* a preppy black boy, wearing penny loafers and argyle socks exposed by a pair of flooding whale-print lime-green pants, and armed with a bucket of whitewash, stood bravely in front of a wall splashed in gang graffiti, while a pack of ragamuffin hoodlums looked on menacingly.

When Foy snatched *Tom Soarer* from my hands, it felt like I'd fumbled away a game-winning touchdown catch. "This book, I'm not ashamed to say, is a WME, a Weapon of Mass Education!" Unable to contain his excitement, Foy's voice rose two octaves and took on a Hitlerian fervor. "And just as he inspired me, the character of Tom Soarer will galvanize a nation to whitewash that fence! To cover up those frightful images of racial segregation that the

Wheaton Academy represents. Who's with me?" Foy pointed at the front door. "I know these great African-American heroes are down with the cause . . ." Legally, I'm not allowed to say who Foy name-dropped, because when I turned my head toward what I thought would be Foy's invisible hallucinations, standing in the Dum Dum Donuts doorway were three of the world's most famous living African-Americans, the noted TV family man _ i _ _ _ _ _ b _ and the Negro diplomats _ o _ _ _ _ o _ _ _ and _ _ n _ _ _ e e _ _ _ _ _ c _. Sensing the Dum Dum Donut Intellectuals were dying, Foy had pulled out all the stops and called in who knows what favors. Somewhat surprised the crowd was so small, the three superstars cautiously sat down and, to their credit, ordered coffee and bear claws and participated in the meeting, most of which was spent with Jon McJones regurgitating the usual Republican Party bullshit that a child born into slavery in 1860 was more likely to be raised in a two-parent household than was a baby born after the election of the U.S.A.'s first African-American president. McJones was a snobby Negro who covered up his self-hatred with libertarianism; I at least had the good sense to wear mine on my sleeve. He went on to cite statistics that, even if true, were completely meaningless when you consider the simple fact that slaves were slaves. That a two-parent antebellum household wasn't necessarily a bond of love but a forced coupling. He didn't mention that some two-parent slave marriages were between sister and brother, mother and son. Or that, during slavery, divorce wasn't really an option. There was no "I'm going out for cigarettes" and never coming back. What about all the two-parent households that were childless because their kids had been sold off to who knows where? As a modern-day slave owner, I was insulted that the venerated institution of slavery was not given the viciousness and cruelty which it was due.

"What a load of crap," I said, interrupting McJones with a schoolboy raise of the hand.

"Like you wouldn't rather be born here than in Africa?" C _ _ _ n _ _ w _ _ _ snapped back with a streetwise inflection that belied his curriculum vitae and his V-neck sweater.

"What, here?" I pointed at the floor. "Like in Dickens?"

"Well, maybe not a hellhole like Dickens," McJones said, giving the other guests a "Don't even bother, I got this" glance. "Nobody wants to live here, but you can't even pretend to tell me that you'd rather be born in Africa than anywhere else in America."

You'd rather be here than in Africa. The trump card all narrow-minded nativists play. If you put a cupcake to my head, of course, I'd rather be here than any place in Africa, though I hear Johannesburg ain't that bad and the surf on the Cape Verdean beaches is incredible. However, I'm not so selfish as to believe that my relative happiness, including, but not limited to, twenty-four-hour access to chili burgers, Blu-ray, and Aeron office chairs is worth generations of suffering. I seriously doubt that some slave ship ancestor, in those idle moments between being raped and beaten, was standing knee-deep in their own feces rationalizing that, in the end, the generations of murder, unbearable pain and suffering, mental anguish, and rampant disease will all be worth it because someday my great-great-great-great-grandson will have Wi-Fi, no matter how slow and intermittent the signal is.

I said nothing and let King Cuz do my fighting for me. In twenty years, I'd never heard him say anything in a meeting more substantive than acknowledging the fact that the iced tea could use more sugar, but there he was, facing off with a man with four advanced degrees who spoke ten languages, none of them black except French.

"Nigger, I refuse to let you impugn Dickens like that!" Cuz said sharply, standing up and pointing a freshly manicured nail at McJones. "This is a city, not a hellhole!"

Impugn? Maybe twenty years of Dum Dum Donuts rhetoric hadn't all gone to waste. To his credit, McJones, despite Cuz's tone and size, didn't back down. "I may have misspoken. But I must take exception to your implication that Dickens is a city, when it's clearly a locale, nothing more than an American shantytown. A post-black, post-racial, post-soul flashback, if you will, to a time of romanticized black ignorance . . ."

"Hey, look, fool, save that post-soul, post-black bullshit for somebody who gives a fuck, 'cause all I know is that I'm *pre*-black. Dickens born and raised. Homo sapiens OG Crip from the goddamn primordial giddy-up, nigger."

King Cuz's little soliloquy seemed to impress Ms. R _ _ _, because she uncrossed her ankles, opened her legs just enough to show off some right-wing inner thigh, and then tapped me on the shoulder.

"That big motherfucker play any football?"

"A little running back in high school."

"Мои трусики мокрые," she said in lip-licking Russian.

I'm no linguist, but my best guess is that it meant Cuz could penetrate her secondary anytime he wanted. The old veterano strode into the middle of the donut shop, the rubber soles of his canvas sneakers squeaking with every step. "This, you proudly uncool motherfucker, this is Dickens," and to some beat that only he could hear, he broke into the complex gangster soft shoe known as the Crip Walk. Never turning his back to the crowd, he pivoted on the balls and heels of his feet. His knees together and his hands free, he skipped around the room in tight concentric circles that collapsed upon themselves as quickly as they expanded. It was as if the floor was heated, and too hot for him to stop in one spot for even a second. King Cuz was debating with McJones the best way he knew how.

Want some, get some, bad enough, take some . . .
Velis aliquam, acquīris aliquam, canīnus satis, capīs aliquam.

As the sparse crowd gathered around the two foes, I did what I'd come to do. I removed my daddy's picture from the wall and tucked it under my arm. Segregating the city with his photo up would be like having sex in the room next to your parents' bedroom. Not being able to concentrate. Not being able to be as loud as you wanted to be. I quietly dipped out as King Cuz was teaching McJones, _ _ _ l C _ _ _ y, _ _ _ _ n P _ _ _ _ _, and a dreamy-eyed _ o n d _ _ _ _ z z _ _ _ _ e the Crip Walk. And they were picking it up like pros. Strutting around like old-school bangers. It figures, because passed down from the Masai and stolen from the Cherokee war dances you see on old Westerns, the C-Walk is an ancient warrior dance. One that designates its baggy-pants *danseur noble* as target. It's a dance that says, "You may fire when ready, Gridley." And any nigger in the limelight, even those conservative shills, knows what it's like to have the bull's-eye placed squarely on your back.

I was untying my horse when Foy placed a father-figure arm around my shoulder. There was an uptight and nervous look to his goatee that I'd never seen before. His neck was caked with dirt, and a deep stench of body odor wafted over me.

"You riding off into the sunset, Sellout?"

"I am."

"Long day."

"That crap about being better off under slavery is too much even for you, isn't it, Foy?"

"At least McJones cares."

"Come on, he cares about black people like a seven-footer cares about basketball. He has to care because what else would he be good at."

Knowing I was never coming back to the Dum Dum Donut Intellectuals, Foy gave me the same sorrowful look the missionaries must've given the jungle heathen. A look that said, It doesn't matter if you're too stupid to understand God's love. He loves you regardless, just hand over the women, the distance runners, and the natural resources.

"You're not worried about that all-white school?"

"Naw, white kids need learnin', too."

"But white kids aren't going to buy my books. Speaking of which—" Foy handed me a copy of *Tom Soarer*, then signed it without me asking him to.

"Foy, can I ask you something?"

"Sure."

"I know it's probably urban myth, but is it true that you own the really racist *Little Rascals* movies? Because if you do, I can make you an offer."

Apparently I touched a nerve. Foy shook his head, pointed to his book, then lumbered back inside. As the glass doors opened, I could hear King Cuz, the nation's wealthiest black man, and two legendary Negro ministers plenipotentiary rapping the lyrics to NWA's "Fuck tha Police" at the top of their lungs. Before placing *Tom Soarer* in the saddlebag, I read the inscription, which I found vaguely threatening.

> To the Sellout,
>> Like father, like son . . .
>> Foy Cheshire

Fuck him. I galloped home. Drove the horse hard down Guthrie Boulevard, inventing some inner-city dressage along the way as I ignored the traffic cop and ran the horse through a series of figure eights by dashing in and out of the orange construction barrels in the shut-down center lane. On Chariton Drive, I latched onto a tiring skateboarder and, with one hand on the reins, pulled her along like a long board cabriolet from Airdrome to Sawyer, whipping her into a sharp turn onto Burnside. I don't know what I expected from trying to restore Dickens to a glory that never existed.

Even if Dickens were to one day be officially recognized, there'd be no fanfare or fireworks. No one would ever bother to erect a statue of me in the park or name an elementary school after me. There'd be none of the head rush Jean Baptiste Point du Sable and William Overton must've felt when they planted their flags in Chicago and Portland. After all, it wouldn't be like I founded or discovered anything. I was just brushing the dirt off an artifact that had never really been buried, so when I arrived home to Hominy, he excitedly unsaddled my horse. Eager to show me some newly disambiguated entry in an online encyclopedia written by some anonymous scholar:

> Dickens is an unincorporated city in southwest Los Angeles County. Used to be all black, now there's hella Mexicans. Once known as the murder capital of the world, shit ain't as bad as it used to be, but don't trip.

Yes, if Dickens ever became a real place again, in all likelihood Hominy's wide smile would be all the reward I'd ever receive.

Twenty

Keep this under your hat, but over the next few months the reseg-regation of Dickens was kind of fun. Unlike Hominy, I've never had a real job, and even though it didn't pay, driving around town with Hominy as the African-American Igor to my evil social scientist was sort of empowering, even though we were mocking the notion of being powerless. Monday through Friday at exactly one o'clock he'd be out front standing next to the truck.

"Hominy, you ready to segregate?"

"Yes, master."

We started small, Hominy's local fame and adoration proving invaluable. He'd soft-shoe his way inside, bust out an insanely in-tricate song-and-dance routine from old Chitlin' Circuit days that would've made the Nicholas Brothers, Honi Coles, and Buck and Bubbles green with blackface envy:

> *'Cause my hair is curly*
> *Just because my teeth are pearly*
> *Just because I always wear a smile*
> *Like to dress up in the latest style*
>
> *'Cause I'm glad I'm livin'*
> *I take these troubles all with a smile*

Just because my color's shady
Makes no difference, maybe
Why they call me "Shine"

Then, as if it were part of the act, he'd stick a COLORED ONLY sign in the storefront window of a restaurant or beauty shop. No one ever took them down, at least not in front of us; he'd worked too hard for it.

Sometimes in homage to my father, if Hominy was on his lunch break or asleep in the truck, I'd enter wearing Dad's white lab coat and carrying a clipboard. I'd hand the owner my card and explain that I was with the Federal Department of Racial Injustice, and was conducting a monthlong study on the effects of "racial segregation on the normative behaviors of the racially segregated." I'd offer them a flat fifty-dollar fee and three signs to choose from: BLACK, ASIAN, AND LATINO ONLY; LATINO, ASIAN, AND BLACK ONLY; and NO WHITES ALLOWED. I was surprised how many small-business people offered to pay me to display the NO WHITES ALLOWED sign. And like most social experiments, I never did the promised follow-up, but after the month was up, it wasn't unusual to get calls from the proprietors asking Dr. Bonbon if they could keep the signs in the windows because they made their clientele feel special. "The customers love it. It's like they belong to a private club that's public!"

It didn't take long to convince the manager of the Meralta, the only movie theater in town, that he could cut his complaints in half if he designated floor seating as WHITE AND NON-TALKERS ONLY, while reserving the balcony for BLACKS, LATINOS, AND THE HEARING IMPAIRED. We didn't always ask permission; with paint and brush we changed the opening hours of the Wanda Coleman Public Library from "Sun–Tue: Closed, Wed–Sat: 10–5:30" to "Sun–Tue: Whites Only, Wed–Sat: Colored Only." As word started to spread of the success Charisma was having at Chaff Middle School, every now and then an organization would seek me out for a little personalized segregation. In looking to reduce the youth crime rate in the neighborhood, the local chapter of Un Millar de Muchachos Mexicanos (o Los Emes) wanted to do something other than midnight basketball. "Something a little more conducive to the Mexican and Native American stature," a sporting endeavor that didn't require a lot of space where the kids could compete on equal footing. Name-dropping the hoop success of Eduardo Nájera, Tahnee Robinson, Earl Watson, Shoni Schimmel, and Orlando Méndez-Valdez did nothing to dissuade them.

The meeting was brief, consisting of two questions on my part. First: "Do you have any money?"

"We just got a $100,000 grant from Wish Upon a Star."

Second: "I thought they only did things for dying kids?"

"Exactly."

During the height of the government enforcement of the Civil Rights Act, some segregated townships filled in their municipal pools rather than let nonwhite kids share in the perverse joy of peeing in the water. But in an inspired act of reverse segregation, we used the money to hire a lifeguard who posed as a homeless person and built a "Whites Only" swimming pool surrounded by a chain-link fence that the kids loved to hop, so they could play Marco Polo and hold their collective breaths underwater whenever they spotted a patrol car passing by.

When Charisma felt that her students needed a counterbalance to the onslaught of disingenuous pride and niche marketing that took place during Black History and Hispanic Heritage Months, I came up with the one-off idea for Whitey Week. Contrary to the appellation, Whitey Week was actually a thirty-minute celebration of the wonders and contributions of the mysterious Caucasian race to the world of leisure. A moment of respite for children forced to participate in classroom reenactments of stories of migrant labor, illegal immigration, and the Middle Passage. Weary and stuffed from being force-fed the falsehood that when one of your kind makes it, it means that you've all made it. It took about two days to convert the long-out-of-business brushless car wash on Robertson Boulevard into a tunnel of whiteness. We altered the signs so that the children of Dickens could line up and choose from several race wash options:

Regular Whiteness:	Benefit of the Doubt
	Higher Life Expectancy
	Lower Insurance Premiums
Deluxe Whiteness:	Regular Whiteness Plus
	Warnings Instead of Arrests from the Police
	Decent Seats at Concerts and Sporting Events
	World Revolves Around You and Your Concerns
Super Deluxe Whiteness:	Deluxe Whiteness Plus
	Jobs with Annual Bonuses
	Military Service Is for Suckers
	Legacy Admission to College of Your Choice
	Therapists That Listen
	Boats That You Never Use
	All Vices and Bad Habits Referred to as "Phases"
	Not Responsible for Scratches, Dents, and Items Left in the Subconscious

To the whitest music we could think of (Madonna, The Clash, and Hootie & the Blowfish), the kids, dressed in bathing suits and cutoffs, danced and laughed in the hot water and suds. Ignoring the amber siren light, they ran under the waterfall of the not-so Hot Carnauba Wax. We handed them candy and soda pop and let them stand in front of the drying blast of the hot-air blowers for as long as they wanted. Reminding them that having a warm wind blowing in your face was what it felt like to be white and rich. That life for the fortunate few was like being in the front seat of a convertible twenty-four hours a day.

It wasn't necessarily a case of saving the best for last, but as Hood Day approached, Hominy and I had managed to install some form of segregation in nearly every section and public facility in Dickens except for the Martin Luther "Killer" King, Jr., Hospital, which is paradoxically located in Polynesian Gardens. Polynesian Gardens, aka P.G., being a majority-Latino neighborhood that carried a rumored reputation for being hostile toward African-Americans. In fact, local legend had it that the injuries black Dickensians suffered while driving through P.G. to the hospital were often more severe than the afflictions that had caused them to seek medical attention in the first place. Between the police and the gangs, navigating the streets of any neighborhood in L.A. County, especially any section not familiar with you, can be dangerous. You just never know when you're going to get rolled up on for being or wearing the wrong color. I'd never had any problems in Polynesian Gardens, but if I were to be honest, I never went there at night. And the evening before our planned action on the hospital, there'd been a shoot-out between Varrio Polynesian Gardens and Barrio Polynesian Gardens, two gangs with a long-standing blood feud over spelling and pronunciation. So to ensure Hominy and I got in and out with our asses intact, I attached two small purple-and-gold Lakers pennants to the front fenders of my pickup truck and, for good measure, flew a giant Iwo Jima–sized, 1987 Championship Lakers flag from the roof. Everybody, and I mean everybody in Los Angeles, loves the Lakers. And driving down Centennial Avenue, even behind slow-moving lowriders that refused to go faster than ten miles an hour, the Lakers flags billowed majestically in the night wind, giving the pickup truck an ambassadorial vibe that allowed us to cruise through with a temporary diplomatic immunity.

The director of Martin Luther "Killer" King, Jr., Hospital, Dr. Wilberforce Mingo, was an old friend of my father's and had given me permission to segregate the place when I explained to him that it'd been me who painted the borderlines, put up the exit sign, and conceived the Wheaton Academy. He leaned back in his chair and said that for two pounds of cherries I could segregate his hospital in any way I saw fit. And under the cover of "no one gives a fuck" darkness, Hominy and I painted the words *The Bessie Smith Trauma Center* in thick, drippy, blood-red horror-movie-poster letters on what was until then a nameless glass-door emergency entrance to King Hospital. Then we drilled a plain black-and-white metal placard into the middlemost concrete pillar. It read, WHITE-OWNED AMBULANCE UNITS ONLY.

I can't say I did this without trepidation. The hospital was the one large-scale place I'd segregated where there was a decent likelihood that outsiders would see my work. Scared to proceed inside, I asked Hominy to hand me one of the fresh carrots I'd picked the night before.

"What's up, Doc?" I teased, nibbling on the carrot tip.

"You know, massa, Bugs Bunny wasn't nothing but Br'er Rabbit with a better agent."

"Did the fox ever catch Br'er Rabbit, because I'm pretty sure the white boys going to catch us after this one."

Hominy straightened the Sunshine Sammy Construction sign on the side of the truck, then grabbed the paint cans and two brushes from the back.

"Massa, if any white people do come through here and see this shit, they going to think what they always think, These niggers crazy, and carry on about they business."

A few years ago, before the Internet, before the hip-hop, the spoken-word poetry, the Kara Walker silhouettes, I'd have been inclined to agree with him. But being black ain't what it used to be. The black experience used to come with lots of bullshit, but at least there was some fucking privacy. Our slang and debased fashion sense didn't cross over until years after the fact. We even had our own set of top-secret sex techniques. A Negro kama sutra that got passed down on the playground, the stoop, and by drunken parents intentionally leaving the door open just a crack so "the little niggers might learn something." But the Internet proliferation of black pornography has given anybody with a twenty-five-dollar-a-month membership pass, or a lack of regard for intellectual property rights, access to our once-idiosyncratic sexual techniques. And now, not just white women, but women of all creeds, colors, and sexual orientations, have to suffer through their partners humping them at a mile a minute and yelling, "Who owns the pussy?" every two strokes. And even though they've never fully appreciated Basquiat, Kathleen Battle, and Patrick Ewing—and still haven't discovered *Killer of Sheep*, Lee Morgan, talcum powder, Fran Ross, or Johnny Otis—these days mainstream America's nose is all up in our business, and I knew eventually I was fucking going to jail.

Hominy pushed me through the automatic doors. "Massa, no one gives a fuck about the hood until they give a fuck."

Hospitals don't have the rainbow of directional lines anymore. In the days of butterfly bandages, sutures that didn't dissolve, and nurses without accents, the admitting nurse would hand you a manila folder and you'd follow the Red Line to Radiology, the Orange to Oncology, the Purple to Pediatrics. But at Killer King, sometimes an emergency room patient tired of waiting to be seen by a system that never seems to care, and holding a plastic cup with a severed finger swimming in long-since-melted ice or staunching the bleeding with a kitchen sponge, sometimes out of sheer boredom they'll slip over to the glass partition and ask the triage nurse, Where does that brackish-colored line lead to? The nurse will shrug. And unable to ignore the curiosity, they set out to follow a line that took Hominy and me all night to paint, and half the next day to make sure everyone obeyed the WET PAINT signs. It's a line that's as close to the Yellow Brick Road as the patients will ever get.

Though there's a touch of cornflower blue in the shade, Pantone 426 C is a strange, mysterious color. I chose it because it looks either black or brown, depending on the light, one's height, and one's mood. And if you follow the three-inch-wide stripe out of the waiting room, you'll crash through two sets of double doors, make a series of sharp lefts and rights through a maze of patient-strewn corridors, and then down three flights of filthy unswept stairs until you come to a dingy inner vestibule lit by a dim red bulb. There, the painted line pitchforks into three prongs, each tine leading to the threshold of a pair of unmarked, identical double doors. The first set of doors leads to a back alley, the second to the morgue, and the third to a bank of soda pop and junk-food vending machines. I didn't solve the racial and class inequalities in health care, but I'm told patients who travel down the brown-black road are more proactive. That when their names are finally called, the first thing they say to the attending physician is "Doctor, before you treat me, I need to know one thing. Do you give a fuck about me? I mean, do you really give a fuck?"

Twenty-one

It used to be that to celebrate Hood Day, King Cuz and his latest crew, the Colosseum Blvd et Tu, Brute Gangster Munificent Neighborhood Crips 'n' Shit, would roll into the territory of their archenemies, the Venice Seaside Boys, caravanning down Broadway Street, four cars and twenty fools deep, the sun at their backs, looking for action. For most of them, unless they were being carted off to jail, it was the one time during the year they left the neighborhood. But since the advent of the variable-rate home loan, most of the VSBs have been priced out of their turf by wine bars, holistic medicine shops, and edgy movie stars who've erected fifteen-foot-high cherrywood walls around quarter-acre bungalows turned into $2 million compounds. Now, whenever the vast majority of the Venice Seaside Boys want to "put in work" and defend their turf, they have to commute from faraway places like Palmdale and Moreno Valley. And it's no fun anymore when your enemy refuses to fight back. Not for lack of bravery or ammunition, but from fatigue. Too tired from fighting three hours of freeway traffic and road closures to pull the trigger. So now the two once-rival hoods celebrate Hood Day by staging their version of a Civil War reenactment. They meet at the sites of the great battles of the past, fire blanks and Roman candles at each other while innocent sidewalk café civilians duck and run for cover. They pile out of their hot rods and hoopties, and like frat boys playing a rough game of two-hand touch in the mud, the misbegotten sons of the Westside chase each other up and down the Venice Beach boardwalk, paying homage to the rumbles of old by "squabbing," throwing blows from the shoulder, as they act out and relive the gang fights that changed history: the Battle of Shenandoah Street, the Lincoln Boulevard Skirmish, and the infamous Massacre at Los Amigos Park. Afterward they meet up with friends and family at the rec center, a demilitarized softball field in the middle of town, and reaffirm the peace over a barbecue and beer.

Unlike all the police departments who credit "zero tolerance" policies for every dip in the crime rate, I don't want to simply assume my six-month campaign of localized apartheid had everything to do with the relative calm Dickens experienced that spring, but that year Hood Day was different. As Marpessa, Hominy, Stevie, and I plied our trade from the visitors' dugout, we were running out of fruit slices much quicker than usual. People were overpaying for eighths. Normally each gang, each hood, uses the park on the day designated to rep their "hood." For instance, the Six-Trey Street Sniper City Killers reserve the park for June 3, because June is the sixth month of the year, and trey means three. Los Osos Negros Doce y Ocho have dibs not on December 8, like you might expect, but on August 12, because contrary to popular belief, California is cold as fuck in winter. I was at the rec center on that balmy March 15, because for the Colosseum Blvd et Tu, Brute Crips, Hood Day is the same day as the Ides of March. When else would it be?

Back in the late eighties, before the word "hood" had been appropriated to refer to any location from the upscale enclaves of the Calabasas Hills, Shaker Heights, and the Upper East Side to the student zoo at your state university, when a Los Angeleno mentioned the hood, as in "I'd watch that motherfucker if I were you. He or she's from the hood!" or "I know I didn't visit Abuela Silvia on her deathbed, but what'd you expect me to do? She lives in the hood!" it referred to one place and one place only—Dickens. And there, on the rec-center baseball field, congregated under the Hood Day banner slung over the home team dugout, were gang and family members of all colors and stripes. Since the riots, Dickens, a once-united neighborhood, had balkanized into countless smaller hoods, and now, like Yugoslavia in reverse, King Cuz and Panache, the erstwhile Tito and Slobodan Milošević of the city, were celebrating the reunification by tromping across the makeshift stage in their Oakley sunglasses, their Doris Day perm curls bouncing off their broad shoulders as they rapped fiendishly to the beat.

I hadn't seen Panache in years. I didn't know if he knew Marpessa and I were sleeping together. I never asked for permission. But seeing him do his signature stage tricks with Lulu Belle, his pump-action twelve-gauge equivalent to B. B. King's guitar, which, considering that like some criminal-minded baton twirler he could throw high in the air, catch, reload, and blast a hubcap out of the air like a clay pigeon, all with one hand, maybe I should've. King Cuz yelled into the microphone, "I know at least one you niggers had to have brought some Chinese food!"

Two dudes, whom the police, and anyone else with a Street Smart IQ of 50, might refer to as "suspicious Hispanic males," stood at the first-base line just outside the festivities, their arms folded across their chests. Although they looked, more or less, like everyone else at the park, from the way they eyed everyone with such disdain, it was hard to tell if they were from Dickens. Like Nazis at a Ku Klux Klan rally, they were comfortable ideologically, but not in terms of corporate culture. Word spread that they were from Polynesian Gardens. Nevertheless, the irresistible smell of hickory-smoked barbecue and the cloud of dank billowed over them, drawing the duo farther and farther into the infield. When the men arrived at the on-deck circle, Stevie, who was slicing the pineapples with a machete, asked, "You know them niggers?" Never taking his eyes off the two homies as they made their way down the dugout steps. Both dudes wore khakis whose baggy leggings spilled over two pairs of Nike Cortez sneakers so fucking new that if they had taken one shoe off and placed it to their ear like a conch shell, they'd hear the roar of an ocean of sweatshop labor. Stevie exchanged prison stares with the guy in the bucket hat, football jersey, and *Stomper* stenciled along his jawline. In the hood men don't wear sporting-club jerseys because they're fans of a certain team. The color, the logo, the jersey numbers all mean something gang-related.

When you're fresh out of lockup everything is racial. It's not like there aren't Mexicans in predominantly black Crip and Blood sets, and blacks in mostly Latino cliques. After all, on the street it's all proximity and propinquity. Your alliance is to the homies and to the hood, regardless of race. Something happens to the identity politics in prison. Maybe it's like movies where it's white versus black versus Mexican versus white, no ifs, ands, or buts, and I do hear tell of some hardcore, color-blind thugs who roll into lockup and dance with the niggers or the vatos who brung 'em. *Fuck La Raza. Chinga black power. This nigger's mother used to feed me when I was hungry, so later for the stupid shit.*

The fool in the ice-cap-white T-shirt and *Puppet* tattooed vertically down his gullet nodded to me first.

"¿Qué te pasa, pelón?"

Us fellow baldheads don't share in all the racial animosity. We've come to accept that, regardless of race, all newborn babies look Mexican, and all baldheaded men look black, more or less. I offered him a hit of my joint. His ears turned deep red and his eyes glazed over like Japanese lacquerware.

"What the fuck is this, dog?" Puppet coughed.

"I call it Carpal Tunnel. Go ahead, try to make a fist."

Puppet tried to ball his hand, but failed. Stomper looked at him like he was crazy, then angrily took the joint from his hand. I didn't need a program to tell me that despite appearances, Puppet and Stomper weren't on the same side. After a long puff, Stomper twisted his fingers into all sorts of dexterous gang signs, but he couldn't knuckle up no matter how hard he tried. He removed his nickel-plated gat from his waistband. He could barely grip the gun, much less pull the trigger. Stevie laughed, and it was cold pineapple slices all around. The homeboys took bites, and the unexpected surge of sweetness with a slightly minty finish caused them to wince and giggle like little kids. Then to the hard glares of the other hoodlums, the two cholos walked into deep center field, calmly scarfing down pineapple and sharing the last of the marijuana.

"You know that NK on Johnny Unitas's neck don't stand for 'Nice Kid'?"

"I know what it stands for."

"Stands for Nigger Killer. Both them niggers from different sets, though. Barrio P.G. and Varrio P.G. Not like them to be chilling like that."

Hominy and I shared a smile. Maybe the signs that we'd posted in Polynesian Gardens on the way home from the hospital job were working. We'd made two signs. Hammered them into two telephone poles on opposites sides of Baker Street, where the rusted train tracks divided the neighborhood between Varrio and Barrio P.G. We placed them in such a way that if folks on one side of the street wanted to know what the sign on their side said, they'd have to cross the tracks to read it. So they had to venture into enemy territory, only to discover that the sign on the north side of the street was exactly the same as the one on the south; they both read THE RIGHT SIDE OF THE TRACKS.

Marpessa pulled me out of the dugout and toward home plate. King Cuz and a delegation of aging thugs and wannabes were standing in the batter boxes, grubbing on ribs and pineapple. Panache was chewing his pineapple slice down to the rind, telling stories about a musician's life on the road, when Marpessa inter-rupted him.

"I just want you to know I'm fucking Bonbon."

Oblivious to the thorns, Panache stuck what remained of the pineapple, skin and all, into his mouth, slurping and sucking out every last drop of juice. When the fruit was dry as a desert bone, he walked up to me, tapped my chest with the tip of Lulu Belle's barrel, and said, "Shit, if I could get some of this pineapple every morning, I'd fuck the nigger, too."

A gunshot rang out. In center field, Stomper, apparently still feeling the effects of the Carpal Tunnel, was barefoot, lying on his back, aiming the gun with his feet, laughing his ass off and shoot-ing with his toes at the clouds. It looked like fun, so most of the men and a few women went to join him, puffing on their joints, weapons out, and hopping through the dirt infield, one shoe on, one shoe off, hoping to spark a few rounds before the cops came.

Twenty-two

Black people pop. "Pop" being Hollywood slang for having a dynamic camera presence, for being almost too photogenic. Hominy says it's why they rarely shoot black and white buddy movies anymore; the bigger stars get washed out. Tony Curtis. Nick Nolte. Ethan Hawke does a film with some African-American and it becomes a screen test to see who's really the Invisible Man. And has there ever been a buddy movie featuring a black woman and anyone? The only ones with the cinematic magnetism to hang were Gene Wilder and Spanky McFarland. Anyone else—Tommy Lee Jones, Mark Wahlberg, Tim Robbins—is just hanging on to the mane of a runaway horse.

Watching Hominy at the L.A. Festival of Forbidden Cinema and Unabashedly Racist Animation, on the Nuart big screen, trading one-liners with Spanky, it wasn't hard to see why back then all the trades thought he'd be the next big pickaninny. The sparkle in his eyes, the gleam in his cherubic cheeks were magnetic. His hair was so kinky and dry it looked as if it might spontaneously combust. You couldn't take your eyes off him. Dressed in raggedy overalls, wearing black high-top sneakers ten sizes too big, he was the ultimate prepubescent straight man. No one could take it like Hominy. It amazed me how he withstood the onslaught of uncensored and unforgiving watermelon and my-daddy-in-jail jokes. Welcoming each insult with a heartfelt and throaty "Yowza!" It was hard to tell whether he was demonstrating cowardice or grace under fire, because he'd perfected that bug-eyed, slack-jawed dumbfounded look that to this day passes for black comedic acting chops. But the modern-day black entertainer has to do it only once or twice a movie. Poor Hominy had to pull off the coon reaction shot three times a reel and always in extreme close-up.

When the lights went up, the host announced that the last living Little Rascal was in the house and invited Hominy onstage. After a standing ovation, he wiped his eyes and took a few questions. When talking about Alfalfa and the gang, Hominy's incredibly lucid. He explained the shooting schedule. How the tutoring worked. Who got along with whom. Who was the funniest off camera. The meanest. He lamented how no one ever notices Buckwheat's emotional range and rhapsodized about how much his mentor's speech and diction improved in the MGM days. I kept my fingers crossed that no one would ask about Darla, so I wouldn't have to hear about a take-five reverse cowgirl under the bleachers in "Football Romeo."

"We have time for one more question."

From the back, directly across the aisle from me, a group of blackfaced coeds stood in unison. Dressed in Victorian bloomers with the Greek letters *N I Γ* stitched across their chests, and their hair haphazardly set in thick plaits with wooden clothespins, the women of Nu Iota Gamma looked like dolls you'd see at an antiques auction. In unison they tried to ask a question.

"We wanted to know . . ."

But they were beaten back by a chorus of boos and a hail of paper cups and popcorn containers. Hominy hushed the audience. The room grew silent, and as it turned its self-righteous attention back to him, I noticed the woman closest to me was African-American, the tininess of her ears giving her ethnicity away. It was

a rare sighting on Sunday afternoon, a true female coon, black as
seventies funk, black as a C+ in organic chemistry, black as me.

"What's the problem?" Hominy asked the crowd.

A tall, bearded white boy in a fedora a couple of rows in front
of me stood up and pointed a finger at the line of sorority Topsies.
"They are in non-ironic blackface," he said defiantly. "That's not
cool."

Hominy shielded his eyes with his hand and peered blindly
into the audience and asked, "Blackface? What's blackface?"

At first the audience laughed. But when Hominy didn't crack a
smile, the guy stared back at him with a doltish wide-eyed look of
bewilderment not seen since the days of great buffoons like Stepin
Fetchit and George W. Bush, the first coon president.

The white dude respectfully called Hominy's attention to some
of the films we'd just seen. "Sambonctious," where Spanky pours
ink on his face and pretends to be Hominy so his dusky friend can
pass the spelling test and join the gang on the school trip to the
amusement park. "Black Rascallion," where Alfalfa dinges up so
that he can audition to be the lead banjo picker in an all-Negro jug
band. "Jigga-Boo!" where Froggy turns the tables on a ghost by
stripping down to his skivvies and covering himself from head to
toe in fireplace soot, shouting "Boo-ga! Boo-ga! Booooo!" Hominy
nodded his head, laced his thumbs in his suspenders, and rocked
back on his heels. Then proceeded to light and smoke an invisible
cigar, which he switched from one side of his mouth to the other.
"Oh, we didn't call it blackface. We called it acting."

He had the audience eating out of his hand again. They
thought he was being funny, but he was dead serious. For Hominy
blackface isn't racism. It's just common sense. Black skin looks
better. Looks healthier. Looks prettier. Looks powerful. It's why
bodybuilders and international Latin dance contestants blacken
themselves up. Why Berliners, New Yorkers, and businessmen,
Nazis, cops, scuba divers, Panthers, bad guys, and Kabuki stage-

hands wear black. Because if imitation is indeed the highest form of flattery, then white minstrelsy is a compliment, it's a reluctant acknowledgment that unless you happen to really be black, being "black" is the closest a person can get to true freedom. Just ask Al Jolson or the slew of Asian comedians who earn their livings by acting "black." Just ask those sorority girls, who were settling back into their seats, leaving the lone black member to fend for herself.

"Mr. Hominy, is it true? Does Foy Cheshire really own the rights to the really racist *Little Rascals* movies?"

Damn, don't get this nigger started about that Foy Cheshire bullshit.

I stared at the black-faced woman in blackface, wondering if she, too, was acting, if she felt free. If she was aware that the natural color of her skin was actually blacker than her "blackface." Meaning technically she was in somewhat-lighter-than-blackface. Hominy pointed me out in the crowd, and when he introduced me as his "master," a few heads turned around to see what a real live slave owner looked like. I was tempted to tell them that Hominy meant to say "manager" and not "master," but I realized that in Hollywood the two words amounted to the same thing. "I believe it to be true. And I believe my master's going to get them back for me, so that one day the world will see my best and most demeaning and emasculating work." Thankfully, the houselights began to dim. The racist cartoons were starting.

I like Betty Boop. She has a nice body, is free-spirited, loves jazz, and apparently opium, too, because in a hallucinogenic short titled "Ups and Downs," the moon is auctioning off a Depression-era Earth to the other planets. Saturn, an old, bespectacled Jewish orb complete with bad teeth and a heavy Yiddish accent, wins and rubs his hands greedily. "I gottum. I gottum da whole vorld. *Mein Gott,*" he gloats, before removing gravity from the Earth's core. It's 1932 and Max Fleischer's metaphorical Jew is making an already chaotic global situation even worse. Not that Betty cares, because

in a world where cats and cows fly, and the rain falls up, priority
number one is to keep your skirt line from ascending to the heavens and exposing your form-fitting panties. And who's to say that
Ms. Boop isn't a member of the tribe? For the next sixty minutes a
few drunken, droopy-feathered Native Americans fail to catch the
Warner Bros. rabbit, much less assimilate. A Mexican mouse tries
to outwit the gringo pussycat, so he can sneak across the border
and steal the *queso*. A seemingly endless lineup of African-American
cats, crows, bullfrogs, maids, crap shooters, cotton pickers, and cannibals act a gravelly-voiced Looney Tunes fool to the strains of
"Swanee River" and Duke Ellington's "Jungle Nights in Harlem."
Sometimes a shotgun blast or dynamite explosion turns a nominally white character like Porky Pig into a gunpowder-colored
minstrel. Bestowing upon him honorary-nigger status, which allows him to sing merry melodies like "Camptown Races" over the
closing credits with impunity. The program ends with Popeye and
Bugs Bunny taking turns single-handedly winning World War II
by flummoxing bucktoothed, four-eyed, gibberish-speaking Japanese soldiers with giant mallets and geisha subterfuge. Finally,
after Superman, supported by gongs and a cheering audience, pulverizes the Imperial Navy into complete submission, the lights
come back on. After two hours of sitting in the dark laughing
at unmitigated racism, in the brightness the guilt sets in. Everyone can see your face, and you feel like your mother caught you
masturbating.

Three rows in front of me a black guy, a white guy, and an
Asian guy prepared to leave, gathering their jackets and trying to
shake off the hatred. The black kid, embarrassed at having been
debased and ridiculed in cartoon classics like "Coal Black and de
Sebben Dwarves," and still hiding behind Superman's cape, playfully attacks his Asian homeboy. Shouting, "Get Patrick! He's the
enemy!" as Patrick raises his hands in self-defense, protesting, "I'm
not the enemy. I'm Chinese," Bugs Bunny's *Jap, monkey, slant-eyes*

slurs still ringing in his ears. The white kid, unscathed and un-
fazed from the skirmish, laughs and flips a cigarette into his mouth.
Smoke 'em, if you got 'em. It's crazy how quickly an evening of
Little Rascals shorts and Technicolor cartoons, some nearly a century old, can raise the ire of racial antipathy and shame. I couldn't
imagine anything being more racist than the "entertainment" I'd
just witnessed, that's why I knew the rumors about Foy owning a
portion of the *Our Gang* catalogue had to be false. What could be
more racist than what we'd just witnessed?

I found Hominy in the lobby signing memorabilia, much of it
having nothing to with the Little Rascals. But old movie posters,
Uncle Remus collectibles, and Jackie Robinson memorabilia, anything dating to before 1960, would do. Sometimes I forget how
funny Hominy is. Back in the day, to avoid the succession of booby
traps laid by the white man, black people had to constantly be
thinking on their feet. You had to be ready with an impromptu
quip or a down-home bromide that would disarm and humble a
white provocateur. Maybe if your sense of humor reminded him
there was a semblance of humanity underneath that burrhead, you
might avoid a beating, get some of that back pay you were owed.
Shit, one day of being black in the forties was equal to three hundred years of improv training with the Groundlings and Second
City. All it takes is fifteen minutes of Saturday-night television to
see that there aren't many funny black people left and that overt
racism ain't what it used to be.

Hominy posed for a group photo with the blackfaced women
of Nu Iota Gamma. "Do the curtains match the naps?" Hominy
said dryly, before delivering a wide smile. Only the real darkie in
the group got the joke, and try as she might, she couldn't stop
smiling. I sidled up to her. She answered my questions before I
could ask them.

"I'm pre-med. And why? Because these white bitches got the
hookup, that's why. The old girls' network exists, too, now, and it's

no fucking joke. If you can't beat 'em, join 'em. That's what my mama says, because racism's everywhere."

"It can't be everywhere," I insisted.

The future Dr. Topsy thought a moment, twisting a runaway plait around her finger. "You know the only place where there's no racism?" She looked around to make sure her sorority sisters weren't within earshot and whispered, "Remember those photos of the black president and his family walking across the White House lawn arm-in-arm. Within those fucking frames at that instant, and in only that instant, there's no fucking racism."

But there was more than enough racism in the theater lobby to go around. A stoop-shouldered white cat flipped the bill of his baseball cap over his right ear, and then slung his arm around Hominy, bussed him on the cheek, and exchanged skin. The two did everything but call each other Tambo and Bones.

"I just want to say, all those rappers running off at the mouth about being 'last of the real niggers,' don't have jack shit on you, because you, my man, are more than the last Little Rascal, you're the last real nigger. And I mean 'nigger' with the hard *r*."

"Why, thank you, white man."

"And do you know why there aren't any more niggers?"

"No, sir. I don't."

"Because white people are the new niggers. We're just too full of ourselves to realize it."

"The 'new niggers,' you say?"

"That's right, both me and you—niggers to the last. Disenfranchised equals ready to fight back against the motherfucking system."

"Except that you'll get half the jail time."

Topsy was waiting for us out in the Nuart parking lot, still in costume and blackface, but wearing a pair of designer sunglasses and excitedly digging through her book bag. I tried to rush Hominy into the truck before he could see her, but she cut us off.

"Mr. Jenkins, I want to show you something." She took out an oversized three-ring binder and opened it on the hood of the pickup. "These are copies I made of the ledgers for all the *Our Gang* and *Little Rascals* movies shot at Hal Roach Studios and MGM."

"Holy shit."

Before Hominy could look at them, I snatched the notebook and scanned the columned entries. It was all there. The titles, dates of principal photography, cast and crew, shooting days and total production costs, the profits and losses for all 227 films. Wait, 227?

"I thought there were only 221 movies?"

Topsy smiled and flipped to the second-to-last page. Six consecutive entries for films shot in late 1944 were completely blacked out. Which meant that two hours of prepubescent hijinks that I'd never seen might still exist somewhere. I felt like I was looking at some top-secret FBI report about the Kennedy assassination. I yanked open the binder and held the sheet up to the sun, trying to see through the redaction's blackness and back into time.

"Who do you think did this?" I asked her.

From her book bag Topsy took out another photocopy. This one listed everyone who'd checked out the ledger since 1963. There were four names on it: Mason Reese, Leonard Maltin, Foy Cheshire, and Butterfly Davis, which I presumed was Topsy's real name. Before I lifted my eyes from the paper, Hominy and Butterfly were sitting in the cab. He had one arm around her and was leaning on the horn.

"That nigger got my movies! Let's be out!"

From West L.A. the drive to Foy's Hollywood Hills abode took longer than it should have. When my father used to force me to accompany him to his black brainiac confabs with Foy, no one knew about the north–south shortcuts from the basin into the hills. Back then Crescent Heights and Rossmore used to be side streets and smooth sailing; now they're two-lane, bumper-to-bumper major thoroughfares. Man, I used to swim in Foy's pool while they talked politics and race. Not once did my father ever show any bitterness toward the fact that Foy had paid for that estate with money he earned from "The Black Cats 'n' Jammin Kids," the original storyboards of which still hang on my bedroom wall. "Dry off, motherfucker!" Dad would say. "You're dripping water on the man's Brazilian cherrywood floors!"

Most of the ride up, Butterfly and Hominy bonded over photos of her and her sorority sisters celebrating the joys of multiculturalism. Denigrating the city of Los Angeles ethnicity by ethnicity, neighborhood by neighborhood. In violation of every traffic law and social taboo, she sat in his lap, their seat belts unbuckled. "This is me at the Compton Cookout . . . I'm the third 'ghetto chick' from the right." I stole a glance at the snapshot. The women and their dates blackened and Afro-wigged, toting forties and basketballs, smoking blunts. Their mouths filled with gold teeth and chicken drumsticks. It wasn't so much the racist ridicule as the lack of imagination that I found insulting. Where were the zip coons? The hep cats? The mammies? The bucks? The janitors? The dual-threat quarterbacks? The weekend weather forecasters? The front-desk receptionists that greet you at every single movie studio and talent agency in the city? *Mr. Witherspoon will be down in a minute. Can I get you a water?* That's the problem with this generation; they don't know their history.

"This was the Bingo *sin* Gringos night we held for Cinco de Mayo . . ." As opposed to the Compton Cookout, it wasn't hard to spot Butterfly in that one: this time she sat next to an Asian woman, the two of them, like the other sisters, wearing gigantic sombreros, ponchos, *bandoleras*, and droopy foot-long Pancho Villa mustaches, while drinking tequila and daubing their cards. *Be-ocho . . . ¡Bingo!* Butterfly flicked through her photos. The titles of each bash a dress code unto itself: Das Bunker: The Pure Gene Pool Pool Party. The Shabu Shabu Sleepover! The Trail of Beers— Hiking and Peyote Trip.

Sitting just off Mulholland Drive, on the crest overlooking the San Fernando Valley, Foy's house was bigger than I remembered. A massive Tudor estate with a circular driveway, it looked more like an English finishing school than a home, despite the giant foreclosure sign bolted to the entrance gate. We piled out of the car. The mountain air was brisk and clean. I took in a deep breath and held it, while Hominy and Butterfly sauntered up to the gate.

"I can smell my movies in there."

"Hominy, the place is empty."

"They in there. I know it."

"What, you going to dig up the yard like in 'Unexpected Riches'?" I asked, invoking Spanky's *Our Gang* swan song into the mix.

Hominy rattled the fence. And then I remembered the code like you remember your best friend's childhood phone number. I punched 1-8-6-5 into the security box. The gate buzzed, the roller chain tightened and slowly pulled the gate open. 1865, black people are so fucking obvious.

"Massa, you coming?"

"Naw, you two have at it."

Across Mulholland was a scenic overlook.

Facing north, I timed my run and sprinted between a speeding Maserati and two teenagers in a birthday BMW convertible. A dirt trail peeled down the mountainside and through the chaparral for about a mile or so, eventually leading to a side street and Crystalwater Canyon Park, a small but immaculately kept recreation area featuring a few picnic tables, some shade trees, and a basketball court. Ignoring the sap dripping down its trunk, I sat underneath a thick fir tree. The ballplayers limbered up for an after-work run or two before the sun set. A lone black man, in his mid-thirties, light-skinned and shirtless, paced at center court. He was one of those semiskilled hoopsters who frequented the white courts in ritzy neighborhoods like Brentwood and Laguna, looking for a decent game, an opportunity to dominate, and who knows, maybe even a job prospect.

"Any niggers out here for the attention, get the fuck off the court," the brother yelled to the delight of the white boys.

The philosophy professor on sabbatical inbounded the ball. A personal-injury lawyer hit a corner jumper. Displaying a surprisingly good handle, a fat pharmacist crossovered a pediatrician, but bricked the layup. The day trader air-balled a shot that sailed out of bounds and rolled toward the parking lot. Even in L.A., where luxury cars, like shopping carts at the supermarket, are everywhere you look, Foy's '56 300SL was unmistakable. There couldn't have been more than a hundred left on the planet. Near the front fender, Foy sat in a small lawn chair, dressed in only his boxers, a T-shirt, and sandals, chatting into his phone and typing on a laptop almost as old as his car. He was drying his clothes. His shirts and pants hanging from hangers hooked onto the car's gull-wing doors, which were in full flight and hovering above like wings on a silver dragon. I had to ask. I got up and walked past the basketball game. Two players vying for a loose ball tumbled by. Arguing over possession before they got to their feet.

"Who's that off of?" a player in beat-up sneakers asked me, his outstretched arms a silent plea for mercy. I recognized the guy. The mustachioed lead detective in a long-canceled but still-in-syndication cop show—big in Ukraine. "That's off the dude with the hairy chest." The movie star disagreed. But it was the right call.

Foy looked up at me from his chair, but didn't stop talking or typing. Speaking in rapid-fire, unintelligible word salad into the phone, he wasn't making much sense, something about high-speed rail and the return of the Pullman porter. The Mercedes coupe's Pirelli whitewall tires were bald. Yellow foam oozed from the cracked and blistered leather seats like pus. Foy was probably homeless, but he refused to sell his watch, or a car that, at auction, even in its fucked-up condition, was worth several hundred thousand dollars. I had to ask.

"What are you writing?" Foy dropped the phone to his shoulder.

"A book of essays called *Me Talk White One Day.*"

"Foy, when's the last time you had an original idea?"

Absolutely unoffended, Foy thought for a second, then said, "Probably not since your dad died," before returning to his phone call.

I returned to Foy's old house to find Hominy and Butterfly skinny-dipping in the pool, a little surprised that no nosy neighbors had bothered to call the police. One old black man looks like all the rest, I suppose. Night fell, and the underwater light flicked on automatically and quietly. The soft light-blue of a pool lit up at night is my favorite color. Hominy, pretending he couldn't swim, was in the deep end, holding on to Butterfly's ample flotation devices for all he was worth. He hadn't found what he was looking for, his movies, but what he had managed to secure seemed to tide him over. I stripped down and slid into the water. No wonder Foy was broke, the temperature had to have been at least 90 degrees.

Floating on my back, I saw the North Star flicker through the steam rising from the water, pointing to a freedom that I didn't even know if I needed. I thought of my father, whose ideas paid for that bank-owned property. I turned over into a dead man's float and tried to position my body in the posture he was in when I found him dead in the street. What were my dad's last words before they shot him? *You don't know who my son is.* All this work, Dickens, the segregation, Marpessa, the farming, and I still don't even know who I am.

You have to ask yourself two questions: Who am I? and How may I become myself?

I was as lost as I ever was, thinking seriously about tearing out the farmland, uprooting the crops, selling off the livestock, and putting in a big-ass wave pool. Because how cool would it be to surf in the backyard?

Twenty-three

About two weeks after seeking the Lost Film Treasure of Laurel Canyon, the secret was out. The *New*-ish *Republic* magazine, which hadn't had a child on its cover since the Lindbergh baby, broke the story. Above the caption "The New Jim Crow: Has Public Education Clipped the Wings of the White Child?" was a twelve-year-old white boy, posed as the pint-sized symbol of reverse racism. The new Jim Crow stood on the steps of Chaff Middle School wearing a heavy gold chain. Unruly tufts of dirty blond hair peeked out from under his wave cap and noise-reduction headphones. He toted an Ebonics textbook in one hand and a basketball in the other. Gold metal braces flashed through a lip-curling snarl, and the XXXL T-shirt he wore read *Energy = an Emcee²*.

A long time ago, my father taught me that whenever you see a question on the cover of a news magazine, the answer is always "No," because the editorial staff knows that questions with "Yes" answers would, like graphic cigarette warnings and close-ups of pus-oozing genitalia that tend not to deter but encourage smoking and unsafe sex, scare the reader off. So you get yellow journalism like: *O. J. Simpson and Race: Will the Verdict Split America?* No. *Has TV Gone Too Far?* No. *Is Anti-Semitism on the March Again?* No, because it never halted. *Has Public Education Clipped the Wings of the White Child?* No, because a week after that issue hit the news-stands, five white kids, their backpacks filled with books, rape whistles, and mace, hopped off a rented school bus and attempted to reintegrate Chaff Middle School, where Assistant Principal Charisma Molina stood in the doorway, barring entrance to her quasi-segregated institution.

Even if Charisma hadn't counted on all the publicity about how if Chaff continued to improve at its current rate, it would become the fourth-highest-ranked public school in the county within the next year, she should've known that while 250 poor colored kids getting inferior educations will never be front-page news, the denial of even one white student access to a decent education would create a media shit storm. What no one could've foreseen, however, was a coalition of fed-up white parents listening to the advice of Foy Cheshire and pulling their children from underperforming public schools and overpriced private ones. And calling for a return to the forced busing many of their parents had so vehemently protested against a generation prior.

Too broke and embarrassed to provide an armed escort, the state of California watched idly as the sacrificial lambs of reintegration, Suzy Holland, Hannah Nater, Robby Haley, Keagan Goodrich, and Melonie Vandeweghe, exited the bus under the protection of not the National Guard but the magic of live television and the loud mouth of Foy Cheshire. It had been a couple of weeks since I'd seen him living out of his car, and from what I'd heard, no one showed up for the last Dum Dum meeting, even though the noted community organizer _ _ r _ _ _ O _ _ _ _ was scheduled to speak.

Shoulders hunched and arms held up protectively in front of their faces, the Dickens Five, as the quintet would come to be known, braced themselves for the pillory of rocks and bottles as they ran the gauntlet and into history. But unlike Little Rock, Arkansas, on September 3, 1957, the city of Dickens didn't spit in their faces and hurl racial epithets; rather, it begged them for autographs, asked if they already had dates for the junior prom. Yet when the would-be enrollees reached the top of the stairs, there stood Assistant Principal Charisma doing her best Governor Faubus, refusing to budge, her arm ramrod straight against the doorjamb. Hannah, the tallest of the bunch, tried to step around her, but Charisma held firm.

"No Anglos allowed."

Hominy and I were on the other side of the fray. Standing behind Charisma, and like anyone else apart from the custodial and food services staff at Little Rock Central High School or the University of Mississippi in 1962, on the wrong side of history. Hominy was in school that day to tutor Jim Crow. Charisma had summoned me to read the business letter that accompanied the mailed edition of Foy Cheshire's latest reimagined multicultural text, *Of Rice and Yen*, an all-Chinese adaptation of Steinbeck's classic set in the days of the railroad coolie. The book was a carbon copy of the original text sans articles and with all the *l*s and *r*s transposed. *Maybe evelybody in whore damn wolrd scaled, aflaid each other.* I'll never understand why after over a half century of Charlie Chan's Number One Son, the dude in Smashing Pumpkins, dope-ass music producers, skateboarders, and docile Asian wives married to white guys in hardware store commercials, people like Foy Cheshire still think the yen is Chinese currency and that Asian-Americans can't pronounce their fucking *l*s, but there was something unnerving about the message's hurried scrawl:

Dear Pawn of the Liberal Agenda,

I know that you won't implement this backbreaking work of swaggering cleverness, but that's your loss. This book will place me firmly in the autodidactic tradition of authors such as Virginia Woolf, Kawabata, Mishima, Mayakovsky, and DFW. See you this Monday for the first day of school. Class may be on your campus, but you will be auditing my world. Bring a pen, paper, and the nigger-whispering Sellout.

Yours truly,

Foy "Did you know Gandhi beat his wife?" Cheshire

When Charisma asked me why he cited those specific writers, I told her I didn't know, but neglected to mention that the list was composed solely of novelists who had taken their lives. It was hard to say if the statement was some sort of suicidal ideation, but one could hope. There aren't many black firsts left these days, and as much as Foy would be a good a candidate for the position of "first black writer to off themselves," I had to be prepared. If he was indeed an "autodidact," there's no doubt he had the world's shittiest teacher.

Foy stepped to the head of the pack to take over the negotiations, magically producing a small stack of DNA results. Flapping them, not in Charisma's face, but directly into the lens of the nearest TV camera. "I have here in my hand a list of results that show each one of these children has maternal roots tracing their ancestries back thousands of years to Kenya's Great Rift Valley."

"Nigger, whose side you on?"

From inside the unhallowed halls of the school I couldn't see who was making the inquiry, but it was a good question and, judging from the silence, one for which Foy didn't have an answer. Not that I knew what side I was on, either. All I knew was that the Bible, conscious rappers, and Foy Cheshire weren't on my side. Charisma, however, knew where she stood, and with two hands to his chest, she shoved Foy and the children back down the stairs like so many bowling pins. I looked around at the faces on my side of the threshold: Hominy, the teachers, Sheila Clark, each a little bit frightened but full of resolve. Shit, maybe I was on the right side of history, after all.

"I suggest if you want to go to school in Dickens so badly, you wait for that school across the street to open up."

The prospective white students picked themselves up and turned around to gaze at their forebears, the proud pioneers of the mythical Wheaton Academy. With its pristine facilities, effective teachers, sprawling green campus, there was something undeniably attractive about Wheaton, and the youngsters began gravitating longingly toward their scholastic heaven like angels drawn by lute music and decent cafeteria food, until Foy stepped in front of them. "Don't be fooled by that graven image," he yelled. "That school is the root of all evil. It's a slap in the face of anyone who's ever stood for equality and justice. It's a racist joke that mocks the hardworking people of this and all communities by placing a carrot on a stick and holding it up in front of old horses too tired to run. And besides, it doesn't exist."

"But it looks so real."

"Those are the best dreams, the ones that feel real."

Disappointed but not defeated, the group settled on the patch of grass near the flagpole. It was a multicultural Mexican standoff, black-ass Foy and the white kids in the middle, Charisma and the utopian specter of the Wheaton Academy on either side of them.

They say that during their weekend skin games, young Tiger Woods's father, in a cheap attempt to rattle his son, would jingle the change in his pocket while his boy was standing over a six-foot putt for the win. The end result was a duffer who's rarely distracted. I, on the other hand, am easily distracted. Permanently sidetracked, because my father liked to play a game he called After the Fact, where in the middle of whatever I was doing, he'd show me a well-known historical photo and ask, "So what happened next?" We'd be at the Bruins game, and during an important time-out he'd flip the snapshot of Neil Armstrong's footprint in the lunar dust in front of my face. So what happened next? I'd shrug my shoulders. "I don't know. He did those Chrysler commercials on television."

"Wrong. He became an alcoholic."

"Dad, I think that was Buzz Aldrin . . ."

"In fact, many historians think he was wasted when he first set foot on the moon. 'That's one small step for man, one giant leap for mankind.' What the fuck does that even mean?"

In the middle of my first Little League game at bat, Mark Torres, a lanky fireballer whose stuff was hard as a teenage erection and, like that first sexual encounter, preternaturally fast, threw me an 0–2 fastball that neither I nor the umpire saw and only presumed to be high and inside because of the windburn across my forehead. My father came storming out of the dugout. Not to impart any batting advice, but to hand me the famous photo of the American and Russian soldiers meeting at the Elbe River, shaking hands and celebrating the de facto end of World War II in the European theater. So what happened next?

"America and the Soviet Union would go on to fight a Cold War lasting nearly fifty years and forcing each country to spend trillions of dollars on self-defense in a pyramid scheme Dwight D. Eisenhower would term the Military Industrial Complex."

"Partial credit. Stalin had every Russian soldier in this photograph shot for fraternizing with the enemy."

Depending upon how much of a science-fiction geek you are, it's either *Star Wars II* or *V*. But whichever one it is, in the middle of the climactic light-saber duel between Darth Vader and Luke Skywalker, right after the Dark Lord cuts off Luke's arm, my dad snatched the flashlight from an usher's hand, then slammed a black-and-white photo into my chest. So what happened next? In the fuzzy circle of light, a young black woman in an exquisitely ironed white blouse and tablecloth-patterned skirt protectively clutched a three-ring binder to her still-developing chest and psyche. She wore thick dark black shades, but stared past both me and the screaming white women tormenting her from behind.

"She's one of the Little Rock Nine. They sent in federal troops. She went to school. And things ended happily ever after."

"What happened next was that the following year the governor, rather than continuing to integrate the school system as required by law, shut down every high school in the city. If niggers wanted to learn, then no one was going to learn. And speaking of learning, notice they don't teach you that part in school." I never said anything about "they" being teachers like my father. I just remember wondering why Luke Skywalker was tumbling headlong into the starlit abyss for no apparent reason.

Sometimes I wish Darth Vader had been my father. I'd have been better off. I wouldn't have a right hand, but I definitely wouldn't have the burden of being black and constantly having to decide when and if I gave a shit about it. Plus, I'm left-handed.

So there everybody was, stubborn as grass stains, waiting for someone to intervene. The government. God. Color-safe bleach. The Force. Whoever.

Exasperated, Charisma looked over at me. "When does shit ever end?"

"It doesn't," I muttered, and stepped into the breezy perfection that is the springtime California morning. Foy had prepped his troops for a boisterous chorus of "We Shall Overcome." They were joined together arm-in-arm, swaying and humming slowly to the beat. Most folks think "We Shall Overcome" is still in the public domain. That through the generosity of the black struggle, its empowering refrains are free to be sung by anyone anytime one feels the stings of injustice and betrayal, which is how it should be. But if you stood outside the U.S. Copyright Office and protested people profiting from a stolen song by singing "We Shall Overcome," you'd owe the estate of Pete Seeger a nickel for every rendition. And even though Foy, singing for all he was worth, had seen fit to change the poignant "someday" lyric to a screaming "Right Now!" I dropped ten cents on the pavement as a precaution.

Foy lifted his hands high overhead, his sweater popping over his potbelly and exposing a gun handle sticking out of his Italian-leather beltline. That explained the lyric change, his impatience, the letter, and the desperate look in his eyes. And why didn't I recognize it sooner, the absence of angularity in his normally pristine box-cut toupee.

"Charisma, call the police."

No one other than college hippies, Negro jubilee singers, Cubs fans, and other assorted idealists knows verses two through six of "We Shall Overcome," and when his flock started stumbling over the next verse, Foy pulled his weapon and waved it like a .45 caliber cue card. Exhorting his choir through the rough patches, even though their backs were turned to him, and flying past me and Hominy toward the school's entrance, which remained closed to them because Charisma had shut the doors behind her.

Dickens doesn't scatter very easily. Neither does a local media used to gangland slayings and a seemingly endless supply of psycho killers. So when Foy clacked two shots at the back end of his Mercedes crookedly parked on Rosecrans, the crowd only parted wide enough to create a fire lane through which the white kids could reach the relative safety of their school bus, where they lowered themselves into their seats. Desegregation is never easy in any direction, and after Foy fired two more rounds into their civil rights movement, progress would be even slower, because the Freedom Bus had a couple of flat tires.

Foy pumped another shot into the Mercedes-Benz logo. This time the trunk popped open in that slow, majestic way that only Mercedes trunks do, and he grabbed an old bucket of whitewash out of the back. But before I, or anyone else, could reach him, he spun around, warding us off with his strap and his off-key singing. He'd made another lyric change. This time personalizing the tune by changing the refrain to "I shall overcome." What's that the judges always say on those televised singing competitions? You really made the song your own.

The pop of a can of paint opening is always a most satisfying sound. And justifiably pleased with himself and his car keys, Foy, still singing at the top of his lungs, rose to his feet and, with his back to the street, aimed his pistol directly at my chest. "I seen it a million times," my father used to say. "Professional niggers that just snap because the charade is over." The blackness that had consumed them suddenly evaporates like window grit washed away in the rain. All that's left is the transparency of the human condition, and everybody sees right through you. The lie on the résumé has finally been discovered. The reason it takes them so long to write their reports has been unearthed, and the tardiness isn't due to a painstaking attention to detail, but to dyslexia. The suspicions confirmed that the ever-present bottle of mouthwash on the colored man's desk in the corner, near the restroom, isn't filled with "a liquid designed to kill bad breath and provide twenty-four-hour protection against germs that cause gum disease and gingivitis," but peppermint schnapps. A liquid designed to kill bad dreams and provide a false sense of security that your Listerine smile is killing them softly. "Seen it a million times," he'd say. "At least niggers on the East Coast have the Vineyard and Sag Harbor. What we got? Las Vegas and fucking El Pollo Loco." Personally, I love El Pollo, and not that I was totally convinced that Foy was a danger to me or anyone else, but if I got out of this alive, the first thing I'd do was visit the one over on Vermont and 58th Street. Order me a three-piece combo—dark, with flame-grilled corn and mashed potatoes, and one of those delicious red fruit punches that taste like my eight-year-old birthday party.

The sirens were half a town away. Even when the county was flush with property tax revenue on overvalued homes, Dickens never received its fair share of civil services. And now, with the cutbacks and graft, the response time is measured in eons, the same switchboard operators who took the calls from the Holocaust, Rwanda, Wounded Knee, and Pompeii still at their posts. Foy turned the gun away from me and raised it to his ear, then with his free hand dumped the pail of unstirred and semi-hardened stain over his head. In clumpy folds, the paint oozed over the left

half of his face and down the length of that side of his body, until
one eye, one nostril, one shirtsleeve, one pant leg, and one Patek
Philippe watch were washed completely white. Foy was no Tree of
Knowledge, at most he was a Bush of Opinion, but in any case, it
was obvious that, publicity stunt or not, he was dying on the inside. I looked down at his roots. One brown shoe splattered with
paint from the milky waterfall that sluiced through his goatee and
fell from his chin. This time there was no doubt that he'd lost it,
because if there's one thing a successful black man like Foy loves
more than God, country, and his ham-hock-limbed mama, it's
his shoes.

I stepped to him. My arms raised and my hands open. Foy
pressed the gun barrel even deeper into his misshapen Afro, holding himself hostage. Suicide by cop or cop-out, I didn't much care,
but I was glad he'd finally stopped singing.

"Foy," I said, sounding surprisingly like my father, "you have
to ask yourself two questions: Who am I? and How may I become
myself?"

I waited for the expected "I do and do for you niggers, and this
is the thanks I get" diatribe about how no one was buying his
books. How even though he was the producer, director, editor, ca-
terer, and star of a television talk show that's been syndicated on
two continents and brought a droll homogenized and romanticized version of black intellectual thought into tens of homes in
over six countries, nothing has changed about how the world sees
us, much less how we see ourselves. How he was directly responsible for getting a black man elected president and nothing changed.
How last week a nigger won $75,000 on *Teen Jeopardy* and nothing
changed. How in fact things have gotten worse. And how you can
tell things are getting worse. Because "poverty" has disappeared
from the vernacular and our consciousness. Because there's white
boys working at the car wash. Because the women in porn are
better-looking than ever and it's the handsome gay men who are

"straight for pay." Because famous actors do commercials extolling the virtues of the phone companies and the United States Army. You know how you can tell shit is fucked up? Because someone thinks it's still 1950 and sees fit to reintroduce segregation to the American ethos. That someone wouldn't be you, would it, Sellout? Putting up signs? Erecting fake schools like the ghetto was some sort of phony Paris complete with railway stations, Arc de Triomphes, and Eiffel Towers built during World War I to fool the German bombers. Like the Germans, who, in turn, in the next war, built fake stores, theaters, and parks in Theresienstadt to dupe the Red Cross into believing that no atrocities were taking place, when the entire war was a series of fucking atrocities—one bullet, one illegal detention, one sterilization, one atom bomb at a time. You can't fool me. I'm not the Luftwaffe or the Red Cross. I didn't grow up in this hellhole . . . Like father, like son . . .

When it's your blood running through your fingers, the amount can only be described as "copious." But writhing in the gutter, clutching at my innards, I began to feel something akin to closure. I never heard the shot, but for the first time in my life I had something in common with my father—we'd both been shot in the gut by gutless motherfuckers. And there was a certain satisfaction in that. I felt as if I'd finally paid my debt to him and his fucked-up notions of blackness and childhood. Daddy never believed in closure. He said it was a false psychological concept. Something invented by therapists to assuage white Western guilt. In all his years of study and practice, he'd never heard a patient of color talk of needing "closure." They needed revenge. They needed distance. Forgiveness and a good lawyer maybe, but never closure. He said people mistake suicide, murder, lap band surgery, interracial marriage, and overtipping for closure, when in reality what they've achieved is erasure.

The problem with closure is that once you have a taste of it, you want it in every little aspect of your life. Especially when you're bleeding to death, and your slave, who is in full rebellion, is scream- ing, "Give me back my *Little Rascals* movies, motherfucker!" and pummeling your assailant with such knobby-knuckled fury that it takes half the L.A. County Sheriff's Department to pull him off, while you attempt to stanch the bleeding with a waterlogged copy of *Vibe* magazine someone has left in the gutter, you don't have time to let anything slide. Kanye West has announced, "I am rap!" Jay-Z thinks he's Picasso. And life is fucking fleeting.

"The ambulance will be here soon."

Things had finally settled down. Hominy, who couldn't stop crying, had taken off his T-shirt, rolled it into a pillow, and cradled my head in his lap. A sheriff's deputy squatted over me, poking gently at my wound with the butt end of her flashlight. "That was a fucking brave thing you did, Nigger Whisperer. Can I get you any- thing in the meantime?"

"Closure."

"I don't think you'll need stitches. It doesn't look like a belly shot; it's more like you've been hit in the love handle. It's superficial, really."

Anyone who's ever described a bullet wound as being superfi- cial has never been shot. But I wasn't about to let a little lack of empathy get in the way of total closure.

"It's illegal to yell 'Fire!' in a crowded theater, right?"

"It is."

"Well, I've whispered 'Racism' in a post-racial world."

I told her about my efforts to restore Dickens and how I thought building the school would give the town a sense of identity. She patted me sympathetically on the shoulder and raised her super- visor on the radio, and while we waited for the ambulance, the three of us haggled about the severity of the crime. The county reluctant to cite me with anything more than vandalism of state property and me trying to convince them that even if crime had gone down in the neighborhood since the Wheaton Academy went up, what I did was still a violation of the First Amendment, the Civil Rights Code, and, unless there's been an armistice in the War on Poverty, at least four articles of the Geneva Convention.

The paramedics arrived. Once I'd been stabilized with gauze and a few kind words, the EMTs went through the standard assessment protocol.

"Next of kin?"

As I lay, not exactly dying but close enough, I thought about Marpessa. Who, if the position of the sun high in the gorgeous blue sky was any indication, was at the far end of this very same street taking her lunch break. Her bus parked facing the ocean. Her bare feet on the dashboard, nose buried in Camus, listening to the Talking Heads' "This Must Be the Place."

"I have a girlfriend, but she's married."

"What about this guy?" she asked, pointing a ballpoint pen at a shirtless Hominy, standing just off to the side, giving his statement to a sheriff's deputy, who was writing in a notepad and shaking her head incredulously. "Is he family?"

"Family?" Hominy, overhearing the paramedic and somewhat insulted, wiped down his wrinkly underarms with his T-shirt and came over to see how I was doing. "Why I is something closer than family."

"He says he's his slave," the deputy chimed in, reading from her notes. "Been working for him, according to this crazy fucker, the last four hundred years."

The EMT nodded, running her powdered rubber-gloved hands down the length of Hominy's saggy-skinned back.

"How did you get these welts?"

"I was whupped. How else a no-account, shiftless nigger like me going to get whip marks on his back?"

Having handcuffed me to the stretcher board, the sheriff's

deputies knew they finally had something to charge me with, though we still couldn't agree on the crime as they carried me through the crowd and to the ambulance.

"Human trafficking?"

"Nah, he's never been bought or sold. What about involuntary servitude?"

"Maybe, but it's not like you're forcing him to work."

"It's not like he's working."

"Did you really whip him?"

"Not directly. I pay some people . . . It's a long story."

One of the EMTs had to tie her shoes. They set me down on a wooden bus stop bench while she adjusted her laces. From the seat-back a photo of a familiar face comforted me with a soothing smile and a red power tie.

"You got a good lawyer?" the deputy asked.

"Just call this nigger right here." I knocked on the advertisement. It said:

Hampton Fiske—*Attorney at Law*
Remember, there are four steps to acquittal:
1. Don't say shit! 2. Don't run! 3. Don't resist arrest!
4. Don't say shit!
1-800-FREEDOM Se Habla Español

He showed up late to the grand jury indictment, but Hampton's services were worth every dime. I told him I couldn't afford to do jail time. I had crops coming in and one of the mares was scheduled to foal in about two days. With this knowledge in tow, he strolled into the hearing, brushing leaves off his suit jacket and flicking twigs from his perm, carrying a bowl of fruit and talking about "As a farmer, my client is an indispensable member of a minority community well documented for being malnourished and underfed. He's never left the state of California, owns a twenty-year-old pickup truck that runs on fucking ethanol, which is next to impossible to find in this city, and thus he's not a flight risk . . ."

The California attorney general, flown in from Sacramento just to prosecute my case, leaped to her Prada-shod feet. "Objection! This defendant, evil genius that he is, has through his abhorrent actions managed to racially discriminate against every race all at the same time, to say nothing of his unabashed slaveholding. The state of California feels that it has more than enough evidence to prove that the defendant is in abject violation of the Civil Rights Acts of 1866, 1871, 1957, 1964, and 1968, the Equal Rights Act of 1963, the Thirteenth and Fourteenth Amendments, and at least six of the goddamn Ten Commandments. If it were within my power, I'd charge him with crimes against humanity!"

"This is an example of my client's humanity," Hampton countered calmly, gently setting the fruit bowl on the judge's bench, then backing away with a deep bow. "Freshly picked from my client's farm, your honor."

Judge Nguyen rubbed his tired eyes. He selected a nectarine from the offering and rolled it in his fingers as he spoke. "The irony is not lost on me that we sit here in this courtroom—a female state's attorney general of black and Asian lineage, a black defendant, a black defense counselor, a Latina bailiff, and me, a Vietnamese-American district judge—setting the parameters for what is essentially a judicial argument about the applicability, the efficacy, and the very existence of white supremacy as expressed through our system of law. And while no one in this room would deny the basic premise of 'civil rights,' we'd argue forever and a day about what constitutes 'equal treatment under the law' as defined by the very articles of the Constitution this defendant is accused of violating. In attempting to restore his community through reintroducing precepts, namely segregation and slavery, that, given his cultural history, have come to define his community despite

the supposed unconstitutionality and nonexistence of these con-
cepts, he's pointed out a fundamental flaw in how we as Americans claim we see equality. 'I don't care if you're black, white,
brown, yellow, red, green, or purple.' We've all said it. Posited as
proof of our nonprejudicial ways, but if you painted any one of us
purple or green, we'd be mad as hell. And that's what he's doing.
He's painting everybody over, painting this community purple
and green, and seeing who still believes in equality. I don't know if
what he's done is legal or not, but the one civil right I can guarantee this defendant is the right to due process, the right to a speedy
trial. We convene tomorrow morning at nine. But buckle up, people, no matter the verdict, innocent or guilty, this is going to the
Supreme Court, so I hope you ain't got nothing scheduled for
the next five years. Bail is set"—Judge Nguyen took a big bite out
the nectarine, then kissed his crucifix—"Bail is set at a cantaloupe
and two kumquats."

UNMITIGATED
BLACKNESS

Twenty-four

I expected the air-conditioning in the Supreme Court to be for shit, like it is in all the good courtroom movies: *Twelve Angry Men* and *To Kill a Mockingbird*. Movie trials always take place in humid locales in the heat of summer, because the psych books say crime goes up with the temperature. Tempers run short. Perspiring witnesses and trial attorneys start yelling at each other. The jurors fan themselves, then open four-paned windows looking for escape and a breath of fresh air. Washington, D.C., is fairly muggy this time of year, but it's mild, damn near frigid, inside the courthouse, yet I have to open a window anyway—to let out all the smoke and five years of judicial system frustration.

"You can't handle the weed!" I shout at Fred Manne, courtroom artist extraordinaire and film buff. It's the dinner break to what has amounted to the longest Supreme Court case in history. We're sitting in a nameless antechamber passing time and a joint back and forth, butchering the climax of *A Few Good Men*, which isn't a great movie, but Jack Nicholson's disdain for the actors and the script and the way he delivers that last monologue carry the film.

"Did you order the Code Red?"

"I might have. I'm so fucking high right now . . ."

"Did you order the Code Red?"

"You're goddamn right I did! And I'd do it again, because this pot is fucking unbelievable." Fred's breaking character. "What's it called?" It being the joint he's holding in his hand.

"It doesn't have a name yet, but Code Red sounds pretty good."

Fred has sketched all the important cases: same-sex marriage, the end of the Voting Rights Act, and the demise of affirmative action in higher education and, by extension, everywhere else. He says that in his thirty years of courtroom artistry, this is the first time he's ever seen the court adjourn for dinner. First time he's ever seen the Justices raise their voices and stare each other down. He shows me an artist's rendering of today's session. In it a conservative Catholic Justice flips off a liberal Catholic Justice from the Bronx with a surreptitious cheek scratch.

"What does '*coño*' mean?"

"What?"

"That's what she whispered under her breath, followed by '*Chupa mi verga, cabrón.*'"

My colored-pencil caricature looks terrible. I'm in the lower-left-hand corner of the drawing. I can't speak to the Court allowing for unregulated corporate spending on political campaigns, or the burning of the American flag, but the best decision it's ever made was to prohibit the use of cameras in the courtroom, because, apparently, I'm one ugly motherfucker. My bulbous nose and gigantic ears protrude from my bald Mount Fuji–shaped head like fleshy anemometers. I'm flashing a yellow-toothed smile and staring at the youngish Jewish Justice like I can see through her robe. Fred says the reason they don't permit cameras has nothing to do with maintaining decorum and dignity. It's to protect the country from seeing what's underneath Plymouth Rock. Because the Supreme Court is where the country takes out its dick and tits and decides who's going to get fucked and who's getting a taste of mother's milk. It's constitutional pornography in there, and what did Justice Potter once say about obscenity? I know it when I see it.

"Fred, do you think you could at least shave down my incisors? I look like fucking Blackula."

"*Blackula*. Underrated movie."

Fred unclips the press laminate from his lanyard and uses the metal fastener as a makeshift roach clip to finish the rest of the weed in one mighty toke. His eyes and nasal passages closed tight, I ask him can I borrow a pencil. He nods yes, and I take the opportunity to remove all the brown-colored implements from his fancy pencil case. Fuck if I'm going down in history as the homeliest litigant in Supreme Court history.

During social studies, otherwise known in Dad's curriculum as the Ways and Means of the Indefatigable White People, my father used to warn me about listening to rap or the blues with Caucasian strangers. And as I got older, I'd be admonished not to play Monopoly, drink more than two beers, or smoke weed with them either. For such activities can breed a false sense of familiarity. And nothing, from the hungry jungle cat to the African ferryboat, is more dangerous than a white person on what they think is familiar ground. And as Fred returns from exhaling a cloud of smoke out into the D.C. night, he has that Ain't-I-a-Soul-Brother glint in his eyes. "Let me tell you something, my man. I've seen them all come through here. Racial profiling, interracial marriage, hate speech, and race-based set-asides, and you know what the difference is between my people and yours? As much as we both want seats at the 'table,' once you get inside, you motherfuckers never have an escape plan. Us? We're prepared to leave at a moment's notice. I never enter a restaurant, bowling alley, or an orgy without asking myself, If they choose this moment to come get me, how in the fuck am I getting out of here? Cost us a generation, but we learned our fucking lesson. They told you people, 'School's out. Ain't no more lessons to be learned,' and you dumb fucks believed them.

Think about it, if the damn storm troopers were to knock on the door right now, what would you do? What's your exit strategy?"

There's a knock on the door. It's a court officer gulping down the last of a prefabricated spicy tuna roll. She's wondering why I have one leg dangling out of the window. Fred simply shakes his head. I look down. Even if I were to survive the three-story fall, I'd be trapped in a tacky marble courtyard. Walled in by thirty feet of overblown Colonial architecture. Surrounded by lion heads, bamboo stalks, red orchids, and a silty fountain. On our way out, Fred points to a small, Hobbit-sized side door behind a potted plant that presumably leads to the Promised Land.

I reenter the chambers to find an insanely pale white boy in my seat. It's like he's waited until the fourth quarter of the ball game to move down from the upper deck, sneak past the ushers to take a courtside chair vacated by some fan who's left early to beat the traffic. I'm reminded of the black stand-up trope about white patrons returning to find "niggers in they seats" and drawing straws to decide who's going to ask them to move.

"You in my seat, dude."

"Hey, I just wanted to tell you that I feel like my constitutionality is on trial, too. And you don't seem to have many people in your cheering section." He waved his invisible pompoms in the air. *Ricka-rocka! Ricka-rocka! Sis! Boom! Bah!*

"I appreciate the support. Much needed. But just slide over one."

The Justices file back into the courtroom. No one mentions my newfound tag-team partner. It's been a long day. Bags have appeared under their eyes. Their robes have wrinkled and lost their sheen. In fact, the black Justice's garment seems to be stained with barbecue sauce. The only two people in the courtroom who look fresh are the Jeffersonian Chief Justice and a mackadocious Hampton Fiske, each with not a hair out of place or displaying the slightest sign of fatigue. However, Hampton has one-upped the Chief

Justice with a costume change. He's now resplendent in an argumentative bell-bottomed, ball-hugging, chartreuse jumpsuit. He doffs his homburg, cape, and ivory-handled cane and adjusts his bulge, then stands aside, as the Chief Justice has an announcement to make.

"I know it's been a trying day. I know that in this culture 'race' is especially hard to talk about, in that we feel the need to defer . . ."

The white kid next to me coughs an *Animal House* "bullshit" into his hand. And I softly ask this ghostly motherfucker his name, because it's only right to know who's fighting next to you in the trench.

"Adam Y___."

"My man."

I'm high as hell, but not high enough not to know that race is hard to "talk about" because it's hard to talk about. The prevalence of child abuse in this country is hard to talk about, too, but you never hear people complaining about it. They just don't talk about it. And when's the last time you had a calm, measured conversation about the joys of consensual incest? Sometimes things are simply difficult to discuss, but I actually think the country does a decent job of addressing race, and when folks say, "Why can't we talk about race more honestly?" What they really mean is "Why can't you niggers be reasonable?" or "Fuck you, white boy. If I said what I really wanted to say, I'd get fired even faster than you'd fire me if race were any easier to talk about." And by race we mean "niggers," because no one of any persuasion seems to have any difficulty talking out-of-pocket shit about Native Americans, Latinos, Asians, and America's newest race, the Celebrity.

Black people don't even talk about race. Nothing's attributable to color anymore. It's all "mitigating circumstances." The only people discussing "race" with any insight and courage are loud middle-aged white men who romanticize the Kennedys and Motown, well-read open-minded white kids like the tie-dyed familiar sitting next to me in the *Free Tibet and Boba Fett* T-shirt, a few freelance journalists in Detroit, and the American hikikomori who sit in their basements pounding away at their keyboards composing measured and well-thought-out responses to the endless torrent of racist online commentary. So thank goodness for MSNBC, Rick Rubin, the Black Guy at *The Atlantic*, Brown University, and the beautiful Supreme Court Justice from the Upper West Side, who, leaning coolly into her microphone, has finally asked the first question that makes any sense: "I think we've established the legal quandary here as to whether a violation of civil rights law that results in the very same achievement these heretofore mentioned statutes were meant to promote, yet have failed to achieve, is in fact a breach of said civil rights. What we must not fail to remember is that 'separate but equal' was struck down, not on any moral grounds, but on the basis that the Court found that separate can never be equal. And at a minimum, this case suggests we ask ourselves not if separate were indeed equal, but what about 'separate and not quite equal, but infinitely better off than ever before.' *Me v. the United States of America* demands a more fundamental examination of what we mean by 'separate,' by 'equal,' by 'black.' So let's get down to the nitty-gritty—what do we mean by 'black'?"

The best thing about Hampton Fiske, other than that he refuses to let seventies fashion die, is that he's always prepared. He straightens a pair of lapels that sit atop his chest like giant tent flaps, and then clears his throat; a purposeful gesture he knows will make some people nervous. And he wants his audience on edge, because if nothing else, it means they're attentive.

"So what is blackness, your honor? That's a good question. The exact same one the immortal French author Jean Genet posed after being asked by an actor to write a play featuring an all-black cast, when he mused not only 'What exactly is a black?' but added the even more fundamental inquiry, 'First of all, what is his color?'"

Hampton's legal team pulls cords, and the drapes fall over the windows, while he walks to the light switch and douses the courtroom in pitch black. "In addition to Genet, many rappers and black thinkers have weighed in. An early rap quintet of puerile white poseurs known as Young Black Teenagers asserted that 'Blackness is a state of mind.' My client's father, the esteemed African-American psychologist F. K. Me (may the genius motherfucker rest in peace), hypothesized that black identity is formed in stages. In his theory of Quintessential Blackness, Stage I is the Neophyte Negro. Here the black person exists in a state of preconsciousness. Just as many children would be afraid of the total darkness in which we now find ourselves immersed, the Neophyte Negro is afraid of his own blackness. A blackness that feels inescapable, infinite, and less than." Hampton snaps his fingers, and a giant photo of Michael Jordan shilling for Nike is projected on all four walls of the courtroom, but it's quickly replaced by successive photos of Colin Powell sharing his recipe for yellowcake uranium before the United Nations General Assembly shortly before the potluck invasion of Iraq and Condoleezza Rice lying through the gap in her teeth. These are African-Americans meant to illustrate his point. Exemplars of how self-hatred can compel one to value mainstream acceptance over self-respect and morality. Images of Cuba Gooding, Coral from *The Real World*, and Morgan Freeman all flit by. With references to such long-forgotten pop icons, Hampton is dating himself, but he continues his pitch: "He or she wants to be anything but black. They suffer from poor self-esteem and extremely ashy skin." A portrait of the black Justice smoking a cigar and lining up a ten-foot putt splashes across the walls. Causing everyone, including the black Justice himself, to have a good laugh. "Stage I Negroes watch reruns of *Friends*, oblivious to the fact that whenever a white sitcom male dates a black woman on television, it's always the homeliest white guy in the bunch getting some love from the sisters. It's the Turtles, the

Skreeches, the David Schwimmers, and the George Costanzas of the group . . ."

The Chief Justice meekly raises his hand.

"Excuse me, Mr. Fiske, I have a question . . ."

"Not right now, motherfucker—I'm on a roll!"

And so am I. I pull out my rolling machine and, as best as I can in the dark, fill the tray with moist product. They can hold me in contempt, *le mépris* of everything. I don't need anyone to tell me what Stage II blackness is. It's "Capital *B* Black." I already know this crap. It's been drilled into my head ever since I was old enough to play One of These Things Just Doesn't Belong and my father made me point out the token white guy in the Lakers team photo. Mark Landsberger, where are you when I need you? "The distinguishing feature of Stage II blackness is a heightened awareness of race. Here race is still all-consuming, but in a more positive fashion. Blackness becomes an essential component in one's experiential and conceptual framework. Blackness is idealized, whiteness reviled. Emotions range from bitterness, anger, and self-destruction to waves of pro-Black euphoria and ideas of Black supremacy . . ." To avoid detection I go under the table, but the joint's not hitting right. I can't get any intake. From my newfound hiding place I struggle to keep the ember burning, while catching odd-angled glimpses of photographs of Foy Cheshire, Jesse Jackson, Sojourner Truth, Moms Mabley, Kim Kardashian, and my father. I can never get away from my father. He was right, there is no such thing as closure. Maybe the weed is too sticky for a clean burn. Maybe I've rolled it too tight. Maybe I don't have any weed in there at all and I'm so high I've been trying to smoke my finger for the past five minutes. "Stage III blackness is Race Transcendentalism. A collective consciousness that fights oppression and seeks serenity." Fuck it, I'm out. I'm ghost. I decide to sneak out quietly so as not to embarrass Hampton, who's been working like a champion of justice on this never-ending case. "Examples of Stage III black folks are people like Rosa Parks, Harriet Tubman, Sitting Bull, César Chávez, Ichiro Suzuki." In the dark I cover my face, and my silhouette cuts across a movie still of Bruce Lee fixing to kick some ass in *Enter the Dragon.* Thanks to Fred, the courtroom artist, I have an exit plan and can make my way in the dark. "Stage III black folks are the woman on your left, the man on your right. They are people who believe in beauty for beauty's sake."

Washington, D.C., like most cities, is much prettier at night. But as I sit on the Supreme Court steps, making a pipe out of a soda can, staring at the White House lit up like a department store window, I'm trying to figure out what's so different about our nation's capital.

The draw from an aluminum Pepsi can isn't the best, but it'll do. I blow smoke into the air. There should be a Stage IV of black identity—Unmitigated Blackness. I'm not sure what Unmitigated Blackness is, but whatever it is, it doesn't sell. On the surface Unmitigated Blackness is a seeming unwillingness to succeed. It's Donald Goines, Chester Himes, Abbey Lincoln, Marcus Garvey, Alfre Woodard, and the serious black actor. It's Tiparillos, chitterlings, and a night in jail. It's the crossover dribble and wearing house shoes outside. It's "whereas" and "things of that nature." It's our beautiful hands and our fucked-up feet. Unmitigated Blackness is simply not giving a fuck. Clarence Cooper, Charlie Parker, Richard Pryor, Maya Deren, Sun Ra, Mizoguchi, Frida Kahlo, black-and-white Godard, Céline, Gong Li, David Hammons, Björk, and the Wu-Tang Clan in any of their hooded permutations. Unmitigated Blackness is essays passing for fiction. It's the realization that there are no absolutes, except when there are. It's the acceptance of contradiction not being a sin and a crime but a human frailty like split ends and libertarianism. Unmitigated Blackness is coming to the realization that as fucked up and meaningless as it all is, sometimes it's the nihilism that makes life worth living.

Sitting here on the steps of the Supreme Court smoking weed, under the "Equal Justice Under Law" motto, staring into the stars, I've finally figured out what's wrong with Washington, D.C. It's that all the buildings are more or less the same height and there's absolutely no skyline, save for the Washington Monument touching the night sky like a giant middle finger to the world.

Twenty-five

The joke is that, depending on the Supreme Court's decision, my Welcome Home party might also be my Going Away to Jail party, so the banner over the kitchen doorway says, CONSTITUTIONAL OR INSTITUTIONAL—TO BE DECIDED. Marpessa kept it small, limited to friends and the Lopezes from next door. Everyone is in my den, watching the lost *Little Rascals* films, huddled around Hominy, who's the real man of the hour.

Foy was found innocent on attempted murder charges by reason of temporary insanity, but I did win my civil suit against him. It's not like it wasn't obvious, but like most of celebrity America, Foy Cheshire's rumored wealth was just that—rumored. And after selling his car to pay his attorney's fees, the only possessions he had of any real value were the only things I wanted—the *Little Rascals* movies. Stocked with watermelon, gin, and lemonade, and a 16 mm projector, we readied for an enjoyable evening of grainy black-and-white old-time "Yassuh, boss" racism unseen since the days of *Birth of a Nation* and whatever's on ESPN right now. Two hours in and we wonder why Foy went through all the bother. Although Hominy's enrapt with his onscreen image, the treasure trove consists mostly of unreleased MGM *Our Gang* footage. By the mid-forties the series had long been dead and bereft of ideas, but these shorts are especially bad. The late edition of the gang remains intact: Froggy, Mickey, Buckwheat, the little-known Janet, and, of course, Hominy in various minor roles. These postwar shorts are so serious. In "Hotsy Totsy Nazi" the gang tracks down a German war criminal masquerading as a pediatrician. Herr Doktor Jones's racism gives him away, when a feverish Hominy arrives for his checkup and is greeted with a snide "I zee we didn't get all of you during zee var. Take zee arsenic pills und vee zee vat vee can do about dat, ja?" In "Asocial Butterfly," Hominy takes a rare star turn. Asleep in the woods for so long that a monarch butterfly has enough time to weave a cocoon in his wild-flung hair, he panics and doffs his straw hat to show his discovery to Miss Crabtree. She excitedly proclaims that he has "a chrysalis," which the ever-inquisitive gang overhears as "syphilis," and tries to get him quarantined at a "house of ill refute." There are a couple of hidden gems, though. In an attempt to revive the stagnant franchise, the studio produced a few abridged reenactments of theater pieces played totally straight by the gang. It's too bad the world has missed out on Buckwheat as Brutus Jones and Froggy as the shady Smithers in "The Emperor Jones." Darla returns to the fold and gives a brilliant performance as the headstrong "Antigone." Alfalfa is no less engaging as the beleaguered Leo in Clifford Odets's "Paradise Lost." But for the most part, there's nothing in Foy's archives to suggest why he would go to such lengths to keep these works from the public. The racism is rampant as usual, but no more virulent than a day trip to the Arizona state legislature.

"How much is left on the reel, Hominy?"

"About fifteen minutes, massa."

The words "Nigger in a Woodpile—Take #1" flash across the screen over a cord of barnyard firewood. Two or three seconds go by. And—Bam!—a nappy little black head pops up sporting a wide razzamatazz grin. "It's black folk!" he says before batting his big, adorable baby seal eyes.

"Hominy, is that you?"

"I wish it was, that boy's a natural!"

Suddenly you can hear the director offscreen yelling, "We've got plenty of wood, but we need more nigger. C'mon, Foy, do it right this time. I know you're only five, but niggerize the hell out of this one." Take #2 is no less spectacular, but what follows is a low-budget one-reeler called "Oil Ty-Coons!" starring Buckwheat, Hominy, and a heretofore unknown member of the Little Rascals, a moppet credited as Li'l Foy Cheshire, alias Black Folk, an instant classic and, to my knowledge, the last entry in the *Our Gang* oeuvre.

"I remember this one! Oh my God! I remember this one!"

"Hominy, stop jumping around. You're in the way."

In "Oil Ty-Coons!" after a clandestine back-alley meeting with a lanky, chauffeur-driven, ten-gallon-hat cowboy, our boys are seen pushing a wheelbarrow loaded with cash down the crime-free streets of Greenville. The nigger rich trio, now dressed in top hat and tails at all times, treats an increasingly suspicious gang to an endless run of movies and sweets. They even go so far as to buy a destitute Mickey an expensive set of catcher's gear he's been admiring in the sporting-goods-store window. Dissatisfied with Buckwheat's explanation for their newfound wealth—"I'z found a four-leaf clo'ber and done won the Irish Lottery"—the gang trots out a number of theories. The boys are running numbers. They're betting on the horses. Hattie McDaniel has died and left them all her money. Eventually the gang threatens Buckwheat with expulsion if he doesn't tell where the money is coming from. "We'z in oil!" Still harboring doubts and unable to find an oil derrick, the gang follows Hominy to a hidden warehouse, where they discover the nefarious darkies have all the kids in Niggertown hooked up to IVs and, for a nickel a pint, filling oil cans with crude drop by black drop. At the end, a diaper-clad Foy turns and mugs "Black folk!" into the camera before the scene mercifully fades out with the *Our Gang* theme music.

Finally King Cuz breaks the silence. "Now I know why that fool Foy went crazy. I'd go nutty, too, if I had some shit like that on my conscience. And I make my livelihood shooting motherfuckers for no reason."

Stevie, a hardcore gangster as ruthless as the free market and unemotional as a Vulcan with Asperger's, has a tear running down one cheek. He lifts a can of beer to Hominy and offers a toast. "I'm not sure how I mean this, but 'To Hominy. You're a better man than I.' I swear the Oscars need to give a Lifetime Achievement Award to the black actor, because you guys had it hard."

"Still do," says Panache, who I didn't even know was here and I supposed must be back from a long day on the set of *Hip-hop Cop*. "I know what Hominy's gone through. I've had directors tell me, 'We need more black in this scene. Can you black it up? Then you say, 'Fuck you, you racist motherfucker!' And they go, 'Exactly, don't lose that intensity!' "

Nestor Lopez stands up sharply, swaying for a moment as the vodka and weed rush to his head. "At least you people have a Hollywood history. What we got? Speedy Gonzales, a woman with bananas on her head, 'We don't need no stinking badges,' and some prison movies!"

"But they're some great prison movies, homes!"

"At least there were some black Little Rascals. Where was fucking little Chorizo or Bok Choy?"

Though Nestor has a point about there not being a Chorizo, I don't mention anything about Sing Joy and Edward Soo Hoo, two Asian Rascals who, though by no means stars, had better runs than many a snot-nosed brat the studios trotted out in front of the cameras. I'm headed toward the barn to check on my newly purchased Swedish sheep. My baby Roslags are huddled under the persimmon tree; it's their first night in the ghetto and they're afraid the goats and the pigs are going to jack them. One lamb's a scruffy white, the other's a mottled grayish color. They're shaking. I hug them both and plant kisses on their snouts.

Hominy's standing behind me, I hadn't noticed him, and, monkey see, monkey do, he plants a chapped liver-lipped kiss on my mouth.

"What the fuck, Hominy?"

"I quit."

"Quit what?"

"Slavery. We'll talk reparations in the morning."

The sheep are still shivering in fear. "*Vara modig*," I whisper in their quivering ears. I don't know what it means, but that's what the brochure said to say to them at least three times a day during the first week. I shouldn't have bought them, but they're endangered, and an old husbandry professor saw me on the news and thought I'd be a good caretaker. I'm scared, too. What if I do go to jail? Who's going to take care of them then? If the First, Thirteenth, and Fourteenth Amendment violations don't stick, there's talk of an International Criminal Court trial and charging me with apartheid. They never prosecuted a single South African for apartheid and they're going to arrest me? A harmless South Central African-American? Amandla awethu!

"Come inside when you're done out there," Marpessa calls from the bedroom.

There's urgency in her voice. I know she means now; I'll bottle-feed the sheep later. *Eyewitness News* is on. My girlfriend of five years lies facedown on the bed, her pretty head in her hands, watching the weather on the television atop the dresser. Charisma sits next to her. Leaning against the headboard, her stocking feet crossed and resting on Marpessa's ass. I find what little mattress space is left and climb into my dream ménage à trois.

"Marpessa, what if I have to go to jail?"

"Shut up and just look at the TV."

"Hampton made a good point in court when he said that if Hominy's 'servitude' was tantamount to human bondage, then corporate America better be ready to fight a hell of a class-action lawsuit filed by generations of uncompensated interns."

"Will you stop talking? You're going to miss it."

"But what if I go to jail?"

"Then I'll just have to find another nigger to have unimaginative sex with."

The rest of the party is huddled around the bedroom door. Looking in. Marpessa reaches back, grabs my chin, and forces my head to look at the screen. "Watch."

Weatherperson Chantal Mattingly is waving her hands over the L.A. Basin. It's hot. *There's a surge of moisture moving in from the south. The excessive heat warning is still in effect for the Santa Clarita Valley and the interior valleys of Ventura County. For other areas expect seasonal temperatures with cooling until about midnight. For the most part, skies will be clear to partly cloudy, temperatures mild to moderate* [whatever that means] *along the coast from Santa Barbara to Orange Counties and much warmer inland. Now for the local forecasts. Not expecting any major changes from now till late evening.* I always like weather maps. The 3-D effect of the topographical coastline map rotating and shifting as the forecast moves south and inland. The gradations in the colors of the mountain ranges and low-lying plains, they never fail to impress me. *Current temperatures . . .*

Palmdale 103°/88° . . . Oxnard 77°/70° . . . Santa Clarita 108°/107° . . . Thousand Oaks 77°/69° . . . Santa Monica 79°/66° . . . Van Nuys 105/82° . . . Glendale . . . 95°/79° . . . Dickens 88°/74° . . . Long Beach 82°/75° . . .

"Wait, does that say Dickens?"

Marpessa laughs maniacally. I shoulder my way past the homies and Marpessa's kids, whose names I refuse to say. I run outside. The frog thermometer hanging from the back porch reads exactly 88 degrees. I can't stop crying. Dickens is back on the map.

Twenty-six

One night, on the anniversary of my father's death, Marpessa and I drove down to Dum Dum Donuts for open-mike night. We took our usual seats, the far side of the stage, near the bathrooms and the fire extinguisher, bathed in the red haze of the EXIT sign. I located and pointed out the other exits to her just in case.

"Just in case of what? By some miracle somebody actually tells a funny joke and we have to run outside, dig up Richard Pryor and Dave Chappelle, and make sure their corpses are still in the fucking ground and it's not black Easter? These fucking micro-Negro comedians they have today make me fucking sick. There's a reason there ain't no black Jonathan Winters, John Candy, W. C. Fields, John Belushi, Jackie Gleason, and Roseanne Barr out this motherfucker, because a large truly funny black person would scare the bejeezus out of America."

"There aren't many fat white comedians these days, either. And Dave Chappelle isn't dead."

"You believe what you want to believe about Dave. The nigger's dead. They had to kill him."

Someone at the club did make me laugh once. One time my father and I were there together when a stumpy black man, the new host, bounded onstage. He was unpaid-electricity-bill dark and looked like a crazed bullfrog. His eyes protruded wildly from his head like they were trying to escape the mental madness therein. And come to think of it, he was rather fat. We were sitting in our usual spot. Normally, except for when my dad was onstage, I'd read my book and let the sexual jokes and white people/black people bits wash over me like so much background noise. But this man-frog opened with a joke that had me crying. "Your mama been on welfare so long," he bellowed, blithely holding the silver microphone like he didn't need it and was there only because someone handed it to him backstage. "Your mama been on welfare so long, her face is on the food stamp." Anybody who could make me put down *Catch-22* had to be funny. After that, it was me who dragged Pops to open-mike night. If we wanted our usual seats, we had to get there earlier and earlier, because word was spreading throughout black L.A. that a funny motherfucker was hosting the open-mike nights. The donut shop would fill with black belly laughter from 8 p.m.–until.

This traffic-court jester did more than tell jokes; he plucked out your subconscious and beat you silly with it, not until you were unrecognizable, but until you were recognizable. One night a white couple strolled into the club, two hours after "doors open," sat front and center, and joined in the frivolity. Sometimes they laughed loudly. Sometimes they snickered knowingly like they'd been black all their lives. I don't know what caught his attention, his perfectly spherical head drenched in houselight sweat. Maybe their laughter was a pitch too high. Heeing when they should've been hawing. Maybe they were too close to the stage. Maybe if white people didn't feel the need to sit up front all the damn time it never would've happened. "What the fuck you honkies laughing at?" he shouted. More chuckling from the audience. The white couple howling the loudest. Slapping the table. Happy to be noticed. Happy to be accepted. "I ain't bullshitting!

What the fuck are you interloping motherfuckers laughing at? Get the fuck out!"

There's nothing funny about nervous laughter. The forced way it slogs through a room with the stop-and-start undulations of bad jazz brunch jazz. The black folks and the round table of Latinas out for a night on the town knew when to stop laughing. The couple didn't. The rest of us silently sipped our canned beer and sodas, determined to stay out of the fray. They were laughing solo because this had to be part of the show, right?

"Do I look like I'm fucking joking with you? This shit ain't for you. Understand? Now get the fuck out! This is our thing!"

No more laughter. Only pleading, unanswered looks for assistance, then the soft scrape of two chairs being backed, quietly as possible, away from the table. The blast of cold December air and the sounds of the street. The night manager shutting the doors behind them, leaving little evidence that the white people had ever been there except for an unfulfilled two-drink, three-donut minimum.

"Now where the fuck was I before I was so rudely interrupted? Oh yeah, your mama, that bald-headed . . ."

When I think about that night, the black comedian chasing the white couple into the night, their tails and assumed histories between their legs, I don't think about right or wrong. No, when my thoughts go back to that evening, I think about my own silence. Silence can be either protest or consent, but most times it's fear. I guess that's why I'm so quiet and such a good whisperer, nigger and otherwise. It's because I'm always afraid. Afraid of what I might say. What promises and threats I might make and have to keep. That's what I liked about the man, although I didn't agree with him when he said, "Get out. This is our thing." I respected that he didn't give a fuck. But I wish I hadn't been so scared, that I had had the nerve to stand in protest. Not to castigate him for what he did or to stick up for the aggrieved white people. After all, they could've stood up for themselves, called in the authorities or their God, and smote everybody in the place, but I wish I'd stood up to the man and asked him a question: "So what exactly is *our thing*?"

Closure

I remember the day after the black dude was inaugurated, Foy Cheshire, proud as punch, driving around town in his coupe, honking his horn and waving an American flag. He wasn't the only one celebrating; the neighborhood glee wasn't O. J. Simpson getting acquitted or the Lakers winning the 2002 championship, but it was close. Foy drove past the crib and I happened to be sitting in the front yard husking corn. "Why are you waving the flag?" I asked him. "Why now? I've never seen you wave it before." He said that he felt like the country, the United States of America, had finally paid off its debts. "And what about the Native Americans? What about the Chinese, the Japanese, the Mexicans, the poor, the forests, the water, the air, the fucking California condor? When do they collect?" I asked him.

He just shook his head at me. Said something to the effect that my father would be ashamed of me and that I'd never understand. And he's right. I never will.

ACKNOWLEDGMENTS

Thank you to Sarah Chalfant, Jin Auh, and Colin Dickerman.

And a special thank you to Kemi Ilesanmi and Creative Capital. This book wouldn't have happened without your faith and support.

Big hugs to Lou Asekoff, Sheila Maldonado, and Lydia Offord.

Shout-out to my family: Ma, Anna, Sharon, and Ainka. Much love.

Much respect, appreciation, and inspiration is owed to William E. Cross, Jr., whose groundbreaking work in black identity development, particularly his paper "The Negro-to-Black Conversion Experience" in *Black World* 20 (July 1971), I read in grad school and has stayed with me ever since.